Logics of Empowerment

Logics of Empowerment

Development, Gender, and Governance in Neoliberal India

Aradhana Sharma

University of Minnesota Press
Minneapolis
London

Sections of chapters 2, 3, and the Conclusion were previously published in "Crossbreeding Institutions, Breeding Struggle: Women's Empowerment, Neoliberal Governmentality, and State (Re)Formation in India," *Cultural Anthropology* 21, no. 1 (2006): 60–95. Sections of chapters 2 and 3 also appeared in "Globalization and Postcolonial States," *Current Anthropology* 47, no. 2 (2006): 277–307 (coauthored with Akhil Gupta).

Published by the University of Minnesota Press
111 Third Avenue South, Suite 290
Minneapolis, MN 55401-2520
http://www.upress.umn.edu

Library of Congress Cataloging-in-Publication Data
Sharma, Aradhana.
Logics of empowerment : development, gender, and governance in neoliberal India / Aradhana Sharma.
p. cm.
Includes bibliographical references and index.
ISBN 978-0-8166-5452-9 (hc : alk. paper) — ISBN 978-0-8166-5453-6 (pb : alk. paper)
1. Women in development — India — Uttar Pradesh. 2. Mahila Samakhya (Project : Uttar Pradesh, India). 3. Economic development projects — India — Uttar Pradesh. 4. Poor women — Services for — India — Uttar Pradesh. 5. Public welfare — India. 6. Neoliberalism — India. I. Title.
HQ1240.5.I4S53 2008
305.48'969409542 — dc22 2008012328

Printed in the United States of America on acid-free paper

15 14 13 12 11 10 09 08 10 9 8 7 6 5 4 3 2 1

For my grandparents, Champa and Tulsi Das Dhawan,
and my parents, Versha and (late) Sushil Kumar Sharma

Contents

Abbreviations

BDC	Block Development Committee
BDO	Block Development Officer
BSP	Bahujan Samaj Party
CDO	Chief Development Officer
DAWN	Development Alternatives with Women for a New Era
DDO	District Development Officer
DFID	Department for International Development
DM	District Magistrate
DPC	District Programme Coordinator
DWCRA	Development of Women and Children in Rural Areas
EC	Executive Committee
FIR	First Information Report
GAD	Gender and Development
GEM	Gender Empowerment Measure
GONGO	Government-Organized Nongovernmental Organization
ICDS	Integrated Child Development Services
IMF	International Monetary Fund
MDG	Millennium Development Goals
MS	Mahila Samakhya
NGO	Nongovernmental Organization
NPD	National Programme Director
NPE	National Policy on Education
NRG	National Resource Group
NRI	Non-Resident Indians
SAPs	Structural Adjustment Programs
SDM	Sub-District Magistrate
SPD	State Programme Director
SSP	Senior Superintendent of Police
TBA	Traditional Birth Attendant
UN	United Nations
U.P.	Uttar Pradesh
USAID	United States Agency for International Development

WCD	Women and Child Development
WDP	Women's Development Programme
WID	Women in Development

Acknowledgments

Financial support for the research and writing of this project was provided by the following institutions: The Wenner-Gren Foundation for Anthropological Research, Inc.; The National Science Foundation; Stanford University (School of Humanities and Sciences, Department of Cultural and Social Anthropology, Stanford Center on Conflict and Negotiation, and the Institute for International Studies); and Wesleyan University. I am grateful to officials at the Department of Education of the Ministry of Human Resource Development, Government of India, who allowed me to conduct my research on one of their projects, the Mahila Samakhya program.

This book is a product of the labor, love, and critical inputs of many different people, and I want to thank them all.

First and foremost, this project would not have been possible without the support and encouragement of all the women directly or indirectly associated with the Mahila Samakhya program. They opened their lives and hearts to me, and much of what I know about theory, struggle, strength, survival, feminism, politics, and social justice is due to them. This book would not "be" were it not for their inspiration: I owe this to you; *shukriya*.

My mentors, Srilatha Batliwala, John Clarke, Jane Collier, Inderpal Grewal, Akhil Gupta, Susan Hirsch, Ayesha Jalal, Kameshwari Jandhyala, Purnima Mankekar, Sally Merry, Donald Moore, K. Sivaramakrishnan, Elizabeth Traube, and Sylvia Yanagisako, have showered me with brilliant insights and unmitigated support. They introduced me to the writings of Wendy Brown, Partha Chatterjee, Arturo Escobar, James Ferguson, Stuart Hall, Lata Mani, Timothy Mitchell, and Chandra Mohanty, among others, which are now key occupants of my "theoretical backpack." My intellectual debt to all my mentors, "virtual" or not, should be evident in the pages that follow: In awe . . .

My friends, comrades, and coconspirators, who give me food for thought and life, keep me on my toes, and contribute immeasurably, knowingly or not, to my ideas and politics, include Sanjay Bahadur, Kathy Coll, Monica

DeHart, Tejaswini Ganti, Raji Mulukutla, Arzoo Osanloo, Mridu Rai, Mukta Sharangpani, Rana Thomas, Gina Ulysse, and Mei Zhan. I thank them for listening and conversing, for questioning and challenging, and for infecting this sometimes arduous journey with laughter, excitement, and generosity. For allowing me to fret and for reminding me to breathe: My deepest affection.

A special thanks to Megan Greenberg and Sarah Gunther, and Grace Kredell and Rosa Seidelman, former and current students, respectively, at Wesleyan University, for reading through chapter drafts with a sharp analytical and editorial eye. I have benefited a great deal from stimulating interactions with many Wesleyan students. Their passionate engagement with ideas and politics, both inside and outside the classroom, fuels my hope for a better tomorrow: With much admiration.

This book would not have taken final shape without the critical comments of two reviewers and the enthusiastic support and assistance of my editor at the University of Minnesota Press, Richard Morrison, and his team, especially Adam Brunner and Mike Stoffel. I am also grateful to Pavithra Jayapaul at TexTech International for coordinating the copyediting and typesetting of the book and to Sallie Steele for compiling the index. For making my thoughts publishable: My heartfelt appreciation.

Finally, I am most thankful to my family for their love, spiritedness, and unquestioned faith in me. Champa and Tulsi Das Dhawan (my maternal grandparents), Versha Sharma (my mother), Vijay Dhawan (my uncle), Gaurav Sharma (my brother), and Renuka Chitnis (my sister-in-law) have been extremely influential in shaping who I am and in teaching me about life, warmth, compassion, and integrity. Sushil Kumar Sharma (my father), who so enthusiastically initiated me into this scholarly and political quest, is not alive to see it come to partial fruition. And lest I forget, Anaya and Oorjit Sharma (my niece and nephew, respectively) have forced me to hone my culinary and explanatory abilities. I hope they now know what "protest" means; "governmentality" is next. All I can say to this incredible and musical family of mine is: You rock!

These are the people who nurture and energize me, who let me soar and keep me grounded, and who push me in more ways than I can possibly comprehend or communicate. They are reflected on every page of this book. The errors, however, are mine alone.

Introduction

The Politics of Empowerment

India Enters the World Stage

The cover of the March 6, 2006 issue of *Newsweek* featured the Food TV celebrity Padma Lakshmi, in an ethnically marked outfit and hands folded in a *namaste*, the common Indian gesture of greeting. The captions read, "The New India" and "Asia's Other Powerhouse Steps Out." Inside was an article by Fareed Zakaria titled "India Rising." Written in the wake of the 2006 World Economic Forum held in Davos, Zakaria's article outlined India's economic coming of age and extolled some strategies used by the Indian government to mark their arrival on the world economic stage.

> In the decade that I've been going to Davos, no country has captured the imagination of the conference and dominated the conversation as India in 2006. . . . As you got off the plane in Zurich, there were large billboards extolling INCREDIBLE INDIA. Davos itself was plastered with signs. WORLD'S FASTEST GROWING FREE MARKET DEMOCRACY! proclaimed the town's buses. When you got to your room, you found an iPod Shuffle loaded with Bollywood songs, and a pashmina shawl, gifts from the Indian delegation. When you entered the meeting rooms, you were likely to hear an Indian voice, one of the dozens of CEOs of world-class Indian companies. And then there were the government officials, India's "Dream Team," all intelligent and articulate, and all selling their country. (Zakaria 2006, 34)

Zakaria chronicled the recent economic strides that India has taken and credited many of these not so much to the "dream team" of bureaucrats who were at Davos, but to an entrepreneurial society. He contrasted China's authoritarian growth model, a favorite point of comparison I might add, with India's. Unlike China's efficiently planned development, "India's growth is messy, chaotic and largely unplanned. It is not top-down but bottom-up. It is happening not because of the government, but largely despite it" (Zakaria 2006, 36). The author attributed India's economic miracle to innovative individuals who have discovered their potential, and who have the desire to make money and also the "smarts" to overcome bureaucratic hurdles.

Zakaria set up India's recent economic growth as an example of the struggle of society against the state. He noted that 1947 marked

> the birth of India as an independent state. What is happening today is the birth of India as an independent society—boisterous, colorful, open, vibrant and, above all, ready for change. [India] . . . is not a quiet, controlled, quasi-authoritarian country that is slowly opening up according to plans. It is a noisy democracy that has finally *empowered* its people economically. In this respect India, one of the poorest countries in the world, looks strikingly similar to the world's wealthiest country, the United States of America. In both places, *society has triumphed over the state*. (Zakaria 2006, 37–38; emphasis mine)

Zakaria described society as the driving force behind India's bottom-up development and painted the state as a tedious, obstacle-ridden, overgrown entity that needed to be reformed and rid of both its socialist and corrupt elements. He did not, however, deny that the state had a crucial role to play in India's continued economic success but limited it to providing an enabling institutional environment for the proper functioning of markets, to producing a skilled labor force (through its technology schools), and to addressing the environmental and AIDS crises. Therefore, he warned, "If India's governance does not improve, the country will never fully achieve its potential" (Zakaria 2006, 40).

This *Newsweek* article tells a now oft-repeated story about the economic success of neoliberal India as a battle pitting two giant, yet evidently distinct, entities—the state and the society—in which the latter has finally trumped the former. To be sure, the "society" that Zakaria lauded, is not one billion strong. The visionary and entrepreneurial society that he counterposed to the cumbersome and slow-changing state consists of the estimated three hundred million upper- and middle-class urban Indians whose "can do" spirit is credited for firing the economic engine of their country. It is this society, painted as the ideal civil society, that is viewed as being at loggerheads with the Indian state, and if it were not for the persistence and empowerment of this society, as Zakaria suggested, India would not be as "incredible" as the bureaucrats at Davos claimed it was.

Celebratory narratives about economic liberalization in India often gloss over its underbelly—the over three hundred million Indians who eke out a living on less than a dollar a day on the social, economic, and political margins of the country. The exploitation of their labor has enabled the success of the dominant classes. Their survival, meanwhile, has been rendered increasingly tenuous by the very processes of liberalization that have benefited some.

Postliberalization India looks quite different when seen from the margins of society. Whereas Indian elites and middle classes have gained from economic liberalization, those on the fringes have suffered its spectacular unevenness and inequalities. While the dominant classes have successfully avoided bureaucratic hurdles along the path of economic growth, the subalterns have had to contend with bureaucratic agencies that might be avoiding them. How do those left out or cast out of the successes of liberalization understand and address their marginalization? How do they encounter and interpret the changing faces of the state and governance in contemporary India? Finally, if the upper third of Indian society (in terms of income and wealth) is economically *empowered*, as the *Newsweek* article claimed, what is being done to address the simultaneous *disempowerment* of the bottom third?

This book takes up precisely these questions and narrates less-often-told stories about the state, development, gender, subaltern subjects, and popular protest in neoliberal India. I engage these issues through the lens of grassroots "empowerment."[1] I ethnographically detail the paradoxes and politics engendered by an innovative women's empowerment project undertaken by state agencies and feminist groups in partnership with each other. The program, Mahila Samakhya (MS),[2] is structured as a hybrid "government-organized nongovernmental organization" (GONGO), and aims to collectively empower and mobilize low-caste, rural Indian women who have been actively and systematically disempowered by economic forces and by social and political structures.

Empowerment in the Neoliberal Age

In the contemporary neoliberal era, empowerment has emerged as a keyword effectively replacing the now much-maligned term *welfare*. The former U.S. president Bill Clinton (2006) pointed to this transition in an opinion piece titled "How We Ended Welfare, Together." The erstwhile U.S. welfare system, he wrote, urgently needed overhauling and many "Democrats and Republicans wanted to pass welfare legislation shifting the emphasis from *dependence* to *empowerment*" (emphasis mine). Clinton credited the success of his decade-old welfare-reform bill to bipartisan partnerships, a strong economy, and especially "empowerment policies [that] made a big difference." I am interested in exploring the conceptual sleight of hand by which the "end of welfare" (and of "dependence") becomes coded as "empowerment," and discussing the material, discursive, and political implications of the use of empowerment as a state-driven development policy targeting subaltern women in India.

The recent focus on empowerment is an important part of neoliberal transformations taking place around the world, as states attempt to downsize their welfare bureaucracies and reinvent themselves as streamlined and efficient institutions. Along with economic liberalization, austerity programs, privatization, and participatory governance, empowerment is now an accepted part of development orthodoxy. Various development actors, including international agencies, governments, and nongovernmental organizations (NGOs) working at international, national, and local levels, are scrambling to implement grassroots empowerment programs. The United Nations' Millennium Development Goals (MDG), for instance, featured the need to "promote gender equality and empower women" as a key objective of our times (United Nations n.d.); the World Bank's new "human" face is about poverty alleviation and empowerment (Kahn 2000); the United States Agency for International Development (USAID) is facilitating empowerment programs (Leve 2001); and the Government of India declared 2001 as "Women's Empowerment Year" (Menon-Sen 2001).[3] Tempered by the current emphasis on dismantling welfare, exerting fiscal discipline, and privatizing state services, the neoliberally imagined empowerment logic seeks to enable grassroots actors, and especially women, to fulfill their own needs through market mechanisms instead of relying on state largesse. I analyze how and to what effect the move away from welfare-style dependent development toward empowerment-style self-development has manifested itself in the "gender and development" (GAD) policy regime of the neoliberal Indian state. I use the Indian case to explore what happens when the state, in collaboration with NGOs, implements empowerment as a technology of government (Cruikshank 1999) or "a category of governance" (Chatterjee 2004, 69) and the tensions and unexpected results that follow from such usage.

This book elaborates how the mobilization of empowerment is altering the state and governance, reconfiguring the relationships between state and social actors, transforming development, and reshaping citizenship and popular politics under the regime of neoliberal *governmentality*. Michel Foucault (1991) used the term governmentality to describe an important transition in the aim and modes of governance in Europe from repressive sovereign power that was primarily concerned with control over territory to a form of biopower and rule that is centrally focused on the care and well-being of the population living in a particular territory (Burchell et al. 1991). He drew attention to the entire range of practices and institutions of surveillance and governance, including but not limited to state agencies, which regulate the conduct of a population and direct it toward particular ends (Dean 1999). Following Foucault, I deploy the concept of governmentality to signal the diffusion of self-regulatory modes of governance, such as empowerment, throughout society and the imbrication of varied social actors, including individuals and NGOs, in the project of rule; the state, in this frame, is one among several nodes of governance, albeit a ominant, coordinating one.

Recent scholarship on neoliberal governmentality, which is largely focused on the global North, suggests that neoliberal mechanisms of self-governance, such as empowerment and participation, are reforming the state, rule, subjectivity, and resistance (Barry et al. 1996; Rose 1996).[4] I ask whether these shifts in the technologies and entities of governance follow a standard script everywhere and how an ethnographic study of neoliberal developments in one part of the global South might trouble the taken-for-granted homogeneity of their effects. Some scholars have recently highlighted the emergent nature of neoliberalism, its variegated flows, geographies and dynamics, and its contingent results (Clarke 2007; Ong 2006; Peck 2004). Ethnographies that analyze the workings of neoliberalism in those places where this doctrine is not the general, or even the primary, ethic and where it sits in sometimes teeth-gritting harmony (in the Althusserian sense) with other political projects, situated histories, and ethical discourses are important in that they reveal the nonessentialized nature and contested effects of neoliberalism (Ong 2006, 3–9). An inquiry into the "particular" and the "peculiar," in other words, complicates neoliberalism's so-called universal core and consequences and illuminates the cracks in its purported global hegemony.[5]

It is in this spirit that I undertook this study of the governmental workings of empowerment in a specific postcolonial, liberalizing Southern setting. The tale I tell is not one about a one-way localization, or "vernacularization," of global neoliberalism in India. Instead, I offer a situated look at how transnational neoliberal ideologies of development articulate and jostle with histories of state and subject formation and of popular movements in India, producing a spatially uneven and ambiguous terrain of changes not easily captured by the rubric of dewelfarized states, depoliticized existence, and disciplined, consuming, individuated civic actors. I construct a nuanced picture of how neoliberal globalization mutates state identity and practices viz. development and citizen identity and practices viz. the state, and how these mutations impact governance and grassroots activism in contemporary India.

I approach these issues through a detailed analysis of the structure, practices, and effects of the MS program, a part-state, part-NGO subaltern women's empowerment project. The initiation of MS and of empowerment as a matter of state policy was the outcome of several intersecting factors, including the political mobilization of subaltern groups in India by grassroots organizations and political parties, feminist activism directed at Indian state agencies, Southern feminist debates about gender and development issues, and the transnational circulations of Paulo Freire's radical pedagogy. Interestingly, the launch of the MS program coincided with the liberalization of the Indian economy. Facing a balance-of-payments crisis in 1991, the Indian government, under pressure from the IMF, implemented a strenuous program of economic and social adjustment. Although the market-friendly reforms initiated in 1991 are often regarded as having liberalized the Indian economy, many of the restructuring measures were already under way by the mid-1980s, during the Rajiv Gandhi era (Corbridge and Harriss 2000; Khilnani 1999). The temporal conjucture between the implementation of liberalization policies and the MS program does not, in itself, make MS an archetypal neoliberal program. Indeed, MS can be seen as much as a response *to* the growing contradictions and inequalities of capitalist globalization as a selective manifestation of some ideas that have since been co-opted into the hegemonic neoliberal bundle. Even though MS is not a straightforward reflection of global neoliberalism writ large, it does provide striking examples of how certain development initiatives in India *articulate* with neoliberal principles. My book focuses on precisely such awkward confluences and analyzes their consequences for the reconfiguration of the state, governance, and subaltern subjectivities and activism.

Theoretical Groundings and Departures

This book investigates the politics, practices, and paradoxes of state-cum-feminist sponsored subaltern women's empowerment and development strategies with a critical anthropological and feminist eye. I analyze the discursive meanings and material manifestations of the state, empowerment, development, subaltern women's subjectivity, agency and struggles, and feminist praxis under neoliberalism with insights drawn from political economy, poststructuralist theory, feminist theory, and postcolonial studies. Instead of viewing development, empowerment, the state, and identity as definitive or ontological givens, I interrogate their performativity (Butler 1999) and mutual construction as cultural and gendered products of translocal historical processes. My purpose is not to ask whether development, empowerment, the state, or collective feminist politics are necessary or valuable, but rather to interrogate what these ideas mean in practice and how they are brought to life through everyday actions and interactions.

This book, therefore, is not an evaluation of the success or failure of empowerment-style development programs targeting marginalized women relative to the goals that they set for themselves. Such assessments rest on preconceived notions of what success and failure might look like, how it may be measured, and who might be qualified to make such a judgment. Taking a success or failure–oriented approach also forecloses the possibility of digging deeper into the workings of governmental initiatives and examining their unplanned consequences, even in the face of overt achievement or breakdown. My aim, following James Ferguson (1994), is to examine how empowerment is conceptualized and implemented as a strategy of development and governance and what it does on the ground, and to pay particular attention to the unintended results that follow.

Analyzing the inadvertent consequences of governmental projects also requires avoiding quick and easy "good versus bad" judgments about these effects. Here Foucault's assertion that not everything is bad but dangerous (1982, 231) provides a useful frame for my work. Neither development programs nor empowerment initiatives, regardless of their underlying aims or the nature of the agencies implementing them (i.e., states, NGOs, or feminist groups), are self-evidently good or bad; instead, I argue, these projects carry predictable and unforeseen dangers and provoke bitter and often empowering *political* struggles.

One of the key criticisms of development discourse has been that it depoliticizes poverty by rendering it into a technically manageable problem (Escobar 1995; Ferguson 1994; Harriss 2002). Ferguson closes his study of the operations and effects of the development apparatus in Lesotho by asserting that "since it is powerlessness that ultimately underlies the surface conditions of poverty, ill-health, and hunger, the larger goal ought therefore to be empowerment" (1994, 279–280). I take the neoliberal rearticulation of development-as-empowerment as my point of entry. Is empowerment yet another weapon "in the armoury of the 'anti-politics machine' that is constituted by the practices of 'international development'" (Harriss 2002, 2)? Do the professionalization and bureaucratization of empowerment, as a prepackaged development strategy, represent a depoliticization of poverty and powerlessness? Or can this recent reworking of development orthodoxy be interpreted as an attempt to put power back where it belongs?

These questions get to the heart of the "dangers" and murkiness that empowerment presents. I contend that empowerment is a risky and deeply political act whose results cannot be known in advance; it is "a power relationship and one deserving of careful scrutiny" (Cruikshank 1999, 69). Although empowerment has generally been viewed as a good strategy for political mobilization by leftist and feminist groups, it is also a perilous means of governance in the Foucauldian sense. Under neoliberalism, empowerment has quickly become a preferred tool with which to produce self-governing and self-caring social actors, orient them toward the free market, direct their behaviors toward entrepreneurial ends, and attach them to the project of rule (Cruikshank 1999; Dean 1999; Hindess 2004; Rose 1996). While the neoliberal governmentalization of empowerment can connote depoliticization, I argue that it also makes possible political activism and transformation.

Whether radical or mainstream, NGO or state-implemented, projects that aim to empower subalterns are intrinsically political interventions and sites of contestation and, therefore, full of risks for the various actors involved. In a feminist-conceived GONGO program, such as MS, the women undergoing and facilitating empowerment face the ever-present dangers of state regulation, repression, and recuperation of an alternative feminist empowerment agenda. State actors, however, also face the risk that their initiatives might produce results that are contrary to what they had imagined—that empowerment programs will not bring about the orderly and manageable transformation that officials seek but will generate an uncontrollable excess, bitter opposition, disruptive conduct, and imperfect subjects. These lurking dangers compel us to carefully scrutinize the forms of political action (whether banal or exceptional, individual or collective) that bureaucratized empowerment projects open up and foreclose, and this is what my study undertakes. My goal is to shed light on the messy interplay between depoliticization and repoliticization, surveillance and subversion, and regulation and unruliness in the context of governance projects in India today.

In so doing, I heed Partha Chatterjee's call to postcolonial scholars to "dirty [their] hands in the complicated business of the politics of governmentality" (Chatterjee 2004, 23). Modern governmental systems, he argues, are altering the relationships between those who govern and those who are governed, and these relationships, in turn, are defining "political society" struggles in India today.[6] Chatterjee uses the term *political society* to denote underprivileged groups who do not fit the small, elite domain of lawful civil society "citizens" in India and who are constituted as "target populations" by governmental regimes and administrative classifications. He states,

> Most of the inhabitants of India are only tenuously, and even then ambiguously and contextually, rights-bearing citizens in the sense imagined by the constitution. They are not, therefore, proper members of civil society and are not regarded as such by the institutions of the state. But it is not as though they are outside the reach of the state or even excluded from the domain of politics. As populations within the territorial jurisdiction of the state, they have to be both looked after and controlled by various governmental agencies. These activities bring these populations into a certain *political* relationship with the state. . . . It is to understand these relatively recent forms of entanglements [in postcolonial societies] of elite and subaltern politics that I am proposing the notion of a *political society*. (Chatterjee 2004, 38–40)

Chatterjee contends that depoliticizing governmental acts, such as development, ironically foster political identifications and political society mobilizations. This is a politics driven by entitlements, rights, and governmental regimes and often crosses over into the zone of illegalities.[7] Governmentality, Chatterjee further suggests, "always operates on a heterogeneous social field, on multiple population groups, and with multiple strategies" (Chatterjee 2004, 60). Thus the politics that governmentality makes possible is equally festering and ubiquitous: it is dispersed, multitactic oriented, tied to specific needs and exigencies, and fragile in the sense that victory is not given and endings are not always blissful.

I argue in this book that even though NGO and state-partnered, empowerment-based development interventions have the potential to deradicalize empowerment, depoliticize inequality, and reproduce power hierarchies, they also spawn subaltern political activism centered on redistribution and justice. Whereas neoliberal policies aim to deflect poor people's gazes and demands away from the state and toward themselves, their communities, and other civil society bodies, the use of administrative or governance techniques such as empowerment paradoxically ends up producing a critical practice directed at state agencies; this is a politics of citizenship centered on demanding resources-as-rights from government bodies.[8] In the face of neoliberal orthodoxy, which desires to sculpt dewelfarized states, poor people's activism in India today refuses to let the redistributive state fade away. The state, in other words, is remade from "above" (by neoliberal gurus and state managers) as well as "below" (by subaltern struggles).[9]

My book takes a cultural and transnational approach to delineating how the state is discursively transformed through neoliberal rhetoric and strategies and through grassroots praxis (Sharma and Gupta 2006). A cultural framing of the state means that instead of seeing the state as an already-constituted, known, and unified actor, I examine how its discreetness and singularity is defined through development practices and encounters (Mitchell 1999). In so doing, I build on anthropological analyses of the state, which argue that the state is not a thing but a performative effect or a product of everyday bureaucratic work, people's interactions with officials, and public cultural representations (Gupta 1995; Hall 1986; Scott 1998).[10] Such studies, as Steinmetz (1999b) notes, have refocused attention on questions of culture that were insufficiently addressed within dominant, macrolevel Marxist (Lenin 1943; Miliband 1969; Poulantzas 1973), and neo-Weberian analyses of the state (Evans et al. 1985; Skocpol 1979).[11] Enculturing the state means disaggregating the structural unity and "itness" (Abrams 1988) the word connotes and paying attention to how the state manifests in the daily lives of people through specific policies. Here the work of feminists is helpful. Feminist scholars have laid bare the patriarchal or masculinist (Brown 1995) dimensions of state power through examining the gendered assumptions, operations, and results of different state policies (Alexander 1997; Fraser 1989; Sunder Rajan 2003).[12] I draw upon these studies to analyze the MS program's GONGO structure, practices, dynamics, and effects, thereby illuminating the discursive and gendered aspects of state reformation in neoliberal India.

In addition to viewing the state as a cultural artifact conjured up by routine development practices and encounters, I also approach it as a product of processes that cannot be contained within the territorial boundaries of the nation-state. Locating the state in a transnational frame is imperative in the context of globalization (Ferguson and Gupta 2002; Sharma and Gupta

2006; Trouillot 2003). The apparatuses and instruments of transnational governance, such as structural adjustment, environmental accords, military maneuvers, the international development machinery, and the human rights regime, complicate the idea of nation-state sovereignty (Gupta 1998; Sassen 1998). The boundary-transgressing movements of policies, images, capital, the instruments and ideologies of violence, and people have rendered nations transterritorial and citizenship transnational (Basch et al. 1994; Coutin 2003; Grewal 2005; Ong 1999). They have also upended the bounded sanctity of states and the territorial effectiveness and reach of state work. Using a transnational approach, I delineate how the Indian state is fabricated as a shifting effect of development ideologies that operate both above and below the nation-state frame.

Official and popular imaginations of the state in India are inextricably linked with development. Development provided the basis for the nationalist demand for independence from colonial rule (which had caused the underdevelopment of the nation) and continues to serve a crucial legitimating function for the postcolonial Indian state (Chatterjee 1993, 1998; Ludden 1992). Given this ineluctable relationship, discursive productions of the state in contemporary India simultaneously reference development. The meaning of development in such narratives, however, is anything but fixed.

This book emphasizes the performative and heteroglossic nature of development and argues that it does more than simply regulate and suppress. I have gained much from critical analyses, which contend that development functions as an ideological system of domination that defines norms and identities for the nations and peoples of the global South, thereby exerting control over them (Escobar 1995; Esteva 1992; Sachs 1992).[13] However, such an overarching and one-sided picture of development allows little room for examining how various actors engage with development discourse or how they locate themselves in relation to the identity slots made available to them (Cooper and Packard 1997; Moore 1999; Sivaramakrishnan and Agrawal 2003; Walley 2004).[14] In this book I illuminate how subjects and identities are made, political agency enacted, and the meaning of development debated in the context of everyday development encounters; I do so by putting the critical scholarship on development in conversation with the literatures on performance (Kondo 1997; Turner, 1988), performativity (Butler 1999) and (post)colonial modernity (Bhabha 1997; Chakrabarty 2000; Mitchell 2000).

The story I narrate is not so much about a unified and smoothly-functioning hegemonic development discourse but about contestations, ruptures, and counterhegemonic moves; it underscores the point that the process of maintaining the hegemony of dominant development ideas and hierarchies is bitterly contentious and requires an enormous amount of work. My purpose, therefore, is not to replace a critical narrative about development with a celebratory one, but to ethnographically tease out the tensions, contradictions, redefinitions, and, indeed, suppressions that development work generates on the ground. I underscore the ambivalent nature of development that condenses both emancipatory and dangerous possibilities—it engenders a (political society) politics of citizenship that is, to borrow a term Stuart Hall used in another context, without "absolute guarantee" (1989, 72).[15]

I illustrate how development operates not as a moribund discourse, but as a fecund terrain for argumentation, identity formation, and resignification. Although development is indeed a powerful mode through which subaltern subjects are named and normalized, it also enables counteridentifications. Marginalized actors use the development idiom to fashion themselves as morally upright and deserving citizens, to reflect on their rights, and to criticize and reimagine the state. They not only imbue dominant notions of development with new meaning, but also contest neoliberal ideas about self-interested, entrepreneurial citizenship, abstract rights, and dewelfarized states.

I position subaltern women as vital actors on the political society stage and analyze their critiques of powerful ideologies and agents, and struggles with and for development. In so doing, I heed feminist calls to strategically include subaltern women as subjects of history and, I might add, politics (Spivak 1988a, 1988b). This is an enormously important political project, as Chandra Talpade Mohanty suggests, given that poor "third world" women have been largely depicted within development literature as victims who "have 'needs' and 'problems,' but few if any have 'choices' or the freedom to act" (1991, 64). Furthermore, an analytical focus on the lives of marginalized women, as many feminist activists and scholars have suggested, provides a broad and inclusive perspective on social justice and equality,[16] which is a key motivation for and concern of my work.

The women I write about are not timeless beings, subordinated by equally timeless traditions. Rather, they are historically positioned actors who, given their marginalized locations (in relation to class, caste, gender, and geography, for instance), experience disempowerment, inequities, and injustices in and of the modern, capitalist, governmental world. They are also not unidimensional subjects, whose existence can be captured by the single word *oppression* and whose consciousness, if it exists at all, is *prepolitical*. I view and represent subaltern women as the political actors they are. While undoubtedly subjugated by larger forces, they are not passive and fatalistic beings, who unquestioningly accept their lot and cannot imagine a different present or future. They fight to survive against formidable odds, negotiate oppressive situations, and act to bring about change. It is the minutiae of their daily struggles—the micropolitics of routine critique and resistances, as well as mass mobilization conditioned by modern governmental practices—that interest me (see also Chatterjee 2004; Scott 1985; Susser 1982). I set the everyday and exceptional political acts of subaltern women against the backdrop of powerful translocal projects, putting forth an analysis that links "the micropolitics of context, subjectivity and struggle . . . [with] the macropolitics of global economic and political systems and processes" (Mohanty 2002, 501).

Feminist and cultural theories of subjectivity, especially those that focus on subject formation in the context of (post)coloniality and state policy, guide my endeavor to illuminate the "material complexity, reality, and agency of Third World women's bodies and lives" (Mohanty 2002, 510).[17] Rather than assuming that women come into development programs as preconstituted subjects, I delineate the performativity of gendered subjectivities, which are constituted in conflicting and sometimes inequality-producing ways through statist development practices. Subaltern women's identities are neither rigid, nor singular, nor necessarily cohesive but represent a fluid and morphing amalgam of multiple axes. Women are both positioned by various social relations (such as class, gender, caste, kinship, and age) and discourses (such as development) and also negotiate these hegemonic positionings; it is in this interplay that their identities and subjectivities are defined (Hall 1989). This open-ended and ambivalent process of subject formation, as I show, raises thorny problems for a feminist collectivist politics that is rooted in assumptions of a common (gender) identity and naturalized sisterhood and problematizes any easy notions of the inevitably good consequences of collective empowerment.

Ethnographic Design and Locations

This book is based on more than twenty months of multisited ethnographic fieldwork in India, the bulk of which I conducted between July 1998 and September 1999. My research included an institutional and rural-level study of the practices, micropolitics, and effects of the MS program. This meant interacting with a wide variety of rural, program, development, and state actors. I chose as my primary subjects the women associated with MS: those who participated as clients and those who worked for the program. Although clients and functionaries are differently positioned in terms of their class, education levels, and relationship to development, both groups are affected by their participation in MS; they also play equally important roles in shaping the meanings and forms of empowerment, as I demonstrate later.[18]

The rural component of my research took place in the North Indian state of Uttar Pradesh (U.P.) and was set up as a comparative study of the effects of MS on program participants and nonparticipants. In addition to intensively observing empowerment, development, and gender dynamics in two neighboring villages (one where the MS program was operating and one where it was not) and discussing these issues with the residents, I also visited several MS villages in my fieldwork district. I attended village-, block-, and district-level program activities such as meetings, rallies, and training workshops and through these forums met and conversed with over seventy-five MS participants.[19]

The institutional component of my ethnography focused on the organization and practices of the MS program and was carried out at the national, state, district, and block levels. In addition to observing organizational dynamics in U.P., I also visited MS sites in the states of Gujarat, Andhra Pradesh, and Assam, and conducted important parts of my institutional ethnography in New Delhi, Hyderabad, Lucknow, Jaipur, Mumbai, and Mussoorie. I attended staff meetings, accompanied program functionaries on their daily beats, and observed their interactions with one another and with MS clients. I interviewed, both formally and informally, ninety individuals who were directly or indirectly associated with the program or who worked in the field of gender and development. These included MS staff members at all program levels, program advisors, key representatives from the Indian bureaucracy who oversaw MS and other women's programs, NGO functionaries, prominent Indian feminists, representatives from the Dutch government who initially funded MS, and experts affiliated with the Ford Foundation and the United Nations.

I relied on ethnographic methodologies, such as participant observation, household surveys, and both open-ended and structured interviews.[20] My multisited ethnographic study was enriched by a documentary analysis of a variety of cultural texts on gender, empowerment, the state, and development, including newspaper articles and reports published by international development agencies, the Indian government, the MS program, and feminist NGOs.

The Institutional Setting

Well before the mainstream international development regime took up the cause of empowerment, the Indian government, with Dutch funds and in partnership with women's groups, launched the MS program in 1989 as a pilot project in ten districts of U.P., Karnataka, and Gujarat.[21] MS was inspired by the empowerment vision and innovative methods of the Women's Development Programme (WDP), which began in the state of Rajasthan in 1984.[22] The MS program has since expanded to include the following states: Andhra Pradesh, Assam, Bihar, Jharkhand, Kerala, and Uttaranchal.[23]

MS was initiated with the specific goal of realizing the objectives outlined in the Indian government's National Policy on Education (NPE) (1986). The NPE is considered a landmark document, in that it underscored the integral and dialectical relationship between women's empowerment and education: education was a critical means for women's empowerment, and empowerment was a necessary precondition for women's education and gender equality. MS was designed and implemented under the aegis of the Department of Education (Ministry of Human Resource Development) in order to translate the visions of the NPE into practice. Operating under the banner "Education for Women's Equality," MS regards education

> not merely as acquiring basic literacy skills but as a process of learning to question, critically analyse issues and problems and seek solutions. It endeavours to create an environment for women to learn at their own pace, set their own priorities and seek knowledge and information to make informed choices. (Government of India 1997, 3)

MS aims to empower subaltern women through radical pedagogical techniques that help to engender critical thinking or conscientization (Freire 1970) and antioppression struggles. The program uses empowerment as a means to achieving gender equality, development, and social change. It works with low-caste, primarily *Dalit*, poor, landless, rural women, because they are considered to be the most disadvantaged.[24] MS believes that these women's location at the bottom of the social pyramid acts as a formidable barrier, preventing them from knowing their rights and accessing information about government programs. The program, therefore, views social hierarchies and the ignorance they spawn as the main obstacles to just and equitable development. It envisions empowerment as a collective and ongoing process of knowledge production and struggle whereby women learn to reflect on their situations, take action to address their problems, change their self-image, and redefine themselves as agents of development and social transformation. Although adult women's empowering education is the primary focus of the program, MS also runs village preschools and alternative residential schools for young girls.

The main programmatic vehicles for subaltern women's collective empowerment are village-level *mahila sanghas*, or women's collectives.

> The *Mahila Sanga* [*sic*] will provide the space where women can meet, be together, and begin the process of reflecting, asking questions, speaking fearlessly, thinking, analyzing and above all feeling confident to articulate their needs through this collective action. (Government of India 1997, 7)

All program villages have MS collectives and women's participation in them is voluntary. The sanghas are, for the most part, homogenous in terms of caste. While the bulk of MS participants are Dalits and women from other lower castes, some village sanghas do have upper-caste participants. In rare cases, villages have separate groups for upper-caste and lower-caste women to avoid intercaste conflicts among participants. MS collectives generally meet weekly to discuss and take action on various issues such as wage labor, government development programs, violence, laws, local legislative bodies (and women's participation in them), health, and rights. Since the mid-1990s, MS members have also been involved in peer-group savings and loan activities. Program functionaries support their clients' efforts by providing them with relevant information and training.

In its initial years, the program used the *sakhi* [friend] model for collectivization. This process entailed identifying one or two women in each village who demonstrated leadership qualities and training them to organize MS collectives and to take the lead in addressing local problems. Sakhis were expected to attend MS workshops and share the information received with other program participants. They received a small honorarium of Rs 200 per month for their MS-related work. This model is no longer used in the program. MS now relies solely on the sangha model, in which all collective members play active roles in taking up issues. Each sangha has a core committee of *karyakarinis*—women who work on specific issues such as health, law, environment, labor, cleanliness, literacy, and political participation. The Rs 200 that was awarded to sakhis as monthly compensation now goes to the collective fund and is slated for village development.

The activities of village sanghas are overseen by field-level motivators called *sahyoginis*.[25] Sahyoginis play a crucial role in MS—they are the primary link between the participants and the program—and MS pays special attention to enhancing their capacities. Sahyoginis act as facilitators, trainers, information disseminators, mediators, and liaisons between MS participants and other entities, such as government officials, bank employees, health-center functionaries, and the like. They help collectivize village women and assist them in mobilizing around local problems. Each sahyogini is responsible for ten program villages and periodically meets with village sanghas separately in addition to conducting monthly meetings attended by representatives from all her program villages.

The work of sahyoginis in every block is coordinated by an MS block unit or office. This office is managed by a block incharge, who arranges training sessions and block-level meetings for MS participants. The activities of several program blocks are coordinated by district offices managed by district programme coordinators (DPCs) along with a team of resource persons, consultants, and clerical staff. Above the district offices are the state-level MS offices, which oversee the activities of all program districts and are located in the capital cities of their respective states.[26] State offices are headed by state programme directors (SPDs).[27] All staff members at the block, district, and state levels are drawn from the NGO sector and are not considered government employees.[28] The highest level national office of the program is located in New Delhi. This office is under the direct charge of the national programme director (NPD), who is an Indian Administrative Services officer, an elite-cadre civil servant, within the Department of Education. Support staff and consultants at the national office are, however, drawn from the NGO sector.

The primary responsibilities of the national office include communicating with government departments and donors, managing program funds, ensuring that the program fits within the larger policy framework of the state, and providing programmatic support to the different state-level MS offices. Senior bureaucrats in the Department of Education and a National Resource Group (NRG) oversee the work of the national-level team. The NRG is an advisory body comprising of feminist and development activists as well as academics who are appointed on three-year terms. This group meets periodically to discuss MS program issues, challenges, and future directions. Government officials representing relevant ministries and departments also attend NRG meetings. Whereas the NRG operates as a national body, an Executive Committee (EC) supervises the work in each program state.

EC members participate in administrative and financial decisions (such as approving senior hires and releasing program funds) but are not involved in everyday programmatic strategy decisions. Although the ECs are chaired by the state-level Secretaries of Education and include ex officio representatives, the majority of EC members belong to the NGO and academic sectors.[29]

MS is a part-state, part-nonstate GONGO, or what many of my informants dubbed as a "semiautonomous" organization. While MS is considered a central government initiative whose national office is housed within the Department of Education, state-level programs are implemented by independent, nongovernmental MS Societies that are registered under the Societies Registration Act (1860) of the Government of India.[30] According to the people involved with the initial program design, including feminists, NGO representatives, and government officials, the MS program's semiautonomous GONGO structure was put in place to prevent direct government intervention and to ensure relative independence for its staff.[31]

Many of my informants regarded MS as a one-of-a-kind program when compared to other state-sponsored development initiatives, because of its innovative structure and approach. First, it is not a straight-up government organization. Second, MS recognizes social hierarchies as obstacles to women's empowerment and education, and ultimately to equitable national development. The program's objectives, such as enhancing the self-image of women and strengthening their capacities to act as agents of social transformation, are unique. Third, unlike most other government programs, MS is not a target-driven program but takes a process-oriented, flexible approach to addressing a variety of issues in different locations.[32] MS is guided by a set of inviolable principles, such as accountability of the staff to rural women, decentralized management, and bottom-up participatory planning, which must be adhered to at all program stages (Government of India 1997, 6). Fourth, MS is not a delivery program—that is, MS does not give tangible goods to its participants. Instead, it provides women with information about their rights and government programs and raises their awareness through collective organizing around local issues.

Spatial Coordinates

The bulk of my rural-level ethnography took place in three adjacent blocks in eastern U.P.—Seelampur, Chandpur, and Nizabad—where I accompanied MS employees on their regular field visits to villages and participated in internal program evaluations and was thus able to interact with a large cross-section of MS participants and non-participants. The U.P. plains were an unfamiliar territory for me and I therefore sought the assistance of local MS staff members in choosing a primary program area for my study. Most staff members suggested Seelampur block, where the MS program had operated the longest (for over nine years) and was being phased out in 1998–1999. Basing my research in Seelampur, they felt, would give me a good idea of MS activities and of the changes the program had brought about in the lives of participating women. Moreover, Seelampur was a shorter commute from the city of Begumpur, where the MS district office was located and where I was to conduct a significant portion of my institutional ethnography. I left the selection of particular villages up to these program functionaries as well, explaining that I wanted to work in an MS and a non-MS village (with fairly similar socioeconomic indicators) in order to do a comparative study of the effects of the program. The staff members, after some deliberations (in which I did not participate), chose Nimani, an MS village, and Gamiya, a non-MS village that were in close proximity to each other and a relatively short walk from my place of residence.

Seelampur is an agricultural region. Although paddy is the main crop, Seelampur also grows other grains (*bajra* and *jowar*), lentils (particularly *arhar*), and vegetables (potatoes, peas, etc.). Besides agriculture, weaving is an important activity in the area. Seelampur lies adjacent to important carpet- and silk-weaving centers of eastern U.P., and some residents are involved in home-based handloom production. The total population of the block, according to the 1991 census, was 158,541; of this, Dalits constituted approximately 17.5 percent and women 48 percent.[33]

The main Seelampur bazaar and administrative center lies roughly twenty-seven kilometers southwest of Begumpur. After a sixteen-hour train journey from New Delhi, one has to take a bus from the Begumpur railway junction to reach this area. The buses, run by private contractors licensed by the state transportation authority, are profusely decorated with religious imagery, lights, and Bollywood-inspired artwork, and are usually bursting at the seams with people, grain, vegetables, and other kinds of luggage. These vehicles ply the road connecting Begumpur with Seelampur and beyond at intervals of fifteen minutes and take approximately an hour and a half to reach Seelampur bazaar. The fare depends on who you are. If you are a regular commuter (for eg., a schoolteacher), the fare is Rs 2 each way, an occasional commuter, Rs 7 each way, and if you are a local bigwig belonging to a land-owning, politically prominent, upper-caste family, then you ride for free (the bus conductors dare not ask for the fare). The last category of travelers, as I would discover later, are key participants in what local MS women call the "mafia," consisting of men who embody and represent the daunting nexus between caste status, economic capital, and political power against which MS functionaries and clients struggle (see chapter 3).

The village of Nimani is about one and a half kilometers west of the main Seelampur bazaar bus stop. Nimani, like other villages in the area, is made up of various hamlets, or *bastis*. People belonging to different caste groups, including Dalit, *Thakur*, *Brahmin*, *Yadav*, *Kurmi* [agriculturalists], *Gadariya* [shepherds], and *Naat* [street performers], live in segregated hamlets on both sides of the main Begumpur–Seelampur road. The total population of Nimani, according to the 1991 census, was 1,456; the village chief reported that this number had grown to four thousand in 1998 and an estimated 40 percent of the residents were Dalits. Nimani has three Dalit hamlets. The hamlet in which MS operated lies to the south of the Begumpur–Seelampur road, about three hundred yards behind a well-known local temple dedicated to the Hindu god *Shiv*. A significant part of my village-level fieldwork was conducted here. The total population of this hamlet in 1998 was approximately two hundred and almost all households in this hamlet fell within the government-stipulated "below poverty line" socioeconomic category. A tiny proportion of families owned small pieces of land (which were primarily titled to males). Only four families owned concrete brick houses; the remaining residents lived in one- or two-room mud huts. Most adult male residents were literate, whereas most adult women were not (all younger girls, however, had some formal education).[34] Men were involved in weaving, leatherwork, cattle rearing, petty commodity production, agriculture, and clerical work (at a local bank); some had migrated to cities such as Mumbai and Surat seeking employment as auto-rickshaw drivers and textile mill workers. Nimani's female residents were primarily involved in agricultural activities, working as sharecroppers and agricultural laborers on farms owned by upper-caste families. Some women also assisted their husbands with weaving. In addition, women were responsible for most household tasks, including cooking, cleaning, collecting fodder for cattle, and child rearing.

The Dalit hamlet in Gamiya lies close to the main Seelampur bazaar. The total population of this hamlet in 1998 was listed as eighty-two in government records. The literacy levels and other socioeconomic indicators and the activities of Gamiya's residents were similar to the ones in Nimani. MS, however, did not operate in Gamiya.

Chapter Sketches

This book discusses the changes in governance, development ideologies, subject formation, and political struggles taking place in neoliberal India and uses the prism of women's empowerment to explore these issues.

In chapter 1, I ask what empowerment signifies in the world of neoliberal development. It is among those ideas that "can be interpreted in different ways . . . [and are therefore] particularly powerful in 'policy-making' because they provide a spacious . . . hanger on which those of different persuasions are able to hang their coats" (Harriss 2002, 1). I chalk out a layered picture of empowerment as a translocal assemblage, condensing varied meanings and spatiotemporal histories that articulate in contradictory and unexpected ways. The hegemonic frame I examine is that of neoliberalism, using as exemplary the World Bank's discourse on gender, empowerment, and social inclusion. The three counterhegemonic visions of empowerment that I discuss are those put forward by feminist scholars of development, Paulo Freire, and Gandhi. These various frames, regardless of their underlying ideological premises, use empowerment as a governmental technology in that their purpose is to direct the behavior of individuals and collectives toward certain ends. Thus, even though the means and ends they envision are often divergent, both oppositional and mainstream strategies also overlap. The tense articulations of these varied conceptualizations of empowerment overdetermine the context in which MS works; they make for a fraught dynamic and outcomes that cannot be determined in advance, as I unravel in the remainder of the book.

Chapters 2 and 3 reveal the cultural and gendered logics of state formation and the paradoxical effects of neoliberal governance strategies in India that help to regulate gender norms and identities and to simultaneously unbound empowerment from hegemonic and controlled expectations. The governmental use of empowerment in a state-partnered development program, in other words, works in ways other than to simply governmentalize.

In chapter 2, I tease out the discursive shaping of the developmentalist Indian state, through the lenses of the MS program and the transnational neoliberal doctrine, complicating the latter's purportedly universal effects on state transformation. Specifically, I analyze the MS program's innovative cross-bred GONGO form and empowerment goal, its location within the government system, and its definition of marginalized women as the paradigmatic subjects–objects of empowerment and illustrate how the neoliberal Indian state is imagined and gendered as a demarcated, vertically authoritative, if ambiguously masculinist, body. I examine how the process of state reformation in India both *reflects* hegemonic ideologies of transnational neoliberal governmentality that celebrate participation and empowerment and also *deflects* away. Despite the transition to empowerment, the transformed neoliberal Indian state is not a postwelfare state. Not only does the Indian government continue to implement redistributive programs because of populist imperatives, welfarist ideologies also, ironically, continue to define the supposedly post- and antiwelfare empowerment framework. I detail these welfarist incursions and carryovers and delineate their gendered implications through a discussion of the MS program's placement within the bureaucratic hierarchy and its definition of the women who need empowerment. The prevalence of welfare-based programs and welfarist assumptions in India today, as I contend, is an illustration of postcolonial "exceptions" to neoliberalism (Ong 2006, 4), which problematize the latter's global uniformity.

Whereas chapter 2 focuses on the MS program's GONGO position (as neither wholly in the state nor wholly of it) and its representations of the women it targets to unravel the gendered and discursive nature of state formation, chapter 3 illuminates this further by examining the concrete impact of the GONGO form on the identities and empowerment practices of the women who work for MS. I do this by analyzing the constraints and paradoxes that state participation in MS raise for its staff members and how they strategically use the program's hybrid identity—part-state, part-NGO—to skirt around these very dilemmas. I argue that the GONGO nature of MS gives its functionaries "two hats"—a nongovernmental hat and a governmental hat. They switch between these hats to strategically position themselves against official and subaltern perceptions of the state and NGOs. I narrate a series of ethnographic vignettes, explaining how MS representatives are viewed by their interlocutors and, in turn, position themselves in a shifting manner in different contexts. These instances tell us much about how the state and its putative "other" (NGOs) materialize through everyday MS program dynamics and about the kinds of empowering challenges that are thwarted and facilitated in the context of this government-partnered program. I show that the usage of empowerment as a state-sponsored, governmental, development technique, bureaucratizes the everyday lives of the women involved in the program, but it also unleashes unexpected consequences that are indeed empowering for some women.

Chapters 4, 5, and 6 highlight the disciplinary *and* generative aspects of development discourse. I argue that development is neither a totalizing nor a dead discourse; rather, it operates as an argumentative and productive ground on which different sorts of subjects and communities are engineered, agency articulated, and a politics of citizenship enacted. Although development interventions depoliticize poverty by rendering it into a technically solvable matter, they also provoke popular struggles surrounding redistribution and moral citizenship that are directed at the state. Even as development attempts to create and regulate disciplined individual and collective bodies, it also breeds subversive tactics and unruly subjects who protest their subjectification and subjection, who test the state and unbound it from its presumed limits, and who resignify development.

Chapter 4 illustrates the performativity of development and subject formation. Written in the form of a two-act play, this chapter reenacts a development encounter between MS clients, program functionaries, state officials, and World Bank experts in Nimani village. I demonstrate how everyday development encounters operate as reality shows or social dramas where developmental identities, hierarchies, and norms materialize and are subverted, actors are fashioned, dominant scripts are enacted and improvised, and different meanings of development and modernity are proliferated. In scripting this development event as a drama, I unmask development's positivist and mimetic logic, highlighting ethnographically its disciplinary under- and overtones. I also, however, revisit questions of subaltern agency. Unlike antidevelopment critics who assume that the real agency of marginalized people lies in rejecting development, I argue that subaltern struggles are not antidevelopment or antimodern per se; rather they repudiate dominant meanings of development and enunciate discrepant modernities.

I carry these themes forward in chapter 5, where I focus on the trope of *failure*, which was frequently used by state and subaltern actors in their discussions of development. Instead of viewing "arrested development" as a point of closure, however, I use it as a point of entry into analyzing what these widespread narratives about failure enable. I argue that official and subaltern stories of development's breakdown are a form of highly antagonistic, public, and moral "citizenship talk," which explains and criticizes power inequalities, articulates mainstream and oppositional notions of rights and national belonging, and redefines proper statehood and personhood. Although these hegemonic and counterhegemonic narratives share a common conceptual grid—that of development—I pay special attention to their dissonances. Officials blame the failure of redistributive development programs on poor people's lack of maturity, of knowledge, of discipline, and of self-motivated entrepreneurialism; meanwhile, subaltern actors explain it as a matter of official error, cunning, and dishonesty. Officials code self-reliant development as the moral responsibility of common people who have failed in that task and are, therefore, undeserving of rights-bearing citizenship. Subalterns, in contrast, see development as the moral duty of the state. They invoke ethical discourses to contest the socioeconomic inequalities in which they are embedded, to criticize the corruption and self-centeredness of powerful and developed people, to rightfully demand that the state redistribute concrete resources, and to position themselves as morally upstanding, deserving citizens. This, I suggest, is a remoralized form of citizenship politics that attempts to resolve the tensions inherent in the neo/liberal meanings of the term *citizenship* and that contests the ideas of privatized states and dewelfarized development. Subaltern talk and political practices thus put forth alternative, ethically imbued, and experientially grounded understandings of citizenship, personhood, the state, and development.

In chapter 6, I delve into the complex relationships between development, gendered subjectivity, and community. I problematize mainstream and critical analyses of development that view idealistic communities as engines of either development or antidevelopment alternatives. Both these perspectives assume that communities precede development and are essentially homogenous bodies made up of individuals who share identities and interests. In contrast, I demonstrate that modern, governmental practices, such as development, do not act on or confront a tabula rasa—*the* community—but engineer contingent and contentious collectivities. I retell a series of incidents surrounding an issue that the MS women's collective in Nimani village took up—that of building a government-sanctioned village-council house-cum-women's center. This proposition, which was seemingly universally beneficial and not simply "prowomen," turned out to be controversial and brought out class- and kinship-based fissures between MS and non-MS women and among MS women. I use these tensions to critically analyze the assumptions that guide the MS program's focus on collective empowerment. The program mobilizes low-caste women *as women*, on the presumption that their identities are alike, that they constitute an organic community, and that they will, therefore, stand in solidarity with each other. Gender identities, however, are anything but monolithic or necessarily cohesive; rather, they are a shifting and context-specific ensemble of multiple, intersecting axes and are shaped and brought together in contradictory ways by administrative practices, such as development. MS, as I show, inserts itself in this open-ended and already fraught process of identification, altering gender identities and relationships on the ground and instituting new affiliations and hierarchies. The complexities of subject formation and the conditional, ad hoc nature of communities in the context of development makes the MS program's strategy of collectivization—which presumes that women already know their gendered interests, act in accordance with these interests, and automatically struggle against gender subordination—risky and without necessarily happy endings. I use the Nimani case to examine the ambiguous implications of collective feminist transformation that is based on a similarity of identity, not difference . And I ask what an "ephemeral" feminist politics that is attentive to the provisionality of identity and community and that *forges* commonality and solidarity through struggle might look like.

I conclude this book by knitting together the various threads of my story about empowerment and development, the state and governance, neoliberalism and its articulations, subjects and subjection, feminist activism, and grassroots politics. I weave in current events in India, ethnographic vignettes, and popular cultural snippets to highlight the paradoxical workings and uneven, unpredictable, and dangerous effects—both enabling and limiting—of neoliberal governmental mutations and discuss their implications for popular struggles in the postcolonial world.

1

Empowerment Assemblages

A Layered Picture of the Term

State involvement as a key player in women's empowerment in India can be dated back to 1984 when the government of Rajasthan implemented the Women's Development Programme (WDP). WDP had empowerment as its explicit goal and was structured as a tripartite partnership between the government, NGOs, and academic institutions. WDP provided a blueprint for MS, which was launched by the Indian government in 1989 as a pilot project in three states, including U.P.; both programs also shared some key personnel.

The Indian state's turn toward women's empowerment as a desired development strategy and goal is the cumulative result of multiple and intersecting local, national, and transnational processes. These include (1) the rise of peasant, Dalit, Gandhian, leftist, and women's movements around issues of equal rights, citizenship, ecology, land redistribution, and political participation in postcolonial India; (2) the failure of state-initiated modernization strategies to alleviate poverty and address growing inequalities; (3) an increase in the number of NGOs during the late-1970s, including those doing empowerment work; (4) the personal initiative of powerful individuals within the government to blaze a different kind of development trail; (5) the relative success of nonformal education and adult-literacy campaigns in mobilizing women to lead struggles such as the antialcohol movement in the state of Andhra Pradesh; and (6) national-level feminist interactions with state agencies, such as those resulting in the passage of the seventy-third and seventy-fourth constitutional amendments that reserve one-third of the seats in local-level legislative bodies for women.

Supranational forces have also shaped this transition to empowerment. The ideas of Paulo Freire (1970) and of regional feminist groups, such as Development Alternatives with Women for a New Era (DAWN), for instance, have influenced the Indian government's agenda for women's education and empowerment and the MS program specifically (see also Townsend, Porter, and Mawdsley 2004). Feminists working in the field of development played a significant role in globalizing empowerment as a favored strategy for promoting gender-equal and just development. Their ideas have since been reinflected, appropriated, and operationalized by international agencies such as the United Nations (UN) and the World Bank.

Empowerment has become a ubiquitous term and a buzzword in transnational development circles, whose meanings, deployments, and consequences are anything but self-evident. An anti-imperialist, radical, leftist, and feminist language that arose out of social movements, empowerment has now been embraced as a panacea—a means and an end of development—by governments and powerful institutions such as the World Bank. Often articulated as a progressive strategy of activism and resistance, empowerment is also a technology of neoliberal self-government that alters the terrain, modes, and actors of governance, including states (Cruikshank 1999; Dean 1999). Empowerment is therefore linked with a wide variety of ideas and practices, including radical politics, persistent action and reflection, just and liberatory social change, development, participatory and decentralized governance, self-regulation, self-esteem, and self-actualization. The term condenses multiple meanings; it is reinvented and practiced in different institutional settings and in different spatial and historical locations by variously positioned actors.

In this chapter I paint a layered picture of empowerment that captures its collage-like, ad-hoc, and also purposeful, quality. Empowerment is a shifting formation and flexible technology of government rather than a singularly coherent discourse and method. Empowerment, I propose, is a "translocal assemblage." By *translocal* I mean something that is both situated (but not locked in place) and formed in articulation with processes that transcend and crosscut various spatial and temporal registers. I use the term *assemblage* to refer to a conjunctural and evolving ensemble-like formation, which results from the intersections of various ideas and institutional practices (Collier and Ong 2005). An assemblage is made up of heterogeneous elements that are not necessarily internally coherent but are brought together for specific strategic ends (Li 2007, 264).[1] Empowerment, as a translocal assemblage, is such a grafted and changing package of institutions, strategies, goals, and ideas, which is continually remade through transnational circulations and articulations with different histories and cultural formations.

Empowerment was not invented by international organizations such as the UN or the World Bank. Thus, it is not a transnational discourse that gets geographically localized in a straightforward one-way manner. Indeed, the prevailing mainstream global discourse on empowerment is an effect of other, second-order transnational circulations of empowerment ideas. This dominant neoliberal discourse, espoused by agencies such as the World Bank, recuperates and re-spins feminist and social movement dialogues on gender, development, and empowerment. What has become globally hegemonic, then, is a product of complex spatial articulations of varied notions of empowerment. This hegemonic ideology in turn jostles with regionally and historically disparate understandings of empowerment to produce complex and uneven results. Here the meaning of empowerment is as open-ended and unpredictable as the on-the-ground effects of empowerment strategies in particular places. Not only the spatiality, but indeed the very "temporality of an assemblage is emergent. It does not always involve new forms but forms that are shifting, in formation, or at stake" (Collier and Ong 2005, 12).

In this chapter I discuss important counterhegemonic and hegemonic framings of empowerment that have influenced the larger context in which women's empowerment initiatives, such as the MS program, operate. The counterhegemonic concepts I elaborate on are those espoused by feminist scholars of development (whose ideas are entwined with leftist doctrines of mobilization), Paulo Freire, and Mohandas K. Gandhi; and I show how they have inspired the MS program. I then examine empowerment's recent neoliberal avatar, using as iconic the World Bank's discourse on social inclusion and women's empowerment. Finally, I overlay the different temporal and spatial framings of empowerment and analyze how a radical concept that has been understood to shape and be shaped by activist subjects struggling for social change and political liberation in counterhegemonic optics has been absorbed, albeit not without tension, in hegemonic projects that seek to sculpt entrepreneurial, economic "mainstream" actors.

Both counterhegemonic and hegemonic usages of empowerment are, following Foucault (1991), governmental, in that they aim to produce aware and active subject-citizens who participate in the project of governance and to mold their behavior toward certain ends; they all, therefore, involve both subjectification and subjection (Cruikshank 1999). Where these projects diverge is in the kinds of subject-citizens they seek to mold, through what means and institutions, and toward what particular ends. The fissures between the various uses of empowerment open up different possibilities of political action, which I pursue in the remainder of this book.

Empowerment as a Counterhegemonic Idea

Feminist Frames

Empowerment was firmly tabled on the development agenda by feminists. Regional networks of feminist scholars and activists, such as DAWN, used UN-sponsored Cairo (1994) and Beijing (1995) conferences to circulate their ideas among the wider development community.[2] In this section I describe the shifts in feminist frameworks of development that enabled empowerment to emerge as a favored strategy and goal.

Since the 1970s the development world has witnessed some important changes in how women's issues have been conceptualized—from welfare-based frameworks through productivity-focused approaches to empowerment-based strategies. To put it slightly differently, the development paradigms have shifted from the welfare approach to women in development (WID) to gender and development (GAD). These paradigms offer different points of entry into analyzing and addressing women's concerns within development.

Initially women were effectively written out of the dominant modernization paradigm of development. Real development in this model concerned economic growth and market-oriented productive activity; it was about and for men. Women's concerns within development were relegated to the welfare sphere, which defined women according to their reproductive roles as wives and mothers and positioned them as vulnerable, dependent beneficiaries of development charity (see Kabeer 1994; Razavi and Miller 1995; Young 1993). Welfare was itself viewed as a residual and feminized category within the modernization model (see chapter 2). Placing women's issues in this sphere not only emphasized their epiphenomenal status to serious development but also furthered naturalized biologically deterministic notions of gender identities and roles and reinforced an essentialized hierarchy between productive and reproductive work.

This thinking dominated the development field until 1970, when Ester Boserup (1970) showed how modernization had not only ignored but actually harmed women in Asia and Africa. Her work made women's issues visible within the mainstream development arena and inaugurated the WID approach. WID scholars, drawing upon Western liberal feminist ideas, criticized modernization theory's mismanagement of women (see Jaquette 1990; Tinker 1990). Against the welfarist focus on women's reproductive roles and putative passivity, WID theorists highlighted women's productivity. They argued that women were efficient and rational economic actors whose full potential must be tapped for growth; women's inclusion in development would result in an efficient allocation of resources and was a sound economic strategy. While WID did not replace welfare-based ideas or approaches, it shifted the logic for investing in women from need and dependency (welfare) to economic efficiency (merit) (Kabeer 1994; Razavi and Miller 1995). In the 1970s and 1980s WID advocates stressed equal access to education and employment and inaugurated microcredit and income-generation programs for women. The goal behind these strategies was to provide women with skills training and resources so that they could realize their productive potential and become active contributors to and beneficiaries of the modernization efforts of their nations.

WID provided a valuable corrective to the field of development by highlighting how modernization policies had marginalized women and why this subverted the larger goal of growth. However, WID advocates did not unpack the basic paradigm of modernization. They took the ethnocentric and androcentric definition of development as Western-modeled economic growth for granted and used efficiency-based rationales for integrating women into this paradigm. WID strategies did not question the kind of development that women were being asked to contribute to (Kabeer 1994; Moser 1993) and this became a key rallying point for GAD advocates.

GAD criticisms and alternatives arose in the mid-1980s, just as the UN Decade for Women (1975–1985) was ending. Sen and Grown's (1987) classic work, which examined the effects of a decade-long WID programming on poor women's position and status in the global South, can be seen as a turning point in feminist theorizing about development. Building on socialist and Third World feminist ideas and dependency theory (Frank 1969), Sen and Grown argued that WID's integrationist approach had not worked because the paradigm of modernization was fundamentally flawed. The issue was not that women had been excluded from an otherwise beneficial and benevolent process of development but that development, defined narrowly in terms of capitalist modernization, was itself problematic, in that it exacerbated inequalities between nations and between genders, classes, and races. Sen and Grown espoused a feminist-oriented, margin-centered vision of development, connecting it to questions of peace and equality, and argued for a society free of all systems of intra- and international domination.

Sen and Grown's work initiated GAD theorizing. Besides challenging mainstream definitions of development, GAD proponents critiqued WID thinkers for focusing exclusively on women's productive capacities; such a move, they argued, did not challenge hardened welfarist notions about gender identities and roles or about gendered work spheres, and perpetuated the higher valuation of productive work. GAD advocates also contested WID's narrow definition of "women" and argued for a shift to "gender" as a social relation of inequality that took into account women's multiple identities and issues (Kabeer 1994; Moser 1993; Overholt et al. 1991; Razavi and Miller 1995). Furthermore, GAD feminists redefined development. Kate Young, for example, contended that development should be about meeting people's physical, emotional, and creative needs, increasing standards of living, and ensuring a more equal distribution of wealth (1993, 136). Naila Kabeer (1994) argued that "reversed" development must begin from the perspective of the most marginalized and place human life and the enhancement of human well-being and creativity at the forefront. According to Kabeer, production needed to be organized around human needs rather than around market mechanisms because the market was not the most efficient allocator of resources (1994, 83–85); the state, she thus averred, had a key role to play in the area of poverty alleviation and development.

Despite subtle differences in their precise visions of a different regime of development, overall GAD feminists seemed to agree that social inequalities, especially gender hierarchies, were a major hurdle in the path of just and equitable development. Empowerment, they concurred, was an ideal strategy for undoing hierarchies and instituting broad-based social change. Significantly, empowerment connoted a shift away from both old-style welfare and WID-based development policies.

"Empowerment," writes Jo Rowlands, "is nothing if it is not about power—and therefore is a fiercely political issue" (1998, 28). How did GAD advocates conceptualize power, disempowerment, and empowerment? Kabeer differentiated between the powerful and the empowered, arguing that those "who exercise a great deal of choice in their lives may be *very powerful*, but they are not *empowered* . . . because they were never disempowered in the first place" (2001, 19). In a move not unlike the one made by Frank (1969), who distinguished between *un*development and *under*development, Kabeer viewed disempowerment not as an original lack but as the outcome of oppressive forces. Empowerment, thus, concerned overcoming disempowerment and the related inability to make strategic life choices, and challenging unequal power relations.

Much of GAD work used the following classificatory scheme for describing the various modes in which power operates in society: power over, power to, power within, and power with (Batliwala 1994; Kabeer 1994, 224–229; Kabeer 2001; Oxaal and Baden 1997).[3] Briefly, "power over" implies a relation of domination and subordination, such that the life choices of certain people are limited by the actions of others; "power to" indicates the capacity of people to make strategic decisions about their lives; "power within" speaks to the awareness among individuals and groups of how power works and the hierarchies it creates in society and also to their capacity to change the status quo; and finally "power with" references collective organizing based on common goals and interests (Oxaal and Baden 1997, 1). Women's empowerment meant addressing all these modes of power, at the levels of the self, the collective, and society.

However, what constituted women's "common" interests around which they were supposed to mobilize? Here Maxine Molyneux's (1985) work on practical and strategic gender needs and interests proved influential.[4] Using her analysis, GAD feminists argued that empowerment approaches needed to especially (although not solely) address women's strategic gender interests; this implied challenging women subordination through gender and other systems of domination, which would lead to emancipatory outcomes.[5] Empowerment required critically analyzing (both individually and collectively) multiple oppressions, raising consciousness, building solidarity from the ground up, and organizing challenges to entrenched systems and modes of power.

GAD proponents thus envisioned empowerment not as a predetermined, economically defined end point, but as a politically charged *process* of awareness raising and struggle to transform power relations; this process had to be contextually specific and open-ended. Empowerment strategies "must perforce be devised within specific political, economic, social and cultural contexts, regionally, nationally, and locally. This entire process is . . . tentative and experimental . . . [and] it is improbable that there can ever be only one path to empowerment" (Batliwala 1994, 67). Additionally, they stressed that empowerment must be an organic process undertaken *with* women, and not a blueprint strategy imposed on them or something handed to them. "We need to move away from any notion of empowerment, and perhaps even development, as something that can be done 'to' people or 'for' people" (Rowlands 1998, 30). These feminists thus raised the issue of the "how" of empowerment. How were marginalized women to be mobilized to struggle against gender and other forms of subordination? Did empowerment require outside empowering forces, and if so, what sort of interactions needed to take place between those facilitating and those undergoing empowerment? Here Paulo Freire's work provided some answers for GAD feminists and for MS program planners as well.

Freire and Conscientization

The Pedagogy of the Oppressed (Freire 1970) exerted a substantial influence on development activists and scholars, especially those working on education and grassroots empowerment issues. In this text Freire laid out the rationale and methodology for a broadly conceived empowering education that would help the oppressed to become acutely aware of the various systems of subordination and to emancipate themselves and their oppressors through persistent struggles for humanization. This was a project of liberation based on developing a participatory pedagogical praxis "*with*, not *for*, the oppressed . . . in the incessant struggle to regain their humanity" (Freire 1970, 30). Freire argued that no one understood oppression better than those who were most marginalized and thus any struggle for liberation ought to begin from their perspectives (a point that GAD feminists also emphasized). "The conviction of the oppressed that they must fight for their liberation is not a gift bestowed by the revolutionary leadership, but the result of their own *conscientização*" (1970, 49). Because they are enveloped in domination and because they identify with the oppressor, Freire posited, the oppressed "have no consciousness of themselves as persons or as members of an oppressed class" (1970, 28); they are also afraid of the repression that anti-oppression activism may cause. "To surmount the situation of oppression, people must first critically recognize its causes, so that through transforming action they can create a new situation, one which makes possible the pursuit of a fuller humanity" (1970, 29). Thus, it was only through the process of critical "conscientization" undertaken by oppressed groups that revolutionary change could occur.

For Freire a liberatory pedagogy involved constant "reflection and action upon the world in order to transform it" (1970, 33). The oppressed, individually and collectively, needed to reflect upon and recognize their lived realities of alienation and oppression; they then had to collectively intervene in and transform these unjust realities. He detailed an active, intersubjective process of transformation that required altering self-perceptions and changing the society in a dialectical process. Ultimately, when transformation sets in, the pedagogy of the oppressed becomes "a pedagogy of all people in the process of permanent liberation" (1970, 36).

What then was the role of outsiders in this grassroots-level, ongoing process of transformation? Freire argued that liberatory change must emerge from the oppressed and those who stood in solidarity with them. "Solidarity requires that one enter into the situation of those with whom one is solidary; it is a radical posture. . . . [T]rue solidarity with the oppressed means fighting at their side to transform the objective reality. . . . [It is] an act of love" (1970, 31–32). This process had to be a dialogic one, whereby those who stood in solidarity with the oppressed did not give them one-way, "bank deposit" types of explanations of oppression or dictate how to bring about change in a top-down manner; so doing would reduce the oppressed to an object status and would be counterrevolutionary. Outside "converts" had to go through a process of "profound rebirth" (1970, 43) and implement a self-reflexive praxis to support the oppressed as trusted comrades, learners, and cocreators of revolutionary knowledge.

Freire's ideas of empowering education undertaken with the marginalized, such that their concrete situations became the starting point of critical reflection, dialogue, and change, are a critical part of GAD feminist frameworks of empowerment and the MS program. Most obviously, MS embodies the critical connection that Freire made between empowerment and education. Initiated under the banner "Education for Women's Equality," MS was designed to help realize the Indian government's goals regarding women's education, set forth in the 1986 National Policy on Education (NPE). The NPE viewed education and empowerment as a prerequisite to undoing women's marginalization from education (Jandhyala n.d.). MS, a Department of Education program, carried this thinking forward. One program document describes the situation of poor rural women as follows:

> [Women's] well-defined social roles and norms of interaction leave little room for education and critical thinking. [G]oing about their chores in isolation, they are unable to share their experiences of oppression with other women, and are therefore unable to tap their collective strength. [T]hey are denied access to information and alienated from decision-making processes. . . . As a result of these factors, women are caught in a vicious, self-perpetuating cycle; their inability to educate themselves perpetuates the stereotype that education is irrelevant to women. (Government of India 1991, 1–2)

To break this cycle of marginalization, the MS program actively uses Freirian principles of collective conscientization, whereby women critically reflect upon their oppressive situations and struggle for emancipation. Empowerment is a pedagogic process that facilitates a transformation of both the self and society. The MS program also unhinges education from literacy and sees education as a key tool for engendering awareness about subordination and struggle: "the concept of education is much broader, and is based more on general awareness-raising, critical analysis of social, economic and political structures, and acquiring empowering knowledge" (Batliwala 1994, 55). Here both the content and method of education matter. The content has to be relevant, arising from the lived experiences of the women. The ideal method of conscientizing subaltern women is collective, dialogic, supportive, and horizontal. The process of empowerment also involves stimulation by external forces (Batliwala 1994, 25). These agents of change, especially field-level MS workers, called *sahyoginis* [friends or partners], are seen as critical nodes in the empowerment process and as sources of information and support.[6] Such facilitators, in MS and other empowerment projects that build upon GAD and Freirian insights, must be respectful of the experiential knowledge of the subordinated; they should also open themselves to learning from marginalized women and critically reflect upon their own methods of mobilization lest they reinforce structures of domination (Batliwala 1994, 49–66).

Translating Freire's radical ideas into a development program, such as MS, however, is not easy. First, outside leadership is a thorny issue. Although empowerment, following GAD frameworks and Freirian notions, is viewed as a self-defined and self-generated process of change, empowerment initiatives often rely upon external agents to induce and assist the process of conscientization. To what extent the facilitators working for the MS program are able to play the ideal supportive role envisioned for them while avoiding the pitfalls of dominating leadership is a question that I address later in the book.

The second key complication with implementing empowerment concerns achieving a workable balance between open-ended definitions and strategies, on the one hand, and instating measurable indicators of empowerment, which donors demand, that necessarily bring some closure and rigidity. The issue is how to give concrete content to Freire's flexible pedagogical praxis and to empowerment, such that the latter can be quantifiably demonstrated, without compromising on contextual sensitivity and adaptability. Srilatha Batliwala lists the following fundamental components of women's empowerment based on the experiences of programs in South Asia:

(i) Creating critical consciousness (including of the self);
(ii) Access to knowledge and information; (iii) Developing new

> skills; (iv) Collective or organisation-building; and (v) Alternative educational opportunities (especially for women and girls). (1994, 63)

She further emphasizes that empowering knowledge concerns acquiring information about "fundamental rights, legal literacy, public policies and schemes" (Batliwala 1994, 55), which increases women's awareness of how existing power structures operate and how they can be made to work for alternative ends. It entails tutoring women in leadership, management, decision making, bureaucratic procedures, and tactics of resistance, which will transform individual behavior and community relationships besides altering the workings of state institutions. Moreover, conscientization of women needs to result in tangible changes, such as an increase in informed choice-making at family and community levels; an improvement in self-image; an increased awareness of rights and entitlements, which can be recorded and used as evidence of an empowerment program's success—MS activists fully recognize that some of these changes are difficult to quantify.

Gandhi and Self-Rule

The usage and sway of grassroots empowerment and decentralized development and governance in contemporary India cannot be seen as simply a translation of transregional feminist ideas or a localization of Freirian insights. They are, rather, a complex result of the articulation of these translocal forces with local historical trajectories and deployments of similar terms. In India one cannot speak of grassroots empowerment without referencing the work of Mohandas K. Gandhi. His concepts of self-rule, individual upliftment, bottom-up and decentralized governance, and a locally defined just and moral social order have defined the terrain on which social movements and NGOs in postcolonial India operate. MS is not a Gandhian program, and yet, as a grassroots empowerment initiative, it cannot avoid the wider influence of Gandhi.[7] I now analyze how the program's vision and strategies of bottom-up empowerment sit with Gandhi's ideas.[8]

Hind Swaraj, written by Gandhi during his South African days, laid the foundation of his counterhegemonic pedagogical project of creating moral persons and establishing an independent, self-sufficient home rule. This philosophical treatise offered a trenchant critique of modern civilization and civil society (Chatterjee 1986a). It expounded a utopic and locally relevant (although not entirely indigenous)[9] vision of an ethical and just free society premised on the notion of *swaraj* [self-rule] and attainable through the practice of *satyagraha* [the struggle for truth, or passive resistance]. While this text did not explicitly theorize the state, it defined, as I show below, an alternative art of governance to the one then dominant in the West, whose fundamental difference lay in its moral content and spatial conception of rule.

True swaraj, for Gandhi, meant economic, political, and moral freedom, which could only be achieved through a complete rejection of the economic, legal, and political structures of modern civil society (Chatterjee 1986a). He argued against those nationalist leaders who believed that Western, liberal institutions and ideas were basically good (insofar as they enabled the British to achieve their dominance) and should be retained even as the British themselves needed to be expelled. Gandhi dismissed exchange- and consumption-based modes of production that relied upon markets and upon competitive, self-interested, and profit-seeking individuals. He rejected the abstract rationality of modern law and legal institutions, arguing that they were immoral and unjust because they perpetuated inequalities in the name of legal equality. He also dismissed the modern system of representative rule, which, in theory, enabled people to participate in governance, but, in fact, only allowed them to "do so through the medium of their representatives whose actions have to be ratified only once in so many years" (Chatterjee 1986a, 90). This system distanced rulers from their subjects, thus institutionalizing an "abrogation of moral responsibility" on the part of the rulers (Chatterjee 1986a, 91). What India needed, in order to be truly independent from enslavement, was to expel these institutions.

Moreover, swaraj could only be attained when people used satyagraha as a guiding principle and as personal and political practice (Gandhi 1997, 95–96). Satyagraha entailed noncooperation. Governance, Gandhi maintained, required the acquiescence of the governed; however, if they pledged to disobey colonial structures and strictures that were inimical to self-determination, they would fundamentally challenge and destabilize colonial rule. "We cease to co-operate with our rulers when they displease us," declared Gandhi (1997, 95). Satyagraha implied refusing to obey man-made laws that were unjust and that supported the interests of the powerful. It meant not doing that which was "repugnant to our conscience" (1997, 91).

True swaraj did not connote English-style rule carried on without the English (Gandhi 1997, 27–29) but implied a fundamental reconceptualization of rule. "It is swaraj," wrote Gandhi, "when we learn to rule ourselves. . . . But such swaraj has to be experienced by each one for himself" (1997, 73). Swaraj, thus, was a self-making project that cultivated a moral person who exercised self-control over *his* (Gandhi only used male pronouns) mind and body and pursued the path of truth.[10] Because it was a pedagogic process that involved self-transformation, one did not have to rely on others to establish a *swaraji* society. Indeed, such a just and free society would be realized through each individual governing her or his conduct according to local moral principles and following the tactic of passive resistance or love/soul force (which Gandhi counterposed to brute and violent force or repressive power).

In emphasizing the role of the self in rule, Gandhi delegitimized government *over* others. Rule, ideally, did not involve taking over the reins of government but concerned ensuring the happiness and welfare of all and could be achieved through self-governance (Gandhi 1997, 76–77). The ideal model of such a decentralized rule, according to Gandhi, was *ramrajya*—a moral, benevolent patriarchy, where the ruler, in following the moral path of truth, embodied the collective will of the people, thus rendering representative institutions unnecessary (see Bose 1997; Chatterjee 1986a). For Gandhi, this constituted an "enlightened anarchy," a stateless society made up of individuals and communities regulating themselves in accordance with communal moral principles (Chatterjee 1986a, 92). State institutions were superfluous in such a system because "each person will become his own ruler" and "will conduct himself in such a way that his behavior will not hamper the well-being of his neighbors" (Gandhi, quoted in Chatterjee 1986a, 92).

The village occupied a central place in Gandhi's imagination as the locus of truth and freedom. The goal of swaraj, he emphasized, was the uplift and reconstruction of rural India, which remained uncolonized by the immoral forces of modernity. In a letter to Nehru, dated October 5, 1945, Gandhi wrote, "I am convinced that if India is to attain true freedom . . . then sooner or later the fact must be recognised that people have to live in villages, not in towns, in huts, not in palaces. . . ." (Gandhi 1997, 150). Home rule would be meaningful only if it improved the condition of villagers (1997, 70). Gandhi promoted a self-contained, self-sufficient village-based moral economy where people produced primarily for their own consumption and broke their dependence on the market. The village was also the locus of governance. Real swaraj meant decentralizing power in society and giving villages the authority to rule and defend themselves through morally driven cooperation.

But whose duty was it to uplift villages? According to Gandhi, the state was not the ideal entity for undertaking such a task. The proper role of the state, in fact, was to "abdicate its presumed responsibility of promoting 'development' and thus clear the ground for popular non-state agencies to take up the work of revitalizing the village economies" (Chatterjee 1986a, 115).[11] The project of social development needed to be shouldered by dedicated, upstanding, and selfless nonstate volunteers (Chatterjee 1986a, 120). Although *Hind Swaraj* essentially detailed an individual project of self-transformation that would result in a social movement for just social change and that did not require leaders per se, Gandhi later emphasized the need for principled people who could lead the masses down the path of emancipation (Chatterjee 1986a). Real civilization "means 'good conduct' " (Gandhi 1997, 67) directed toward moral ends and achieved through *satyagrahi* practices, and true satyagrahis would lead by setting personal examples for others to follow. Civil disobedience, as explained in *Hind Swaraj*, was a key tactic for attaining self-rule and one that could be used by anyone. However, after observing the troubled ground-level mobilization of this tactic during the agitations surrounding the Rowlatt Act in 1919, Gandhi stated that "he only is able and attains the right to offer civil disobedience who has known how to offer voluntary and deliberate obedience to the laws of the State in which he is living" (Gandhi, quoted in Chatterjee 1986a, 105).[12] Thus, one had to first become a subject of law and of the state and submit to these institutions in order to refuse further subjection. Those individuals who fully comprehended the workings of the state and the oppressive nature of top-down governance were identified as the leaders of satyagraha. Therefore, even though Gandhi's idea of self-governance focused on the role of individuals regulating their everyday practices and behavior according to moral principles, it also retained a notion of trusteeship and tutelage whereby certain individuals could guide this process of self- and social change through their acts and knowledge.[13] This knowledge was not one grounded in rationality and scientific reason but in the local moral universe.

Real knowledge and education, asserted Gandhi, concerned learning to exert proper moral control over the mind, will, senses, and desires; it was patently not about "a knowledge of letters" (Gandhi 1997, 101), acquired through formal schooling. Gaining literacy would not "add an inch" to the happiness of peasants and would only make them "discontented with [their] cottage or [their] lot" (1997, 101).[14] True knowledge, instead, was experiential and gained through personally observing ethical principles on a daily basis. This form of knowledge, unlike its secular counterpart, would enlighten people and enable them to do their duty, and had to be transmitted in local languages (1997, 100–106). Moral education would integrate individuals into the collective ethos of the community, rather than alienating them from it (Chatterjee 1986a, 92).

How does MS engage with Gandhi's ideas of empowerment? The program detaches literacy from education and builds on Freirian and Gandhian concepts of education as a broader process of awareness raising.[15] Its vision of empowerment also articulates with the Gandhian notion of swaraj, in that the program defines empowerment as a simultaneous process of change at the levels of individual subjects and society, which is contextually defined and relevant. MS also stresses the collective nature of this dialectical and ongoing process of self- and social liberation; individual change can only occur through collective conscientization.

This conscientization not only requires raising rural Dalit women's awareness about how unequal social structures subordinate them, but also rests on giving them information about state agencies, laws, and rights. Here one notes a departure from Gandhi, who rejected modern institutions and practices as a means to self-empowerment. Even though he later averred that knowledge of these institutions, laws, and procedures was important for movement leaders, he also maintained that true liberation could not, ultimately, come about through such knowledge. Gandhi was firmly opposed to liberal, rational laws and abstract rights, shorn of their moral content; real rights, for him, did not *precede* duties (as they are envisioned in liberal law) but flowed *from* the "performance of duty" (Gandhi 1997, 82). MS also trains women in the art of petitioning the government for their entitlements and rights. Petitioning, as a method of demanding redress and holding state institutions accountable, was a tactic that Gandhi was uncomfortable with. Whereas petitions did serve an educative purpose in that they informed people about their situation of enslavement and served as a means to "warn the rulers" about the oppressive and unjust nature of their rule (Gandhi 1997, 85), they were limited in scope unless backed by the force of love and by the capability, on the part of supplicants, to suffer fearlessly without being awed by the face of power (1997, 21–22). MS uses peaceful tactics of resistance, such as *dharnas* [sit-ins], a form of passive resistance that Gandhi endorsed. In addition, it relies upon training women, not so much in disobeying laws, but in using available bureaucratic means for demanding justice.

A key part of the MS program's vision is to empower subaltern women so that they can participate in the processes of governance; they are also meant to make government institutions democratic and accountable. Such an education of women, which arguably prepares them to become proper and better-integrated members of civil society, is not what Gandhi had in mind when he wrote about self-rule and rural uplift and reconstruction. His alternative social development project, one with strong pedagogic elements, could not be undertaken by a top-down entity such as the state, but by other social actors. MS, interestingly, is a part-state and part-NGO project, which purports to combine the state's greater resources and reach with the bottom-up participatory techniques of nonstate actors. One thus sees in MS a selective incorporation of Gandhian ideas of self- and social change and a simultaneous engagement with other discourses of empowerment and participatory governance. The program also operates in a context where empowerment has become a mainstream neoliberal technology of governance and development; I now turn to this hegemonic framing of empowerment.

Empowerment as a Hegemonic Idea: Neoliberalism and the World Bank

Contemporary neoliberalism, David Harvey suggests, is premised on the notion that

> human well-being can best be advanced by liberating individual entrepreneurial freedoms and skills within an institutional framework characterized by strong private property rights, free markets, and free trade. The role of the state is to create and preserve an institutional framework appropriate to such practices. . . . It holds that the social good will be maximized by maximizing the reach and frequency of market transactions, and it seeks to bring all human action into the domain of the market. (2005, 2–3)

The neoliberal doctrine views the market is the ideal arbiter of resources and the harbinger of social good and dictates that the state must minimize its interventionist role. Thus, all social welfare programs need to be dismantled because they distort the working of the market and hamper the development of free and autonomous subjects who help themselves by participating in the market rather than relying upon state charity. The proper functioning of the market depends upon and contributes to the making of empowered, entrepreneurial selves, who, by simply pursuing their self-interest and governing themselves, can enhance the well-being of societies as a whole.

It is in the construction of appropriately "liberated" and "aware" individuals and in the privatization of state responsibilities, such as welfare, that empowerment enters the neoliberal picture as a key governmental technology (see Cruikshank 1999; Dean 1999; Hindess 2004). Strategies of empowerment, self-help, and self-esteem are a critical part of the neoliberal development package in that they enable the actualization, to a greater or lesser extent, of the goals of free market, good governance, democracy, and the rule of law and rights.

The languages of empowerment, self-help, and self-esteem, which emerged out of social movements and critical feminist practices (Cruikshank 1996, 238), now function as neoliberal "liberation therapy" (1996, 233) that fashions rights-bearing, entrepreneurial personhood. Barbara Cruikshank proposes that democratic governance has always relied upon strategies that seek to construct new kinds of individuals, who freely subject themselves to citizen-making projects (1996, 247). Empowerment, self-esteem, and self-help are the newest technologies, which help to mold individuals into responsible citizen-subjects who fit the requirements of the prevalent governance regime and who participate in the project of rule by governing themselves. The neoliberal doctrine of limited, small, and participatory government is premised on decentralized power and self-regulating citizens who are not coerced to follow certain regimens but voluntarily submit to a "tutelary power" (Cruikshank 1996, 234), such as a social worker, a program, or a therapist, because it is in their self-interest to do so (see also Rose 1990). Thus "women are convinced to participate in their own 'empowerment' without threats. Governance in this case is something we do to ourselves, not something done to us by those in power" (Cruikshank 1996, 235; Rose 1990).

The neoliberal doctrine links a transformation of the self with a transformation of society. This focus on the inward, individual self is not so much a subversion of collective politics or of the feminist dictum "personal is political," but a new terrain and style of politics that links the personal and social in novel ways (Cruikshank 1996, 236). Here the pursuit of self-interest, individual fulfillment, and self-government are viewed not only as personal goals but as social obligations practiced in the interest of political freedom, participatory democracy, and the free market (1996, 232). Once individuals are taught how to enhance their self-esteem through empowerment techniques and learn to properly govern themselves, it is believed, society will automatically be rid of the ailments that plague it. For instance, poverty, under neoliberalism, is not understood as a consequence of unequal political-economic and social structures, but as a symptom of improper subjectivity and individual failure (see Goode 2002); self-remaking, therefore, constitutes an ethical and democratic attack against such individual and social ills (Cruikshank

1996 and 1999; Rose 1990). Furthermore, confronting poverty, powerlessness, and other lacks is not the job of the state, but the duty of individuals who have been properly inculcated in the ways of the market and political institutions and who have the ability to enact their citizenship in a responsible manner. The material benefit of this logic lies in rearranging the activities and shrinking the costs of an interventionist welfare state. The World Bank's discourse on empowering deprived groups and including them into market-led development exemplifies this neoliberal logic.

The World Bank, Social Inclusion, and Women's Empowerment

Environmental, social, and gender concerns took center stage at the World Bank in the mid-1990s, as it began promoting itself as an entity doing sustainable, people-centered, and equitable development, and working to uplift marginalized groups, such as women and indigenous communities.[16] James Wolfensohn's (1997) speech to the board of governors, "The Challenge of Inclusion," is seen as momentous, for it laid out the World Bank's reworked social development agenda (Serageldin 1998). Fighting poverty and including those at the fringes of societies into the "economic mainstream" were defined as the most serious development challenges, which required integrating social and human concerns into economic development packages (Wolfensohn 1997, 1–4). Whereas poverty alleviation has been part of the institution's core mission since the McNamara years (Finnemore 1997), Wolfensohn effectively incorporated the language of empowerment and inclusion in this mission.[17] "Under the leadership of its visionary president, James D. Wolfensohn [1995–2005], the World Bank has embarked on an effort to mainstream its concern for culture in its drive for poverty reduction, empowerment and social inclusion" (Serageldin 1998, 1).

Women were recognized as a key fringe group that needed to be empowered. "No society has progressed without making a major effort at empowering its women through education and the end of discrimination" (Serageldin 1998, 2). The World Bank lagged behind other international organizations in embracing women as key actors in development, only establishing a "Women in Development" division in 1987 (Murphy 1995). It released its first major WID report in 1994, which, not surprisingly, advocated an instrumentalist approach to women's issues: it used the liberal feminist language of WID to argue that investing in women was the most efficient route, in terms of costs and benefits, to achieving broader development goals (Kardam 1991; Murphy

1995). Thus, educating women was good because it reduced fertility, which, in turn, spurred economic growth (Kardam 1997, 139). Since the mid-1990s, the focus of World Bank shifted away from "women" and it attempted to mainstream "gender" within all of its work.[18]

By 1995 the platform of "gender and empowerment" gained prominence within international development circles, thanks to the work of feminists who circulated their ideas through international conferences. Wolfensohn spoke at the Beijing conference in 1995, endorsing empowerment as an important policy strategy and recognizing the centrality of women to development. "I need no persuading that women are absolutely central to sustainable development, economic advance, and social justice. . . . All the evidence tells us that not to empower women is a tragically missed opportunity—not only to create a more just, but also a more prosperous society" (Wolfensohn 1995). In 1997 he went on to delineate the World Bank's new development paradigm as one of "sustainable development that is people-centered and gender-conscious, that seeks equity for all and empowerment of the weak and vulnerable everywhere so that they may be the producers of their own welfare and bounty, not the recipients of charity or aid" (Serageldin 1998, 4). By 2001 the World Bank had adopted empowerment as a "key pillar" of its development work (World Bank 2001, 7), which demonstrated the institution's commitment to the UN-declared Millennium Development Goals (of which the third is to "promote gender equality and empower women").

In 2002 the World Bank published "Empowerment and Poverty Reduction: A Sourcebook," which reiterated the importance of empowerment: "empowerment enhances development effectiveness . . . through its impact on good governance and growth" (Narayan 2002, 1). This publication defined empowerment as "the expansion of assets and capabilities of poor people to participate in, negotiate with, influence, control, and hold accountable institutions that affect their lives" (Narayan 2002, vi). Rather than viewing itself as one of the "problem" institutions that people might desire to hold accountable, given the disempowering results of policies such as structural adjustment programs (SAPs), the World Bank positioned itself as a problem solver and a key node in empowerment, given its "comparative advantage" in the field of poverty reduction.[19] The institution's comparative advantage flowed from "its relationship with more than 100 governments around the world. [Its] comparative advantage is, obviously, not to work at the community level but to advise governments" (Narayan 2002, 8). The World Bank has since endorsed a collaborative, alliance-based approach to development, which rests on the "full participation of all stakeholders that must be part of the decision making process: the international, regional, national and local governments, the private and public sectors, the civil society and the international agencies, with special attention to the role of women and the empowerment of the poor" (Serageldin 1998, 3). Even though the World Bank promotes participatory development in which the civil society is a key player, it continues to operate on the usual governmental principle that sees the state as the primary and neutral entity for bringing about desired development (see Ferguson 1994). This is in contradistinction to many feminist analyses that view empowerment as the domain of grassroots organizations and not of states or of the World Bank (Kabeer 1994; Moser 1993; Oxaal and Baden 1997; Sen and Grown 1988). Furthermore, what exactly the World Bank means by "international governments," how they are different from "international agencies," and which category it sees itself as belonging to on its list of empowerment "stakeholders" is not readily apparent.

Putting a human face to its much criticized economistic approach and adopting a feminist language of women's empowerment do not represent a decentering of the dominant neoliberal market model of development that the World bank has consistently followed since the 1980s, but can be seen as an attempt to give this model a social and ethical spin (see also Bergeron 2003). This is clearly an important rhetorical move, which has allowed the institution to respond to and incorporate critics from within and without and to label itself as a progressive organization doing legitimate, much needed work.[20] The World Bank now sees social and cultural factors as important "variables" in development: they hinder women's participation in markets and economic growth and need to be overcome for more optimal and efficient outcomes. Bergeron contends that this expanded social mission allows new fields of intervention for the World Bank: "By including social factors (but only those that directly affect capitalist markets), the Bank is widening the scope of its analysis and intervention into the developing economies. It is also attempting to depoliticize the concerns raised by women's social movements . . . by positioning them as clients of development and objects of expert administration" (2003, 164).

These new social concerns get translated through the institutional prism and priorities of the World Bank and the expert-oriented economic model of development that it has always used. This is apparent in the new $24.5 million Gender Action Plan unveiled by Paul Wolfowitz, 2005–2007 president of the organization, which seeks to promote women's economic empowerment because that "is smart economics . . . and a sure path to development" (World Bank 2006b). Wolfowitz claimed that

> Although we see women front and center in areas such as education and health, we need more of it in those areas that support shared economic growth—such as infrastructure, finance, private sector development and agriculture. These are critical areas: women's ability to benefit from investments in roads, energy, water, extension and financial services will profit not only women, but also men, children and societies as a whole, as economies grow and poverty is reduced. (World Bank 2006b).

Whereas one would be hard-pressed to argue against the idea that women need to be included in the processes and benefits of infrastructural and agricultural development, what is interesting is how Wolfowitz conceived of empowerment, economic growth, and women's roles in them. The sectors that drive economic growth are clearly not education and health, but infrastructure, private sector, finance, and agriculture from which women are implicitly excluded; thus the work of women peasants, for example, is immediately erased. Once these critical sectors of growth are defined, women need to be included in them. This is a restatement of the World Bank's WID-derived logic that views women as key means of *economic* development and makes economic efficiency–based arguments to integrate women into development. Indeed, empowerment itself is viewed as economistic and instrumentalist. Accordingly, women need economic empowerment, such as increased access to land, labor, and credit markets, because this will promote real economic growth; moreover, this strategy is economically sound and makes business sense for the World Bank. Women's empowerment is seen as a tool to foster gender equality, which, in turn, shapes the outcomes of development. Development, under this logic, remains firmly tied to economic growth achieved through market mechanisms. In fact, a recent World Development Report clearly states that "making markets work in more gender-equitable ways can significantly raise women's productivity and incomes and contribute to economic growth" (World Bank 2006a).

Women's empowerment is also judged in terms of quantifiable economic success. Thus a key strategy laid out in the new Gender Action Plan is to "improve knowledge and statistics on women's economic participation and the relationships between gender, equality, growth, and poverty reduction"

(World Bank 2006b). More research on how gender inequalities impede economic growth is necessary, but by the same token, women's empowerment projects also need to concretely prove, through statistical evidence, that they indeed make economic sense and help promote growth and reduce poverty. Empowerment, in other words, allows the World Bank to conduct its business as usual, but in a more efficient and apparently social conscious way.

Layerings and Articulations

Hitherto I sketched out four empowerment frames, which stem from different ideological perspectives and arose out of diverse spatial locations and historical moments. These frames are critical to understanding what empowerment means within the world of development today and how it is mobilized on the ground. If empowerment can be seen as a translocal assemblage, then it is important to analyze how its various layers and meanings articulate. I now examine what overlaying the counterhegemonic and hegemonic frames of empowerment reveals about their commonalities and differences.

I want to reiterate that the frames I have delineated so far use empowerment as a *governmental* technique. Whether used as a strategy to engender feminist social transformation, to enable a Freirian liberatory struggle against oppression, to establish a Gandhian order of moral self-rule, or to solve poverty and reduce big government through neoliberal market emphases, empowerment has the overall goal of shaping certain kinds of subjects and remaking society (see also Cruikshank 1999). The disparate ideological framings of empowerment rest on the active participation of subordinated peoples in the project of governance to make it more equitable, just, participatory, and efficient. Even though neoliberal approaches focus more on individual entrepreneurialism and de-emphasize the dialectical relationship between self and society and between the individual and the collective, which is precisely what counterhegemonic frames highlight, they all view technologies of the *self* as a form of *social* intervention. Both counterhegemonic and hegemonic initiatives of empowerment seek to mold behavior toward certain ends and are, therefore, governmental projects. Where these frames diverge, however, is in terms of the social subjects they want to create and the kind of "end" society they seek to establish, and thus in their vision of what empowerment is and how it should come about.

GAD feminists, Freire, and Gandhi define empowerment both as an end in itself and as a revolutionary means to founding a different kind of society. GAD advocates seek an equitable society, free of all social hierarchies, where individuals are able to fully realize their creative potential and make strategic life choices that maximize their well-being and that of society as a whole. Freire's liberated society is also one free of domination, where the oppressor and oppressed roles are not reversed but done away with and where liberatory pedagogy, grounded in lived experiences, is practiced on a continuous basis. Gandhi envisioned an independent, self-sufficient, and self-governing society founded upon collective moral principles. Justice, equality, and agency in the form of liberation of and by the oppressed seem to be the common threads that tie together the various counterhegemonic visions of a new social order. They also envisage a fundamental structural change of social relations and institutions that perpetuate domination and subordination.

The hegemonic neoliberal model is aimed at creating a free, democratic, and participatory society, rid of social inequalities, as well; yet freedom here is defined in narrow individualistic, economic (i.e., the freedom to participate in the market), and political terms (i.e., limited government and people's unforced involvement in representative democracy). There is no questioning of the inherent goodness of economic, political, and legal systems as they exist in the democratic, modern West. However, it is considered imperative that states alter their role so as to allow the unhindered functioning of the market, guarantee property rights and the rule of law, and ensure that individual citizens take part in the institutions of representative democracy.

The market and the state are indeed the very institutions that are opened up to serious inquiry in counterhegemonic frames. GAD feminists critically analyze the inequalities promoted by the market and contend that the main role of empowerment strategies is to challenge the dominant market-oriented and economic growth–based development paradigm. They argue that the market cannot be relied upon as a means to ensure the most equitable social outcomes. Whereas these advocates do not suggest entirely doing away with the market, they challenge its self-regulating character and argue that the market is not the ideal distributor of goods or enhancer of welfare. Thus, Kabeer (1994) claims that production decisions need to be based on human needs and on increasing human well-being and capabilities rather than on market rationality, and names the state as an important player in this process. GAD feminists also recognize that the state aids and abets gender and other hierarchies. According to Batliwala, "the state, with its administrative, legislative and military arms, becomes [an] instrument by which a given power structure sustains and perpetuates its control over society" (1994, 19); the state directs many of the "structures and institutions through which the unequal control and distribution of resources is sustained, and the ideology of dominance perpetuated" (1994, 68). Whereas the neoliberal doctrine espoused by the World Bank sees the state as a key stakeholder and partner in women's empowerment programs, GAD feminists are more cautious in their approach. Moser, for example, directly questions state involvement in women's empowerment programs, arguing that although the state has the wherewithal to provide for women, it also controls them "either directly through legal means, or indirectly through its control over institutional structures and planning procedures. That has shown only too clearly the limitations of both its political will and its ability to confront fundamental issues of women's subordination" (Moser 1993, 191). If the state is part of the oppressive apparatus that empowerment seeks to undo, then GAD feminists' skepticism about its "enabling" role in empowerment makes sense; GAD advocates concur with Freire's contention that it "would be a contradiction in terms if the oppressors not only defended but actually implemented a liberating education" (Freire 1970, 36).[21] Even though there is debate among GAD feminists over whether an entity that helps to perpetuate inequalities can be an ally in women's empowerment and liberation (see chapter 2), there also seems to be some consensus that the state needs to participate in equitable and peaceful development. This requires that state institutions alter their policy priorities to reflect these goals and play a role in the "social management of the market" (Elson 1988) and in social provisioning (Kabeer 1994). Unlike neoliberal ideologies, therefore, the GAD feminist approach does not write off either redistribution-focused development or the state's responsibility to ensure collective well-being and justice through appropriate redistributive policies.

Gandhi, on the other hand, was more obviously opposed to modern state structures and their role in development. Where neoliberalism lauds modern rational legal institutions, Gandhi viewed the abstract rationality and equality of secular law as patently unjust. Where neoliberalism sees empowerment as a mechanism to expose marginalized people to market discipline, Gandhi was against the founding principles of modern markets (such as selfish individualism, limitless consumption, and profit-based exchange). For him, true self-rule and freedom from enslavement meant disengaging from the market model and creating a new, self-sufficient, self-governing moral order. He saw social development not as the duty of the state but of voluntary nonstate actors.

At first glance the neoliberal rhetoric of the World Bank seems to endorse, albeit awkwardly, Gandhi's idea that the government cannot solve social problems of inequality, but people can. Could it be that neoliberal gurus today are talking the same talk about self-rule, self-help, and decentralized government as Gandhi did nearly a hundred years ago? Might this be an example of an insidious appropriation of a radical strategy by a mainstream organization or of a "perverse confluence" (Dagnino 2005, 158)? Whereas both the World Bank and Gandhi use self-rule as a means to transform governance and diminish the state, I argue that Gandhi's vision of distancing the formal institutions of government (such that they become unnecessary for self-rule) and narrowing the role of the state in social development and uplift (indeed its complete absence) is radically different from the neoliberal version of small government-at-a-distance (Rose 1996). The latter notion of decentralized and participatory rule, while seemingly attenuating governance, in actuality knots together distanced social entities in a tighter fashion with formal state apparatuses (Barry et al. 1996). It also seems to retain a pyramid-like, vertical spatial configuration of rule, where the state lies at the apex but partners with civil-society actors and spreads governmental mechanisms throughout society. Gandhi's imagination of self-rule, in contrast, was bottom up, concentric, and expansive. He thought of society and rule in terms of aggregative circles at the center of which lay the village, encircled by the *taluka* [block], then the district, and so on and so forth (Chatterjee 1986a). Each circle was "self-reliant in its own terms, no unit having to depend on a larger unit or dominate a smaller one" (Chatterjee 1986a, 121). Furthermore, Gandhi's model of enlightened anarchy, based on morally charged and self-directed rule by individuals and communities, meant that state structures were ultimately unnecessary for governance, economic production, welfare, and even defense. Anything less would be unjust. This radical (and radial) decentralization of rule, where the state and representative government are rendered irrelevant and governance is re-embedded in communal morality, is quite different from the model of limited democratic governance that neoliberalism celebrates. The neoliberal doctrine sees a noninterventionist state that does not hamper the free working of the rational market and privatizes its development functions. Like current neoliberal orthodoxy, Gandhi too advocated for the state's absence from social development. However, his argument cannot be read as a laissez-faire opposition to state intervention (Chatterjee 1986a); it does not converge with the neoliberal imperative for rolling back the state in the interest of unhindered market operation. Gandhi's vision of governance was firmly grounded in local moral worldviews, which neoliberalism erases, and not in the abstract and rational logics of the market and the state, which neoliberalism endorses. If, according to Gandhi, the state needed to stay out of social development, it certainly could not play a role in grassroots empowerment; empowerment was best left to the people.

How are empowerment and disempowered subjects conceptualized in the various frames I have outlined? Empowerment initiatives do not simply target already constituted group of people, but in fact define these groups (see also Cruikshank 1999). Where counterhegemonic projects seek to create political agents of just, equitable, and moral change, who are trained in the arts of resistance, mobilization, and self-governance, neoliberalism attempts to fashion self-regulating entrepreneurial citizens who know how to function properly in a free-market society. It aims to institute precisely the self-interested, consumptive, competitive, profit-motivated, rights-bearing "homo-economicus" model of personhood that counterhegemonic approaches reject.

Counterhegemonic strategies focus on subaltern subjects who are marginalized, oppressed, or enslaved. They see these subjects as leaders of struggles because their position at the very bottom of society and experiences of multiple oppressions gives them a more expansive perspective on justice or because, as in the case of Gandhi, they are relatively untouched by the forces of modernity and therefore offer alternative models of living and being. However, the three counterhegemonic frames I discussed earlier also display some ambivalence on the issue of leadership and the need for external facilitators. For Gandhi, at least initially, the path of truth, self-rule, and autonomy was one that each person had to walk on their own, using the moral constraints of the society in which they lived as their guides. And yet, later, he emphasized the need for good, upright, selfless leaders, who set examples that other could follow. For Freire the oppressed have to lead themselves and others toward liberation; however, outsiders can stand in solidarity with the oppressed. GAD feminists seem to follow Freire's message and emphasize the need for facilitators who can support the struggles of subaltern women. The World Bank documents I analyzed make no specific mention of outside motivators; interestingly, however, they position the World Bank as a leader in the field of empowerment, given its "comparative advantage."

Counterhegemonic frames view marginalized actors as disempowered, but not powerless. *Disempowerment* is a term that is deliberately used by GAD feminist to emphasize the active processes of subordination carried out by people in positions of dominance and by social, political, and economic structures; this is precisely the element that neoliberal discourses of empowerment write out (see also Cruikshank 1999, 73). Empowerment, under current neoliberal orthodoxy, becomes a benign and programmatic way to train improper and deficient subjects in the ways of the market and civil society and to include them in these institutions. No mention is made of the willful roles that powerful people and institutions play in the disempowerment and subjection of those on the fringes or of the kinds of awareness raising such oppressors might need in order to address their own privilege. Rather, neoliberalism paints a naturalized picture of poverty and powerlessness, where certain people lack the requisite attitudes and means to become rational, economic agents; the solution, therefore, is to supply them with those means and outlooks so that they can contribute to economic growth by helping themselves out of poverty. This represents the tautological thinking whereby some people are poor because they are powerless and they are powerless because they are poor; hence empowerment becomes an obvious and obviously depoliticized, bureaucratic solution to both poverty and powerlessness.

The insertion of the languages of social inclusion and empowerment in the rhetoric of the World Bank, as I argued earlier in this chapter, does not represent a turn away from its economistic conception of development. It is, instead, an example of an "add social issues and mix" strategy whereby tackling social problems becomes important insofar as it enables economic growth. The World Bank, following WID rationales, values both women and empowerment because it sees them as ideal and important tools for achieving efficient and speedy market-centered growth. This also means that empowerment can be specifically defined and measured in terms of its concrete contribution to economic growth. Thus statistics on women's literacy, labor force and informal sector participation, share of earned income, participation in governance institutions, and so on, become "proxy" indicators of empowerment (Malhotra, Schuler, and Boender 2002) and evidence of the success or failure of empowerment initiatives over time.[22] This bureaucratic, quantifiable approach to empowerment negates one of the basic premises of counterhegemonic frames that empowerment is not a fixed point of arrival but ongoing processes of struggle for liberation, equality, truth, and justice. In fact, GAD feminists argued against the very instrumentalist notion of women's empowerment that the World Bank assumes and implements. Rather than seeing empowerment as a quantifiable thing, a universal strategy, or an expert-defined top-down blueprint for change, they stressed its processual, contextual, and self-defined character.

The very term *empowerment* condenses contradictions: between empowerment as individual transformation and empowerment as collective mobilization for change; between empowerment as locally defined, open-ended struggle and empowerment as an expert intervention packaged into a development program that promises to deliver emancipation; between empowerment as a ground-up, organic course of action and empowerment as something that is externally induced by facilitators; and between empowerment as contextual and processual and therefore not measurable by universal standards and empowerment as singularly quantifiable. These are tensions that even nonmainstream, feminist empowerment initiatives, such as the MS program, are unable to completely resolve. Despite their commitment to *collective* conscientization and political activism, and thus their marked distinction from the neoliberal focus on *individual* economic uplift, programs such as MS cannot avoid the general spread of discourses of individualism and unintentionally end up engendering conflicts between their clients (as I show in chapter 6). Even though these alternative projects define empowerment as a sui-generis process undertaken by oppressed actors, their reliance upon outside motivators who can raise awareness, albeit through solidarity-based mechanisms (Freire 1970) or moral means (Gandhi 1997), complicates both the agency and the role of subaltern actors in self-directed change.[23] Using outside change agents means that hierarchies and some elements of top-down planning can enter into even radically envisioned empowerment initiatives (see chapters 3 and 6). Furthermore, whereas such programs emphasize their bottom-up orientation, as externally funded development projects they also have to work with donor priorities and other institutional strictures, which limit the scope of flexibility that they can exert. MS, for instance, explicitly takes an open-ended, process-oriented approach to subaltern women's empowerment and resists defining empowerment according to stringent criteria. But the program's involvement with state agencies and foreign donors has meant that empowerment measures, such as literacy statistics, have crept into the program. Many MS staff members I spoke to complained about this mainstreaming of empowerment and recognized the risks of increased bureaucratization. It is not only the MS program that faces these dangers; other grassroots NGO empowerment efforts that are supported by outside donors have to mold empowerment to cater to funding-agency demands as well. Thus if empowerment is defined as women's increased access to credit, then an emphasis on microcredit programs with measurable success becomes important; and if it is defined as an increase in women's employment, then a focus on quantifiable women's income-generation projects becomes crucial. The mainstreaming and predominance of the language of empowerment within the current regime of neoliberal development means that empowerment is increasingly evaluated according to universal standards set by international development institutions and not autonomously by groups working on the ground. This entails a flattening of the complexities that empowerment is supposed to imply. These are the realities and risks that empowerment programs in today's neoliberal climate, regardless of their ideological orientations, face and have to negotiate.

Conclusion

Empowerment is a contradictory terrain; it is an emancipation tactic that doubles as a technology of government and development. Various empowerment projects, therefore, "share a political strategy: to act upon others by getting them to act in their own interest" (Cruikshank 1999, 68). Regardless of whether it is implemented as an expert bureaucratic program or as a radical project for self- and social liberation, empowerment is firmly political. It denotes relationships of power as well as powerful acts of self-formation and collective struggle. Hence empowerment is neither self-evidently good, nor bad, nor neutral, but dangerous. As a layered translocal assemblage, it encompasses a wide range of definitions, strategies, and actors. Empowerment, as a concept and in its ground-level manifestations, is the resultant and shifting effect of the agglomerations and articulations of various meanings and practices produced by disparate social actors in different institutional and geographical sites. Even a cursory reading of this ensemble reveals its tension-ridden nature.

The complex conjunctions of Gandhian, feminist, Freirian, and neoliberal discourses of self-rule, awareness raising, conscientization, and self-reliance, and the multiple understandings of empowerment they espouse shape the field, workings, and outcomes of Indian empowerment initiatives such as the MS program. If the definition of empowerment, its ground-level implementation, and its evaluation or measurement are themselves sites of contestation, as I have shown, then the results of empowerment mobilizations are equally fraught and not given in advance. The remainder of this book examines the tensions, micropolitics, and effects of a feminist-cum-bureaucratic usage of empowerment as a *means* to uplift subaltern women and establish a just and equal society, and an *end* unto itself.

2

Engendering Neoliberal Governance

Welfare, Empowerment, and State Formation

On a sunny morning in November 1998, I accompanied a team of MS staff members to the block office in Nizabad, a paddy-growing region of the state of Uttar Pradesh (U.P.).[1] Meena Rani, a field-level MS employee, led the group in its mission to introduce the program to local government officials and to garner their support.[2] The block office was abuzz with activity as it was a Friday, the scheduled day for weekly meetings between the block office staff and residents, when they discussed and resolved local development issues. A clerk navigated us through clusters of people and showed us to a sparsely furnished room. MS staffers got busy hanging program posters as we awaited the arrival of the administrators.

Not long after, two women and a group of men joined us. The women were local residents, who came to attend the MS presentation. The men included the block development officer (BDO), Sukhdev Singh, his assistants, and a few elected officials. After brief introductions, the MS team began its presentation with a song describing women's participation and responsibilities in local elected bodies, such as the *panchayat* [village council].[3] The theme of the song had been chosen with care. MS representatives had decided to sing nonconfrontational songs when introducing the program in mixed-gender settings, because songs that directly invoked gender inequality or women's rights might alienate men. Sukhdev Singh nodded approvingly as the women sang. Meena Rani then invited the BDO to describe the steps his office had taken to address the needs of poor women in his block. Singh told us that these women needed income-generating skills and literacy. Earlier, his office had arranged for training in midwifery and vegetable pickling under the government-run Development of Women and Children in Rural Areas (DWCRA) scheme.[4] However, the participating women had failed to transform their newly acquired skills into income-generating work. "It is [the women's] responsibility to do the work," the BDO complained, shaking his head with disappointment, "and not the government's responsibility. But they are not doing [anything]. That is the reason for the failure [of this program]." He asked the MS team to raise women's awareness so that "they can move ahead on their own."

The BDO's comments provided the perfect opening for Meena Rani's program pitch. "MS is a [program] of the Human Resource Development Ministry of the Government of India . . . that attempts to empower women, raise their awareness and make them self-reliant," she stated. One of the BDO's assistants interjected, "What do you mean by *sashaktikaran* [empowerment]? It sounds suspicious."[5] Meena Rani clarified that "Empowerment means giving women information, helping them to move forward, and raising their awareness. Men and people like us," she said, glancing around the room, "have access to information, but women who are illiterate and spend most of their time at home do not have access to information. We all need to be aware." The BDO agreed, adding that "men, women, and the whole family" needed awareness.

As we conversed, a smiling, bespectacled woman wearing a white sari walked into the room. The men rose as she entered, and we followed suit. She was Shahida Banu, the elected block chief of Nizabad and a regular attendee of Friday meetings.[6] The BDO introduced the MS team to Shahida Banu and asked Meena Rani to redescribe the program. She once again identified MS as a government program and explained its purpose. She then sought Shahida Banu's opinion on the needs of women in her block. Shahida Banu agreed with the BDO that literacy and income generation were the two most important needs of women in Nizabad but was not aware of any specific government programs that catered to these needs. When the BDO mentioned the training in pickling, Shahida Banu responded dismissively, "Training in pickle-making is inappropriate." She explained that most women already possessed that skill. Moreover, pickling was not an economically viable activity given the abundant availability of homemade pickles in virtually every house in the area. She then asked Meena Rani whether the MS program gave participating women any tangible resources. Meena Rani's "no" brought forth a disapproving look from the block chief. "So this basically means that women will have to provide 'free' services for your program ['free' *seva karni padegi*]. Women even get money for attending nonformal education programs. People's first priority is their stomachs. It will be better if you people give something to women," advised Shahida Banu. "You will have better success."

Meetings between MS functionaries, local administrators, and elected officials were a common occurrence during my fieldwork in eastern U.P. This particular exchange caught my attention for several reasons. First, the BDO's insistence that the women needed to take responsibility for their own development raised interesting questions in relation to neoliberal critiques of welfare-style development and promotion of competitive entrepreneurialism and self-reliant social actors. Second, his assistant's distrust of women's empowerment raised the issue of why the term *empowerment* was more threatening for some state representatives than the more technical and putatively apolitical term *development* (Ferguson 1994). Third, Shahida Banu's charge that neither the government-run pickling scheme nor the MS program addressed poor women's immediate survival needs alluded to the classist and gendered ideologies underlying bureaucratic practices of development and empowerment. Finally, I was intrigued by Meena Rani's labeling of MS as a government program in the presence of these officials. A few days earlier, she had introduced MS as an NGO to a group of village women who were potential program clients. When the women had asked her what they would receive in return for participating in MS, Meena Rani had responded that they should not expect any material benefits other than information, knowledge, and support. MS was a *sanstha* [NGO] and not a *sarkari* [government] program that distributed goods.

Meena Rani's shifting identification of MS, at times as a state project and at other times as an NGO, raised an interesting conundrum. Was she simply unclear about the MS program's identity? When I posed this question to Sunita Pathak, a senior bureaucrat involved in MS, she clarified that "[MS] is partly governmental, and it is also nongovernmental. . . . The national level [program in New Delhi] is strictly governmental. . . . [But] from the state level onwards, [MS] is an autonomous organization." In the development world, MS would be considered a GONGO, a parastatal entity that is, perhaps, only seemingly contradictory.

Although Pathak's elucidation cleared up my perplexity regarding the program's hybrid identity, it neither explained why a grassroots women's empowerment initiative was structured as a GONGO, nor clarified why program functionaries chose to switch between identities in different situations. In this chapter I take up the first question, examining the MS program's crossbred organization, its location within the government system, and its representation of its target population to reveal the cultural and gendered logics of state transformation and empowerment; in chapter 3 I analyze the shifting identification practices of program personnel.

Whereas grassroots empowerment strategies and GONGOs are not new to India, I ask what their intersection in the MS program, in a context of economic liberalization, reveals about the contemporary workings of neoliberal governmentality. The neoliberal era is witnessing a proliferation of (a) innovative institutional *forms* (such as NGOs and GONGOs), which are taking on development functions usually associated with the state, and (b) novel *mechanisms* of rule such as empowerment (Barry et al. 1996; Clarke 2004; Cruikshank 1999; Rose 1996). The MS program, which combines empowerment strategies with a GONGO form, offers an especially interesting vantage point from which to explore how neoliberally inflected development discourse is transforming the terrain of state and subject formation in India today. My purpose here is not to position MS as a classic example of a neoliberal program; the launch of MS, as I explained in chapter 1, is a complex outcome of the articulation of various translocal processes including, but not limited to, transnational neoliberalism (see Sharma 2006; Gupta and Sharma 2006). The program's hybrid organization and women's empowerment emphasis do, however, point to the ways in which the state and governance are changing in neoliberal India.

In this chapter I illustrate the cultural and gendered dynamics of neoliberal governmentality in India in two interrelated ways. First, I demonstrate how the state is discursively constructed as a separate and arguably masculinist entity through the crossbred design and empowerment focus of the MS program. Here I build on anthropological scholarship on state formation, which, instead of taking the boundaries of the state as self-evident, grapples with how "it" is produced through banal bureaucratic practices, people's encounters with officials, and public cultural representations (Mitchell 1999; Sharma and Gupta 2006; see Introduction). These explorations of the performativity of states have been paralleled by feminist efforts to engender state power (Alexander 1997; Brown 1995; Fraser 1989; Sunder Rajan 2003). I bring feminist analyses to bear on the cultural construction of the state as a means to argue that empowerment techniques and crossbred GONGOs redefine the identity and role of the state as a vertically authoritative (Ferguson and Gupta 2002), yet ambiguously gendered, actor that facilitates self-development. The emphasis of empowerment programs on self-help is supposed to shift focus away from redistributive policies and undo welfare-based ideologies. However, as I demonstrate, welfarist assumptions about women's putative passivity and the "feminized" (read: unproductive) nature of their work continue to underpin the current thinking about empowerment. This is the second move I make to unravel the gendered logic and effects of state-sponsored development practices. Not only do problematic welfarist notions undergird a supposedly distinct, *antiwelfare* empowerment logic, but the Indian government also continues to implement redistributive programs. I postulate that the interpenetration of welfarist and empowerment ideologies and the coexistence of welfare and empowerment programs in India provide an important corrective to a widely prevalent truism that neoliberalism equals dewelfarization. Indeed, the Indian case illustrates the oddities of neoliberalism—the "exceptions" that complicate its uniform dynamics and universal global effects (Ong 2006). In this chapter I offer a nuanced look at how the uneasy articulations of neoliberal ideologies and other political imperatives are reshaping the state and rule in India.

In the following section I discuss why MS was designed as a hybrid GONGO. I show how MS planning practices, in tandem with transnational neoliberal policies, discursively produce and engender the postliberal Indian state. Next, I analyze the MS program's unusual location (as *in* the government, but not *of* it) and its representational practices (that is, how it constructs the ideal female objects–subjects of empowerment) to further unravel the gendered dynamics of state power. Here I demonstrate the persistence of welfarist notions about women's subjectivities and labor within the alternative feminist empowerment framework espoused by MS. Thus, this empowerment program paradoxically entrenches normative class, caste, and gender identities even as it works to challenge these norms.

GONGOs and Empowerment: Enculturing and Engendering the Neoliberal State

Nearly everyone I spoke with described MS as an innovative development program. They considered it unique because of its focus on nonmaterial empowerment and its GONGO form. This hybrid form, as one bureaucrat put it, "is a nice combination of government and nongovernment pluspoints." MS symbolized an unusual partnership between state agencies and local feminist groups. Although representatives of women's movement felt uneasy about collaborating with state actors because of their previous involvement in antistate activism (leftist, student, and/or feminist), they nonetheless agreed to be part of MS's hybrid structure. Some well-known activists explained their participation in MS in terms of the changes in the Indian political scene during the 1970s and 1980s and the concomitant shifts in feminist engagements with state bodies.[7] These women characterized the 1970s Indian state as repressive. Indira Gandhi's declaration of a state of emergency in 1975 and the resultant suspension of civil rights and lack of governmental transparency led to a deep suspicion of the state. Versha Rai, a core member of the MS team, defined the 1970s as a "period of NGOs [and] autonomous groups working totally independently of the state."

Carving autonomous niches did not, however, mean that women's movement activists in India isolated themselves from government agencies (Jandhyala 2001). They critically interacted with state structures on the issues of development, violence, and the law. In 1974, for instance, the Committee on the Status of Women in India published a report entitled *Towards Equality* (Government of India 1974). This committee was set up in response to the Indian government's obligations as a signatory to the UN-sponsored 1967 Declaration on the Elimination of Discrimination against Women (Philipose 2001). *Towards Equality* examined the differential impact of the postcolonial state's modernization policies on women across regional, caste, and class barriers. It documented the extent to which women had been excluded from the benefits of development and called upon the state to fulfill its constitutional duty of guaranteeing equality. This report set in motion dialogues between women's organizations and state agencies on development issues and resulted in the inclusion, for the first time in the history of postcolonial India, of a separate chapter on women and development in the government's sixth Five-Year Plan in 1980 (Agnihotri and Mazumdar 1995). During the late 1970s and early 1980s, women's groups also engaged state agencies on the issue of gendered violence. The Mathura rape case served as a key galvanizing incident. A young tribal girl, Mathura, was raped in custody, and the Supreme Court acquitted the policemen who had committed this crime (Gandhi and Shah 1992). The violence of rape, as women's groups highlighted, was compounded by violence of the judgment passed by a biased judiciary. Not only did this incident display the state's naked, masculinist prerogative power (Brown 1995), which rests on perpetrating violence in the name of "protection," but it also brought to the fore the biases of rape laws. Women's groups used this case to expose gendered forms of oppression and implicated state institutions in their reproduction (Philipose 2001). They also lobbied for increased accountability of state agents and for constitutional and legislative changes that would ensure justice (see Gandhi and Shah 1992).

The mid-1980s saw a shift from this earlier period of antagonistic engagement between women's groups and state bodies. Rajiv Gandhi's entry into politics, his overtures toward cleaning up and innovating government, and his promise to give greater priority to women (Agnihotri and Mazumdar 1995, 1875) played an important role in opening up the state as a possible arena for creative, collaborative feminist work. In the development field, for instance, members of women's organizations participated in re-envisioning government policies on education, population, the informal sector, and empowerment. Feminist involvement in state development projects, albeit tempered with a good dose of wariness and self-reflection, was shaped by a realization that NGO efforts were limited in their reach. As Versha Rai commented

> The women's movement [was] . . . totally anti-state [in the] 1970s. But then . . . [came] a recognition that what is your reach, what are you impacting? If I am working in one hundred villages . . . what difference does it make if I am not doing anything anywhere else. [Our thinking was that] we need to . . . make more impact on mainstream structures. We cannot [work] in isolation. So the question of partnerships, linkages, networks [arose]—this was the . . . language of the 1980s.

When the opportunity to design MS presented itself in the late 1980s, some movement activists saw it as a chance to implement their ideas of gender equality and social change on a larger scale; that is, to reach out to greater numbers of marginalized women, to use state resources for social transformation, and to mainstream gender within government institutions (Jandhyala 2001). The decision to work with the state did not, however, preclude debates about reformist versus radical activism. Many questions were raised about the why and how of feminist partnering with state agencies. Kaveri Mani, a member of the initial MS team, remarked

> When I joined MS, there was horror and outrage from colleagues: "What are you doing! How can you join a government program!" We had never experimented with feminist ideals as part of a huge structure like this. [But] one had a stake in proving that . . . it was possible to go to scale with women's organizations. . . . We created a kind of protective shell around the program . . . as a conscious strategy.

This protective shell materialized in MS's hybrid GONGO structure, which was supposed to give the program operational independence (which remains debatable, as I show in chapter 3) and to also merge the benefits of small NGOs with large government development bureaucracies.

Almost all of my informants cited the state's wider reach and greater resources as the main benefits of state involvement in grassroots development. Some MS activists also described state participation in such efforts as its duty toward its most disadvantaged citizens. Development was a responsibility that the postcolonial state had not only willingly assumed but also periodically reiterated through its populist rhetoric; it could not privatize this duty, especially during a time when the survival of marginalized women was increasingly threatened by the forces of economic globalization. As Versha Rai asserted, "The government *should* take responsibility for its people. NGOs cannot take on the state's job."

An added benefit of state participation in a grassroots project, as far as government officials were concerned, was the authority and legitimacy that the state label carried in government circles. Sunita Pathak, a bureaucrat associated with MS, told me that

> I think where it helps the [MS] program, really, being a government initiative, is . . . the authority it gives it. And . . . legitimacy. Because an NGO has to really prove itself. You write "Government of India," and everybody knows that you are a government program. [It] helps [with] credibility. . . . It is also easier for government departments to work with MS than it is for [them] to work with an NGO because if there is a problem with an NGO, there is no responsibility.

The extent to which the MS program's government affiliation gave it legitimacy within the state bureaucracy, however, was a contested matter, as I reveal later in the chapter.

The government label also had its downsides. "The main problem is that a state, given its very nature . . . says that if program A has three components, program A will have three components forever," explained one bureaucrat, as he discussed the rigidity of the typical bureaucratic way of doing things. Other disadvantages, identified by my informants, included a target-driven top-down approach to development, red tape, inefficiency, political expediency, corruption, and a rule-boundedness that discouraged flexibility, innovation, and motivation.

In addition, Kaveri Mani identified a fundamental contradiction relating to state participation in a grassroots empowerment project. "To be able to question issues is not something that the government and the state would like. It has a class bias. It has an urban bias. It has an elitist mode. So why should it . . . initiate a program which is going to question its own role and interest!" Nina Singh, a bureaucrat who had worked on many state-sponsored gender projects, took Mani's criticism further:

> A government program . . . does not integrate the element of struggle that lies at the heart of empowerment. . . . That is the biggest constraint—that struggle is not understood in a government lexicon. The element of struggle [which] is the basis of empowerment programs . . . is not internalized by bureaucrats. [They] reduce everything to a safe thing called "development."

The government, according to Mani and Singh, could not be trusted as the sole agent for women's empowerment, given the inequalities, such as those of gender and class, it reflected and perpetuated, and given its ability to depoliticize struggle and hijack the radical potential of empowerment.

The activists and bureaucrats who designed MS thus desired a part-NGO program structure that would mitigate the problems of bureaucratic intervention and state development models and bring added benefits. NGO strengths, as described by my informants, included grassroots-level accountability and legitimacy, bottom-up approaches, decentralized and participatory planning, flexible and democratic ways of working, and a motivated workforce. In Mani's words, "While women's groups have the advantages of being small . . . of being close to the people . . . [and] of having a committed staff, the advantage of the state was its outreach . . . and large scale. And so there was this feeling that it is possible to marry the two."

MS's crossbred GONGO structure signifies this interweaving or "marriage." As I explained in the Introduction, at the national level, MS is a central government program, housed within the Department of Education in New Delhi. The national office is run by a team of NGO activists but is headed by a Department of Education bureaucrat. At the level of each state in which it operates, MS is implemented through nongovernmental "MS Societies." State-level MS offices oversee the work of district-level offices, which in turn support the work of block-level offices. MS participants are located at the block or "grassroots" level where program planning is supposed to happen with a "worm's eye view and not a bird's eye view" (Ramachandran 1995, 20) of women's lives; this involves the active participation of program clients, rather than top-down planning on their behalf. MS employees at the state, district, and block levels are drawn from the NGO sector. MS also has advisory bodies at the national and state levels, consisting of both nongovernmental and ex officio members. NGO representatives enjoy at least 51 percent representation in these advisory bodies, which is meant to ensure a critical and continuous activist input into the program, and to avoid a bureaucratic takeover of its daily workings and long-term visions.[8]

The MS program's GONGO organization and my informants' discussions of it reveal the cultural logic of state formation, highlighting how the discreteness and autonomy of the state is constructed as an effect of everyday development practices (Mitchell 1999). In designing MS, planners attempted to fuse state and nonstate structures. However, this effort was premised on the idea that two mutually exclusive "pure" spheres exist in the first place—"crossbreeding" after all assumes distinct breeds. Even as MS's GONGO form attempted to blur and transcend the boundary between state and nonstate arenas, it also solidified that boundary and reified these two zones as essentially set apart. The "N" in GONGO served as the limit at which the difference between state and nonstate spheres could be produced.

MS planners' practices not only helped to draw the line between these two spheres but also to arrange them hierarchically. For instance, my informants characterized the state by its larger scale and authority. In so doing, they reiterated the verticality of the state, a spatial metaphor denoting both the state's higher position and greater dominance vis-à-vis the nonstate realm (Ferguson and Gupta 2002). By drawing attention to the wider reach and resources of the state, these individuals also enforced the spatial metaphor of encompassment (Ferguson and Gupta 2002), which imbues the state with a broader scope and sphere of influence than nonstate actors. Further, my informants defined NGOs by their grassroots-level legitimacy, local-level care-based work, and bottom-up orientation.[9] They thereby implicitly located NGOs as the spatially rooted, micro, dominated and enveloped *Other* of the translocal, macro, vertically authoritative, and spread-out state.

My ethnographic observations also suggest a subtle, if ambiguous, gendering of states and NGOs. At times my informants' representations appeared to feminize NGOs and masculinize the vertically encompassing state, and at other times they turned this gendering on its head.[10] This ambivalence viz. the gender of state and nonstate realms, as I postulate below, reflects popular and subaltern understandings as well as neoliberal images of these spheres.

Public cultural discourses in India often portray the government as "grass without roots," and NGOs as "roots without grass" (Khan 1997, 12)—here scale and spread captures the spirit of the grass-like (unlocalizable?) state, and root-like operations and connectedness to place mark the essence of NGOs. My informants' descriptions of the identity and benefits of NGOs echoed these common understandings. They positioned NGOs as grounded, accountable, authentic, and arguably feminized bodies that take on charitable welfare (read: maternal) and thus apolitical tasks, and whose (feminized) staff and clients are dependent on outside funds and support. At one level these characteristics define the superiority and advantage of NGOs; at another level, they deprivilege NGOs vis-à-vis the public and implicitly political sphere of state activity and rights and the for-profit private sector of productive economic activity.[11] NGOs are seen as social agencies that do altruistic, nonpoliticized, care-based work naturalized as feminine. In contrast, the state is implicitly represented as a masculinist entity. According to Wendy Brown, "The masculinism of the state refers to those features of the state that signify, enact, sustain, and represent masculine power as a form of dominance" (Brown 1995, 167). Verticality symbolically encodes social conventions of masculinity that represent men as dominant and authoritative. Encompassment expresses the ability to define and control particular discursive and sociopolitical terrains. On the one hand, the metaphor of encompassment connotes both masculinist power and the hegemonic image of the state as a sovereign entity with the legitimate power to define, manage, and protect (through violent means, if necessary) territories and populations and to regulate proper subjectivity.[12] On the other hand, encompassment in the North Indian context comes laden with more complex symbolism. It evokes a feminine quality in the popular imagination in that enveloping nurturance is often associated with motherhood. My interlocutors' invocation of the state's encompassing quality perhaps reiterated frequent subaltern characterizations of the state or government as *mai–baap* [mother–father] rather than as a patriarch-writ-large (see chapters 3, 4, and 5). In this "maternal-paternal" metaphor, the state's relationship to its subjects is cast in kinship and generational terms, while the gender opposition is reinscribed as a distinction between the state's functions of care or nurturance, on the one hand, and security or protection, on the other.

My informants' ideas about state and NGO pros and cons both reiterated the state's vertical masculinity and troubled simplistic binaries between masculinized states and feminized NGOs. Their complex gendering of these entities seemed to resonate with the equally ambiguous neoliberal imaginations of privatized states and efficient NGOs. The neoliberal doctrine depicts

NGOs as efficient, trim, disciplined, flexible, knowledgeable, and arguably "ideal" masculinist actors. However, it also reinforces the feminization of NGOs by primarily relegating to them the supposedly maternal tasks of care and welfare. Neoliberal ideologies paint a similarly complex picture of the gender of the state. The overgrown, indulgent, beleaguered, and leaky state that neoliberalism wants to transform and cut to size is an "emasculated" state. What neoliberalism seeks to conjure instead is a strong "hypermasculine" state that is lean and devoid of the excesses, inefficiencies, and "bleeding" tendencies of feminized welfare functions.[13]

The complex articulations of expert and popular local understandings of state and nonstate actors with transnational, neoliberal notions indicate how the (Indian) state is culturally constructed as an effect of translocal discourses that crosscut various spatial registers. MS planners' decision to set up a GONGO for grassroots women's empowerment reflects not just local, regional, and national-level politics and processes, but also transnational shifts in the institutions and modes of governance. The neoliberal emphases on good, small government and on the roll back of welfare states have been accompanied by a global explosion in the numbers of quasi- and nonstate entities, such as GONGOs and NGOs, which perform governmental tasks (Ferguson and Gupta 2002).

These transnational trends are evident in India, which has seen an unprecedented growth in NGOs since the 1980s. Whereas twelve thousand Indian NGOs were registered with the Home Ministry in 1988, the estimated number at the beginning of this century stood at around two million (Kamat 2002).[14] Unlike the early postindependence phase, which was dominated by welfare-based Gandhian or religious organizations, NGOs now are more diversified in terms of their nature, visions and ideologies. The 1960s and 1970s witnessed a burgeoning presence of international NGOs, community-based organizations, and social action groups (Sen 1993). Their goal was not simply relief, but development and, in some cases, empowerment (Khan 1997; Sen 1993). At this time the Indian government also set up large capitalist development-oriented GONGOs or "corporate NGOs" (Garain 1994), which focused on technical and financial assistance for capitalist development rather than on poverty alleviation or empowerment (Kamat 2002; Kothari 1986).

The Indian NGO sector expanded rapidly in the late 1970s and 1980s as a result of several factors including (1) the failure of state-led development planning to reduce poverty and destitution; (2) the violent excesses of Emergency and the squashing of leftist student movements and other radical organizations; (3) the failure of leftist Indian political parties to organize a sustained movement for radical change, making grassroots organizations a viable alternative for mobilization; (4) the post-Emergency promotion of rural-based NGO efforts by the newly elected Janata government, which set up semigovernmental bodies such as the Council for the Advancement of People's Action and Rural Technology (CAPART) to support NGO work; and (5) increased funding made available by the Congress government of the mid-1980s to voluntary organizations doing "nonpolitical" work (Kamat 2002; Khan 1997; Sen 1993). In addition, foreign governments and foundations provided funds for NGOs during this period, encouraging them to take on state development and regulatory functions.

This rapid growth in nonstate and quasistate bodies, when seen in conjunction with the recent emergence of empowerment discourses on the mainstream development stage, sheds further light on the translocal spatiality and transformation of states and governance under neoliberalism. Empowerment is now used as a mechanism of neoliberal self-government and development, and for defining citizenship, as I explained in chapter 1 (Cruikshank 1999; Hindess 2004). It is, in other words, a dominant category of governance (Chatterjee 2004) endorsed by disparate actors, including the World Bank, NGOs, and states. The worlding of empowerment has followed the global diffusion of neoliberal policy instruments such as economic liberalization, deregulation, privatization, and SAPs; these policies, I contend, have fostered state participation in and promotion of grassroots empowerment. As the IMF pushes austerity measures onto the global South, the World Bank advocates small and clean government and funds empowerment programs.[15] The addition of grassroots empowerment to the neoliberal policy package of liberalization, structural adjustment, and small government may seem contradictory; indeed, feminists have amply documented the poverty and inequality-producing consequences of adjustment programs (Sparr 1994). However, this bundle of strategies is not as oxymoronic as it seems. In fact, the World Bank's encouragement of empowerment strategies implicitly acknowledges and attempts to correct for the disempowering effects of SAPs. Furthermore, empowerment initiatives help to facilitate the neoliberal goals of small and good government. Such initiatives can allow postcolonial, developmentalist states to downsize their welfare bureaucracies and redistributive role by educating individuals and communities in the techniques of self-care and self-development and farming out their welfare responsibilities onto empowered people and NGOs.

The numerical increase in quasi- and nonstate actors in India and their conjoining with state-sponsored grassroots empowerment projects reflect, in part, global neoliberal trends that seek to detach or autonomize entities of governance from state institutions by spreading the art of self-government so that the burden of poverty relief and grassroots development may be shifted from state bodies to newly empowered social bodies. This "responsibilization" (Burchell 1996) of nonstate actors is meant to governmentalize society and degovernmentalize the state (Barry et al. 1996).

I argue, however, that these concurrent processes do not signal a complete neoliberal autonomization of governance (Barry et al. 1996) or a straightforward privatization of the state in India. First, the contemporary Indian state cannot fully relinquish its development and welfare functions because its legitimacy rests on precisely such functions. The urgency of and responsibility for national development define the identity and "difference" of the independent nationalist Indian state. The developmentalist imperatives of the state have meant that the Indian government continues to run, and has even expanded some large-scale welfare-based programs, such as the Integrated Child Development Services (ICDS) program, that distribute food and other resources to those sections of the population defined as "at risk" (Gupta and Sharma 2006). The coevalness of welfare and empowerment initiatives in neoliberal India is a consequence of populist activism, which persists in challenging the uneven benefits of economic globalization and liberalization. The Indian state, according to Sushil Chakrabarty, a former bureaucrat,

> . . . is under a major, major constraint—and that is the constraint of democracy. . . . The state will face a continuous demand to expand ICDS, to do more of service delivery, because expansion of service delivery sustains governments and Members of Parliament. So I don't think that the state can ever stop doing programs like ICDS.

Another bureaucrat also stressed the complementarity of welfare and empowerment programs, suggesting that "welfare activities are helpful because they make it possible for women to 'be'," but they "do not help women acquire a voice, much less a say in the affairs of the family and the social system." Hence empowerment programs "that influence [women's] minds become important." The fact that the legitimacy of the Indian state is tied to its redistributive functions and that populist democratic politics pressures the state to come through on its promises means that government bodies cannot step away from implementing welfare programs under neoliberal adjustment.

The Indian case, thus, provides an important corrective to the dominant story about neoliberalism's homogenous global impact that is overwhelmingly antiwelfare and pro-state-privatization (see Ong 2006). First, it illustrates that a selective implementation of neoliberal technologies and their articulation with varied contexts and histories can result in discontinuous consequences, such as the preservation and expansion of state welfare functions in some places. Second, postcolonial states, such as India, have rarely enjoyed the resources or the panoptic reach of metropolitan biopower regimes and welfare states in the West (Ferguson 1994; Gupta 2001). Governments are now supposed to roll back welfare, but one can legitimately ask what exactly are postcolonial states retreating from in the current neoliberal moment. Third, entities such as NGOs, which help privatize the state, always operate within the purview of regulative, governmental regimes. The Indian government monitors NGOs through registration laws and funding stipulations, rendering questionable the independence connoted by the term "nongovernmental."[16] Hence, the autonomization of the NGO sector and the concomitant privatization of state functions are at best partial in India.

While the intersection of GONGOs and empowerment approaches might not allow a complete autonomization of government functions in India, it does enable the state to reenact its verticality precisely at a time when its authority is threatened by supranational forces. The transnational neoliberal development regime, consisting of bodies such as the IMF and the World Bank, wants to reshape the potency of the state by rendering it hypermasculinist; however, it also challenges the vertical masculinism of postcolonial states by directly intervening in their sovereign policy affairs. The implementation of empowerment programs and the establishment of parastate and nonstate organizations are among the ways in which states respond to these neoliberal contradictions. By engaging in grassroots empowerment when its ability to assert sovereign control over national policy affairs and to deliver on the promise of developing all sectors of society is compromised by transnational factors, the Indian state is able to re-present itself as transformed. By taking on the "unstately" task of empowerment, it sends the message that this is not government as usual. Empowerment projects represent the strengthening and inclusion of civil society in governance; they also redefine the state's paternal benevolence and developmental responsibility. Instead of being unambiguously tied to its capacity to directly care for its citizens and provide for their basic needs, the state's commitment to national development is now expressed through its ability to empower marginalized subjects to care for themselves and to participate in the project of self-rule. Moreover, creating a GONGO to implement empowerment sets the state apart as a separate and superior actor, and as a leaner, more efficient, partially dewelfarized, and defeminized masculinist body.

The intertwining of welfare and empowerment, the complexities of neoliberal changes, and the gendered nature of the contemporary state in India are further instantiated by where MS is located within the state system, how it is perceived by officials, and who the program targets, as I demonstrate below.

Placing MS, Locating Gender in the State

MS is implemented by the Department of Education of Ministry of Human Resource Development of the Indian government. The decision to so place MS was a controversial one, because it raised the issue of which state agency should "own" women's development programs. Some officials believed that MS, a women's program, should be implemented by the Women's Bureau of the Department of Women and Child Development (WCD), which also comes under the Ministry of Human Resource Development. Ultimately, the Department of Education won because Anil Bordia, who conceptualized MS in partnership with women's groups, was then Secretary of Education. Debates about which agency ought to control women's programs were rife as I conducted my fieldwork, revealing the contested place of gender within the state. I interviewed bureaucrats who believed that all programs dealing with women or gender should be part of the WCD because this agency was created precisely for that purpose. Other officials and NGO representatives, however, were pleased that MS was not a WCD project because that sent an important message that gender issues should not be confined to a single government department.

WCD was created in the mid-1980s by the Rajiv Gandhi administration. The Ministry of Welfare initially housed women's and children's bureaus; this ministry was split up, and the two bureaus were placed in the Ministry of Human Resource Development. This move of women's issues from the Ministry of Welfare (which has since been renamed Social Justice and Empowerment, itself a significant move in the liberalization context) to the Ministry of Human Resource Development denotes a small but significant conceptual shift in how women are viewed within the state; it parallels changes in the feminist development frameworks I outlined in chapter 1. Rather than being viewed as passive welfare recipients women are currently seen as a critical human resource whose potential must be harnessed for development (see also Gupta 2001).[17]

While the purpose behind the creation of WCD was to mainstream *gender* issues across the bureaucratic apparatus, in effect it incarcerated *women's* issues in one department. WCD literally "houses" women's concerns. Bijoy Roy, a former WCD official, contended that

> I wouldn't even say gender—the women's question was DEFINITELY ghettoized. Everyone used to throw things at WCD—"this is a women's issue; you people deal with it" [*yeh to women's issue hai; yeh aap dekh lo*]. Someone would talk about the effect of the green revolution on women and the agriculture ministry would tell us, "take the information from us, but you reply." WCD had the responsibility of the parliamentary response [on all women's issues].

WCD's mandate is to monitor various ministries' records on gender issues and to undo the gender blindness of their policies. But WCD officials are unable to meaningfully carry out their duties because, as Roy explained,

> WCD is under-funded, under-budgeted, and under-technically qualified. . . . [It] is left with a larger than life mandate and smaller than life resources. The women's bureau is weak; it is located within a weak department. . . . Weak means that you are seen as a "soft" ministry, dealing with "soft" areas. Your cabinet minister will never be really powerful, if you had a cabinet minister at all. Most of the time you have a minister of state who is junior to a cabinet minister.

Roy's statements reveal the low priority given to women's issues and to WCD within the ministerial hierarchy.

It is also worth noting that WCD represents both women and children. Why is it that the state regards women and children as forming one constituency? While women's and children's concerns do overlap in certain instances, relegating these groups into one agency naturalizes motherhood as the primary identity of women.[18] Additionally, this move reinforces the ideology of protection within which women and children are represented as vulnerable populations and the state is portrayed as a masculinist protector (Brown 1995; Gupta 2001). Powerful gender norms, which underwrite such a naming, are thus institutionalized within a single government body.

Such state practices encode patriarchal assumptions and reveal the reductionist notion of gender that operates through state agencies. Women's concerns become metonymic of gender, and are consigned to a women-specific department. This department, however, does not have adequate resources or the clout to influence the gender components of government policies. It lacks the power to effectively monitor larger ministries' track records on addressing gender issues, let alone force these ministries to integrate gender into their everyday policymaking.

Given these issues and the relative weakness of WCD, many of my informants were relieved that MS was placed within the Department of Education. Indeed, if the agenda of the state is to mainstream gender at all levels, then locating a women's empowerment program within the Department of Education sends a strong signal; it represents the efforts of at least some individuals within the government to broaden and address women's issues and gender concerns through channels other than the WCD. The question then arises whether MS has been able to influence government policies generally or whether it remains a unique icon of an imaginative approach to gender and development issues within the larger state system.

Nearly all my interlocutors believed that MS was perceived as a poster child by the government, which encapsulated a creative, gender sensitive approach to development. A former MS employee complained that even though MS is considered an important program within the Department of Education, one that the government cannot afford to ignore precisely because of its international prestige, the program was nevertheless tokenized during her tenure.

> Whenever there was any note to write about women's education or gender issues in education, it used to be dumped straight on MS. And when you had to make a presentation about women's education, since MS is the flagship program, it was always taken out and waved around. So [there was] appropriation in that sense. . . . And tokenism—a great bit.

This again unmasks the contradictory practices of state agents vis-à-vis gender. The MS program's placement in the Department of Education was an attempt to widen gender concerns within the state apparatus, but the program became the sole example of the Department's gender sensitivity.

Even though MS was used as a poster child when necessary, this did not automatically translate into respect or legitimacy for the program within government circles. My informants belived that development programs that distribute tangibles and thus have larger budgets have more clout. Anu Chopra, a New Delhi–based development activist, told me that the MS program's budget was too small to make any significant impact on the rest of the government. She compared MS with other big state initiatives, such as the ICDS program,[19] stating that

> ICDS is all about the *delivery* of inputs. . . . "What do you have to give?" is what every [government] department asks. So if you do not have anything to give, in the government's eyes, you have no budget. You are not important. Your mandate . . . is not significant at the government level.

This indicates the extent to which welfare programs with tangible deliverables remain significant for the state despite the shift toward empowerment. A program that does not distribute material benefits to people is considered relatively unimportant in the context of delivery-based development projects that are used as a system of patronage by local officials and politicians (see also chapter 5). Welfare-style programs are critical for the survival and legitimacy of state actors in the context of populism. There is thus a contradiction between the neoliberal denigration of welfare and its use by politicians, elected officials, and local administrators to garner political support and maintain their dominant socioeconomic positions.

My ethnography also points to the conflicts that can arise between various levels of the state with respect to gender, development, and empowerment issues. State agents occupying the lower ranks of the bureaucracy and working at district and block levels are enmeshed in populist politics; their interests and stakes are different from higher-placed bureaucrats and those who work for the New Delhi–based central government.[20] How do officials at the national, state, and local levels of the development administration perceive the MS program and women's issues? And what do these perceptions tell us about the place of gender within the state?

In the opening narrative of this chapter, I introduced an official at the Nizabad block office who was overtly suspicious of the notion of women's empowerment. Meena Rani tried to placate this man by defining empowerment as awareness raising and information dissemination rather than as a challenge to patriarchal ideologies and practices. A Water Department official I met in Nizabad expressed similar doubts about women's empowerment.

Upon learning that the goal of the MS program was to provide women with information about their rights, he retorted, "But providing women with information on their rights will lead to fights between women and men!" Sameera, an MS employee who was with me, immediately responded, "We are not here to break families." Clearly, some state functionaries were uncomfortable with women's empowerment because they interpreted it as a threat to the stability of the family and the established gender order. MS staff members had to mediate in such situations and depoliticize empowerment in order to render it more palatable for local administrators, whom they often encountered in their daily work.

Other local officials considered MS as unworthy of their attention. When I asked the BDO of Seelampur block, Ram Kumar, whether he knew about the "Mahila Samakhya" program, his brow furrowed. "Mahila *Ka*makhya?" he asked. I repeated the correct name of the program, but it still did not ring a bell. I persisted, mentioning that MS was a Government of India program. But Kumar shrugged. He had not heard of MS because program personnel had never visited him; however, he stated, they would get more respect and recognition if they were to contact him. Kumar had been in office for over a year, serving as the highest administrator in the block, and yet he did not know about the existence of a nine-year-old government-initiated women's program in his area. Moreover, he gave the impression that it was not his responsibility to find out about such programs.[21] I discovered that the district development officer (DDO) of Begumpur district, in which Seelampur block is located, did not know about MS either. The chief development officer (CDO), who oversees all development activities in a district, was aware of MS but complained that MS staffers had not called on him for a while; thus, he could not be blamed for not knowing about the current needs of the program.

MS, as I discovered through my interactions and interviews, was considered as relatively insignificant by local administrators because it was a program managed by and targeted at women, did not distribute any tangible resources to its clients and had a relatively small budget over which local officials had no direct control. Therefore, the representatives of the local-level administration whom I met either ignored MS or were threatened by its feminist goals. Higher-ranked, state- and national-level civil servants were more ambivalent in their responses to the program: some showed full support, some took little interest, and some were completely against women's empowerment.

The launch of MS was made possible because of the backing and vision of a key senior national-level bureaucrat, Anil Bordia. He not only brought together a core group of NGO activists to design and implement MS, but also insulated the program from intervention by unsupportive government officials during his tenure as Secretary of Education. When I met Bordia in the summer of 1999, he had retired and was skeptical about continued support for MS. "It would be a rare thing if a [government] successor provided that kind of protection. An astute and far-sighted civil servant will create a system, to the extent possible, for the continuation of the program. . . . [But] when, in which state, which person will destroy the program?" Bordia shrugged, "It will be destroyed." He added, matter-of-factly

> The inherent problem [arises] because programs like this are working in a very simmering or overt manner against a system that is rallied totally against [them]. And here is a person who stands between those forces and empowering processes. If you remove that person, a dismantling [of the program] can happen. . . . If there is an assault on the program, and if the assault is itself led by the government, then there is very little chance of its continuance. Particularly on gender issues—it is a very serious matter. Because most men just don't see the point. Their straight [accusation is that such programs are] destroying family values, destroying ancient Indian values. . . . Can you imagine these people! And a fair number of women are also [thinking like that].

According to Bordia, women's empowerment was ill understood and thus considered dangerous by a largely gender insensitive state system; consequently, MS faced a constant threat of co-optation and subversion. For instance, Ramesh Dubey, a senior state-level bureaucrat in charge of the MS program in U.P. during its early years, was not only unsympathetic toward the program, but also belittled feminists. "Dubey . . . slandered us," recalled Rita Kumari, an MS manager. "During one of the [MS] Executive Committee meetings he scoffed at feminists. He told us, in a very pointed manner, that there are two kinds of dogs—the domesticated ones who wear golden chains and eat biscuits, and stray ones who roam the streets. And all of us women at the meeting kept quiet. We needed money to run the program and he was our director." By drawing these analogies, did Dubey mean to liken MS workers to "kept" animals, who are controlled by a benevolent master (in this case the state) and are "chained" by funding exigencies? Or did he mean to imply that they were like stray dogs roaming the streets and scavenging for their rights? Although insulted, violated, and angry, MS staffers could not overtly refute Dubey because they depended on him to disburse program funds. The ironies and contradictions of their own limitations as representatives of a government-implemented feminist program and as women undergoing empowerment in their own lives were not lost on these MS staffers.[22]

The gender of officials did not seem to matter significantly where attitudes toward MS and women's empowerment were concerned, as Bordia and some MS functionaries emphasized. Rita Kumari informed me about a female official who oversaw the state-level MS program in U.P. for a short while. "She was a woman who did not support us as a woman but only as a *sarkari* [government] officer. She did not give us the kind of support that is needed in MS. . . . " I met another senior female bureaucrat, Rajni Gupta, who showed little sensitivity toward subaltern peasant women's workloads. I was present at a village-level meeting with her where she expressed concern about the fact that girls were not going to school. The village women reported that the local school was too far and that their daughters were afraid to walk alone because of the threat of violence from upper-caste men. Rather than discuss how power disparities result in gender and caste violence or how state agencies could positively intervene in such cases, Gupta instructed the women to escort their daughters to school. It did not matter that the school was four kilometers away or that women would have to spend precious time away from work to escort the girls. Gupta assumed that these women were housewives, not peasants or agricultural laborers, with "free" time on their hands, and that chaperoning their daughters was their duty as mothers. Some female government representatives I met were neither more supportive of women's struggles against gender subordination nor more critical of the gendered assumptions that underlie state practices. Rita Kumari's comments indicated that these officials' identities as state functionaries and as women were perhaps contradictory; their gendered interests were complicated by their positions as officers of a masculinist state.

Bordia also highlighted the unenlightened masculinism of state structures, which made it difficult to support and sustain innovative women's empowerment efforts from within. The continued existence of empowerment projects, Bordia contended, depended on the farsightedness and strength of certain individuals within the government to do something different and to shield their efforts from co-optation. Many of my informants appreciated the sheltering that MS received from some senior civil servants, such as Bordia. They explained that it is not too difficult for high-ranking officials in New

Delhi to defend women's empowerment because they are removed from the cauldron of local power politics and thus have less at stake. Lower-level officials, on the other hand, are deeply entangled within such politics and hence generally not in favor of seemingly radical programs for social change.

By providing a stratified picture of what administrators at different levels within the state system thought of the MS program, I do not want to suggest that all high-ranking New Delhi-based bureaucrats are gender aware while their counterparts in state- and local-level administrations are not. In fact, Nina Singh, a civil servant herself, told me about some senior colleagues who had different ideas about gender and the place of women. She gave an example of one such individual who wanted the MS program shut down because it was misleading and inciting women ["*Yeh log auraton ko bharkate hain; isko bund karo*"]. Singh echoed Bordia's sentiment that because MS posed a real threat to the social and state order, it would, in all likelihood, get appropriated and depoliticized by the government. She described MS as a "hot-house plant," which needed insulation and care from a hostile environment in order to survive and grow.

> In the larger environment, there is nothing to sustain projects [like MS]. . . . You have these beautiful flowers blooming in a hothouse. . . . The point is that the bureaucratic environment is the biggest hurdle to cross. . . . If the average politician [or bureaucrat] doesn't understand [the program] and thinks that it is bad for women, [then] how do you sustain this in a governmental context? The real thing is the political level, the political layers which have to approve projects, sanction funds; it is they whom I see as the biggest threat.

Singh's and Bordia's statements iterated GAD feminist ambivalence about state involvement in grassroots empowerment (see chapter 1). Partnering with state agencies on such projects is dangerous for NGO activists because barring a few enlightened officials, government actors, both appointed and elected, tend to not support programs that envision radical liberation, equality, and social transformation.

The preceding discussion of the antagonisms surrounding the issues of gender and empowerment across various governmental layers offers a disaggregated and polyphonic picture of the state (Gupta 1995). Different state arms and layers do not necessarily work in concert with each other and this necessitates that the state be "viewed in terms of the actual contradictions of its institutions—interstate rivalries, political parties' conflicts, center-state relations . . .—and in terms of its functionaries' status, provenance, attitudes, and attributes (which include to a significant extent their class, caste, and gender identities)" (Sunder Rajan 2003, 227). I demonstrated that individuals working at different levels of the administration and for different state agencies have varied perceptions of MS and of women's empowerment. Whereas some regard women's empowerment as a crucial aspect of development and social change, others regard it as antifamily and, therefore, as bad for society; while the latter group espouses patriarchal notions about the place of women within society, the former group's endorsement of empowerment does not necessarily mean that they are guided by nonpatriarchal ideologies. The empowerment framework is itself traversed by welfarist norms about gender, as I show below. Even though the state is not a coherent actor with unified interests, I argue that its practices of development can produce a coherence of *effects* where gender hierarchies are concerned, reproducing normative, patriarchal notions of women's proper place and face.

Gendered Logics of Welfare and Empowerment: Mahila Samakhya Targets

MS works with marginalized, landless, rural women belonging to low-castes (primarily Dalit). A program document explains their oppression in the following manner:

> Women are caught in a vicious circle . . . Daily struggle for food, fuel, water, fodder for their cattle, child birth and child rearing saps them all of their energy. Their social interaction is determined by cultural traditions, taboos and superstitions. Their social and family roles are well defined. They are socially and physically oppressed. They do not have access to information beyond their immediate present. Alienated from decision making processes, they relate to Government's schemes and programmes as passive recipients. They do not have any information about their rights and thus they view their environment with suspicion and fear. All these factors reinforce a low self-image. Women are ultimately trapped in their own perception of themselves and in the way society perceives them. (Government of India 1988, 2)

The paradigmatic oppressed woman, as defined by MS, is poor, passive, uninformed, fearful, and trapped. Interestingly, this description overlaps with welfarist images of marginalized women, which empowerment approaches were supposed to have moved beyond. However, where feminist empowerment frameworks diverge from welfare ideologies is in seeing disadvantaged women as potential agents; that is, they believe that welfare objects can become empowered subjects. Thus MS strategies, include

> 1. To initiate a process where women will perceive the need to move from a state of passive acceptance of their life situation to one of active self determination of their lives and their immediate environment. (Government of India 1988, 3)
>
> 2. To create an environment where women can seek knowledge and information and thereby empower them to play a positive role in their own development and development of society. (Government of India 1997, 5)

What do these statements reveal about the program's approach to women's empowerment? First, subaltern women are projected as both powerless, passive objects and as actively disempowered subjects, oppressed by social and state structures; one thus sees borrowings from both welfarist and GAD concepts. Second, they either lack a critical awareness of their subordination (false consciousness?) or have passively accepted it or do not have the ability to change it because of internalized fear or lack of information; this seems to be an adaptation of Freire's ideas (see chapter 1). Third, subaltern women do not contribute to their own, their communities', and the nation's development. What they require, therefore, is a benevolent, sympathetic and empowered hand (the state? NGO activists?), which will help them become aware agents of positive change. They need knowledge and information to fulfill their development and social duties in a responsible manner and to promote gender equality; and these are the goals the MS program hopes to achieve.

Governmental representations of subaltern women's lives and subjectivity raise some thorny issues. MS program documents seem to enforce a problematic "divide between false, overstated images of victimized and empowered womanhood [that] negate each other" (Mohanty 2002, 528). This move, as Mohanty claims, enacts a form of discursive colonization of marginalized women. For example, what is achieved by counterposing empowerment and victimhood as temporally and spatially separate states—where a woman can be either one or the other—rather than as coeval processes that shift based on particular contexts? Why depict subaltern women as always-already victims who lack awareness of their oppression? I do not wish to suggest that rural, landless Dalit women do not experience class, caste, and gender subordination of the worst kinds. However, instead of emphasizing these women's agency in negotiating multiple oppressions (Mani 1989b) or highlighting the contextual interplay between empowerment and disempowerment in their lives, state-authorized MS documents define subaltern women as victims of men, of society, and of tradition, who are therefore unable to partake in the progress of the nation. The work that these women do and the agency they exert as peasants, petty commodity-producers, mothers, and wives is thereby overlooked: their productive labor is erased and reproductive labor is naturalized as nonwork that does not contribute meaningfully to development. Their daily struggles for food, fuel, fodder, water, and in child rearing are mentioned, but lamented because they drain women's energy that could have been better channeled toward self and social development; these everyday struggles for survival, moreover, are not considered political. Program documents also position subaltern women as would-be liberators of themselves and others. Like Freire, MS sees the oppressed as potential political/revolutionary actors. I see this as a positive move. Yet, I question why subaltern women should bear the sole responsibility of undoing hierarchies and spearheading change and ask what kinds of antioppressive and solidary roles (in the Freirian sense) dominant state and social actors might be impelled to play in such liberatory and progressive social projects.

What does the preceding discussion reveal about the gendered dynamics of state-partnered women's empowerment and about the gender of the developmentalist state? I argue, following Nancy Fraser (1989), that the Indian state's development imaginary is implicitly gendered: it designs masculine and feminine programs and targets them at people who are differently positioned in terms of class, caste, and gender. Feminine programs include both welfare and empowerment (which are considered social, and therefore apolitical, programs), whereas masculine programs include agricultural and infrastructural development programs (which are purportedly gender neutral). Welfare programs have always focused on the uplift of the poor; here the category of the poor is not only caste and class specific, it is also feminized in that "the poor" are assumed to be passive and in need of benevolent help. Empowerment programs, by assuming a needy, ignorant, and oppressed female subject, also partially reiterate the welfarist logic. Programs belonging to the masculine category, on the other hand, assume a middle class, lower/upper caste, male subject. Agricultural development programs, for example, which seek to provide technical skills, knowledge, and credit to farmers, target men. They position men as productive, aware, knowledgeable, and responsible citizens, who can learn and apply technology in innovative ways. Meanwhile feminine programs position their feminized, primarily female, targets as needy, vulnerable, and unproductive dependents. The postcolonial Indian state's discourse on development and empowerment is thus a gendered one.

If welfare and empowerment programs are both feminized, as I have just argued, then how does empowerment differ from the welfare approach? Even though GAD-advocated empowerment was supposed to have revised and replaced welfarist notions of women's identities, as I discussed in chapter 1, this alternative strategy unwittingly reproduces some of the very gender norms that underlie welfarism. At first glance, empowerment seems to highlight women's agency in self-development. The goal of grassroots empowerment projects is to turn supposedly unproductive, ignorant, and passive subaltern women into responsibilized social actors and productive citizens. By emphasizing women's productivity, the empowerment logic builds on WID feminist ideas laid out in the previous chapter. However, by highlighting women's *latent* productivity, it also indexes welfare-based ideologies about women and work. The Indian state's version of empowerment is founded on subaltern women's passivity in the face of oppression. They need outside motivating forces to build awareness, maximize their productive capacity, and minimize their reproductive drain. This nurturing entails a management of women's perceptions and attitudes, and an enhancement of their knowledge and abilities. Admittedly, this is not the same kind of *care* promoted by old-style welfare strategies, which did not even consider poor women capable of real, productive work. However, despite their desire to liberate women's potential and emancipate societies, empowerment programs grounded in radical conscientization and feminist frameworks can, ironically, also serve to regulate and discipline subaltern women quite like welfare and WID programs, albeit in different ways.

Welfare and empowerment logics are interwoven, and yet, for MS employees and some Indian government officials, empowerment strategies represented a stark break with welfarism. They alleged that the MS program was unique, because unlike welfare-based programs, MS did not give women *handouts*, which supposedly create dependency. A program document clearly states that MS "is not involved in the delivery of services and resources" (Government of India 1997, 9). Instead of giving tangibles such as sewing machines, MS delivers intangible empowerment to women. The program's amazing achievement, according to MS-associated people, was that poor women participated even in the absence of material incentives. As Anita Joshi, an MS staff member, described,

> I think the edge that MS has . . . is the fact that it is not a delivery program; and [it is] indeed possible then, to look at the process of women mobilizing for change in an altruistic sense. In a sense [all] we are saying [to the women is] that we will help you find your feet. That is not an incentive. I doubt whether I would participate in a program if somebody were to say that [to me].

The MS clients I met with spoke excitedly about the nonmaterial benefits, such as knowledge and information [*buddhi aur gyan*], they derived from their participation in the program. But they also often expressed a desire for tangible things (see chapters 5 and 6). Many development NGOs offered their clients resources such as free medicines, sewing machines, and money. MS had to compete with such projects in order to establish its legitimacy and this was no easy task given that MS did not distribute tangible good to women. The program's focus on intangible consciousness-raising was also frowned upon by some local leaders, such as Shahida Banu in Nizabad, who exhorted MS functionaries to reconsider their approach and to make poor women's survival needs a priority.

MS clients' desire for concrete benefits and resources from the program complicates the subaltern altruism that Anita Joshi so admired. Joshi, a middle class, urban activist, indicated that she would not participate in a program that gave no tangible incentives; she nonetheless expected poor women to do so. Her use of the ideology of voluntarism to explain subaltern women's participation in MS problematically reinforced caste, class, and gender norms. Altruistic social work imagines a middle- or upper-caste and class housewife as its paradigmatic subject (see de Alwis 1995). It presupposes that (a) as housewives women only do housework, (b) housework is *natural*, reproductive female work, and (c) housewives have leisure time to do social work, which is an extension of their natural work and is hence unpaid. By defining subaltern women's labor for social change as altruistic (and therefore nonremunerative), Joshi implicitly reinstated the privileged, altruistic housewife norm and erased these women's daily survival work and desire for material improvement.

Expecting voluntary work from poor women who do not have any time to spare is a form of patriarchal exploitation that has been institutionalized and naturalized within the state's development framework. This thinking also seeps into the MS program as revealed by the ways in which it imagines the identities and roles of marginalized women and represents them as the ideal objects–subjects of empowerment. A focus on voluntarism regulates poor, lower-caste women's identities by normalizing the ideal of a middle- or upper-class and caste housewife, and furthers patriarchal ideas about women's work. Voluntarism squares with the neoliberal doctrine of pulling oneself by the bootstraps, but paradoxically also fosters the ideology of women's dependence on men and on state largesse. The Indian state's vision of empowerment continues to rely upon gender-, class-, and caste-based ideas about welfare. Examining who is defined as the classic client of an empowerment project and how she must participate in it helps to unravel the contradictions inherent in the logic of state-partnered women's empowerment. MS intends to undo gender power hierarchies but simultaneously re-inscribes these hierarchies.

Conclusion

In this chapter my purpose was to tease out the cultural and gendered logics of neoliberal governmentality and state formation, through analyzing the hybrid organization of the MS program, its location within the governmental structure, and the assumptions about disempowered subjects that guide it. That neoliberalism is altering the nature and working of states is now an established fact. What is less commented on is the complicated process of articulation through which these changes are affected in particular places and thus the subtle (or not) differences in the consequences of neoliberal globalization. An ethnographic study of state formation under neoliberalism highlights the contextual specificity of neoliberal transformations and adds conceptual depth to governmentality and state theories (see Introduction).

I revealed the cultural and gendered nature of state formation in postliberalization India by focusing on (a) the discursive construction of the state, and (b) the concurrence of welfare and empowerment ideologies in the present moment. Instead of taking the contours of the Indian state for a given, I illustrated how "it" materializes as a distinct, vertically authoritative, and encompassing, if ambiguously masculinist, entity through translocal policy instruments and empowerment ideologies, and through local planning discussions about the MS program's hybrid GONGO form. A GONGO is an oddity: it interweaves two supposedly distinct and very different entities, states and NGOs, in a single organization. My work shows that GONGOs are only apparently oxymoronic, and that GONGOs and NGOs are as intricately involved in the project of rule as the state is. Richa Nagar and Saraswati Raju comment on this governmentalization of society, claiming that in contemporary India, not only have "NGOs . . . become an arm of the government [but also] the government has become the biggest NGO" (Richa and Raju 2003, 3). This blurring of the divide between state and nonstate governmental entities underscores the need for practices that restore the distinctiveness and authority of the Indian state and help it to remake itself in a neoliberal image. The hybrid institutional form of a GONGO, ironically, fulfills this function in that it reifies the state as a partly detached and streamlined actor with the authority to create an autonomous GONGO for doing development work. The state's sponsorship of empowerment as a strategy of governance further reconfigures its identity and role as a facilitator of self-actualization and self-development, rather than simply a provider and caretaker.

The neoliberal shifting of responsibility for governmental welfare functions from state agencies to quasi- and nonstate entities in India, however, is partial and contentious. Indian state transformation in the context of neoliberalism cannot be easily captured under the theme of "smaller states rid of their welfare roles." The spread of empowerment programs alongside the increased presence of NGOs and GONGOs do not necessarily imply a shrunken state that has dismantled welfare but point to a multiplication of governmental bodies whose autonomy from the state remains questionable. Empowerment strategies and new institutional entities are increasingly entangled within webs of governance as instruments of rule (see chapter 1). Moreover, the Indian state cannot completely privatize its developmental functions because they are an inseparable part of its postcolonial identity and legitimacy; indeed, the national government continues to design new redistributive projects and expand existing ones (see Conclusion). Even as the neoliberal logic compels states to roll back welfare, growing dissatisfaction with the uneven benefits of liberalization and populist democratic politics in India exert contradictory pressures on state structures, thus resulting in a simultaneous usage of both redistributive and empowerment initiatives. Indeed, the implementation of empowerment programs by governmental entities, such as NGOs and GONGOs, allows for a reconciliation between the developmentalist and neoliberalizing faces of the Indian state: it enables the state to continue performing its legitimizing, if altered, development function, by building the capacities of various actors to care for themselves and by distributing intangible *awareness* in addition to tangible resources. The state can thus appear to become leaner without abandoning its development role.

My work shows that in India, welfare and empowerment strategies are not consecutive but coexistent. Empowerment programs do not replace welfare programs; they also do not dismantle masculinist welfare ideologies but instead retain some key residuals. Although the "gender and empowerment" focus of programs such as MS, building on GAD frameworks, was supposed to have substituted old-style "women's welfare and development," my analysis of the MS program's location within the governmental system and it's representation of subaltern women as classic objects–subjects of empowerment shows the extent to which patriarchal, welfarist notions about women's "proper" identities, place, and work continue to underpin gender and empowerment thinking.

Debates about the placement of MS within the ministerial hierarchy of the Indian government and the range of official reactions to the program and to women's empowerment (from active support, to neglect, to suspicion, to disparagement), underscore the masculinist and polyphonous nature of state structures. The state is not an autonomous and unified actor, speaking with a singular voice, but a complex entity simultaneously constitutive of and constituted by larger social relations. Not everyone who works for the state subscribes to patriarchal ideologies. Their perceptions of and approaches to gender issues are overdetermined by their location and rank within the government, and by the various aspects of their social positioning as members of civil society. Despite the wide-ranging official perspectives on empowerment and gender issues, however, state development practices can fortify existing relations of dominance and subordination. This is a consequence of the masculinist nature of state power and bureaucratic practices (Brown 1995). Therefore, although the state is not a homogenously patriarchal entity with unified gender interests, even "pro-women" governmental practices and policies, such as those of empowerment, can end up producing a coherence of effects where gender inequalities are concerned.

State participation in the MS program's crossbred GONGO form is rife with contradictions. Even though MS has become an icon and a repository of the Indian state's innovative stance on gender issues, it continues to be a marginalized "island" in the governmental structure because of its low budget, women only focus, and lack of redistributable resources. Whereas MS attempts to move away from welfarist definitions of women's subjectivities, it also ascribes to naturalized assumptions about women's passivity, altruism, and essentially reproductive (thus secondary) labor. Finally, even as MS explicitly aims to undo gender and other social hierarchies, it also ends up reinforcing them. In chapter 3 I reveal further the antinomies that state participation in MS raises by focusing on the program's employment arrangements and the work-related practices of the women who staff it. I demonstrate how MS representatives use the program's GONGO form to negotiate the paradoxes of "state sponsored women's empowerment," and to use the not-so-coherent nature of governmental spaces toward alternative and surprising ends.

3

Empowering Moves

Paradoxes, Subversions, Dangers

One of the key reasons why the planners of MS structured it as a GONGO was to use the state's greater reach and resources to empower subaltern women. The GONGO structure also addressed some activists' concerns about state involvement in women's empowerment. These activists believed that the program's partial nonstate identity, characterized by some as its "semi-autonomous" nature, would shield it from bureaucratic co-optation and afford MS functionaries the freedom to interpret and implement empowerment in an open-ended and flexible manner. In this chapter I examine the extent to which these advantages of a hybrid organizational form are realizable by delineating what the MS program's GONGO nature means on the ground for its employees.

Women's empowerment programs impact the lives not only of those who are targeted by them but also of those who work for them. Persons identified as facilitators of empowerment—and in MS they are primarily women—are implicitly positioned between the disempowered (subaltern actors) and the powerful (state and civil-society actors); in occupying a mediating space as go-betweens, however, they also concretize the two seemingly opposing poles on the empowerment continuum. These facilitators are seen as translators of state and donor agendas, feminist goals, and subaltern women's definitions of empowerment, which are often contradictory. The women who help implement projects like MS, however, do not merely translate preset empowerment agendas, but interpret and materially shape these visions through their everyday work practices. Furthermore, they do not simply support marginalized women's struggles but participate in and are directly influenced by them. Hence, it becomes important to examine the practices and predicaments of facilitator-activists. How does mobilizing empowerment on the ground affect the self-image and work lives of MS personnel and alter the very meaning of empowerment?

One of the first things that struck me as I began the rural portion of my research was the perplexing manner in which MS field personnel positioned the program in front of different audiences. I began chapter 2 with a description of how Meena Rani identified MS as an NGO in certain situations and as a government project in others. She was not alone in her vacillation. I observed other field-level functionaries position the program in a similarly mobile fashion. Curiously, they did not identify MS as a GONGO, but chose instead to strategically position the program in an either–or (NGO or government organization) manner.

Prabha Kishore described the dual nature of MS's identity in terms of its "two hats." Kishore was a native of the hilly regions of northern India and had been with MS for many years. Her easy manner belied a steely resolve and a commanding presence—when she spoke in rapid-fire Hindi, people listened with rapt attention. I described to her the confused and varied responses I got from program participants when I asked them whether MS was a government project or not. "How do people perceive it—as a *sanstha* [an NGO] or a government program?" I questioned. Kishore's perfectly round face broke into a knowing smile. "This [confusion] has been one thing that is unique about this program. [The government label] is a [source of] strength but it has also been [the program's] biggest weakness. We have also used [the government label] a lot. When we started this program we never said that this was a government program. . . . In fact, for the first one or one and a half years, we did not even see the face of the government." "Did you know that this was a government program? What was your perception initially?" I asked. "All we knew was that MS was under the Ministry of Human Resource Development but nothing else," Prabha Kishore replied. "Who were the government people involved—we did not know anything about these matters. So we never felt that this was a government program. . . . We used to think that this was an NGO. . . . The program's nature, its way of working is like NGOs." "This program is unique," she continued, after a momentary pause. "It wears two *topis* [hats]—one is a governmental hat and the other is a nongovernmental hat. We have made very good use of both these hats."

In this chapter I examine the dilemmas that MS staff members faced as a result of the program's quasi-state identity. What limits did this partial government nature put on the work identities and empowerment-related efforts of MS employees, and how were they able to successfully skirt around these constraints on occasion and engender unexpectedly empowering results? State participation in MS, as I demonstrate below, raised two key conundrums for its workforce. First, they had to define their work identities. As GONGO functionaries, were they government employees or NGO employees? The latter received less remuneration but had more flexibility in their work, whereas the former earned more but had to work within governmental dictates. Second, MS representatives had to decide on how to identify the program in front of different audiences with varied imaginations of and expectations from state and nonstate actors. I show that although the MS program's hybrid identity raised these dilemmas for its workforce, it also provided a partial resolution. Program employees shifted back and forth in how they positioned MS and themselves, using both aspects of the program's crossbred structure to negotiate the very contradictions that this hybrid form threw in their path.

In the next section I describe the program's employment arrangements and analyze the material impact of its GONGO organization on the women who work for MS. I then illustrate how MS functionaries shift the manner in which they identify themselves and the program, in response to how they are viewed by their interlocutors. I highlight the dialectic between positioning and being positioned (Hall 1989), through a series of ethnographic vignettes, paying particular attention to what these strategies and encounters tell us about the imagined state and state power. Analyzing the program's employment arrangements and practices and the occasions when MS functionaries don different program hats reveals much about how the state materializes through everyday development practices and the kinds of empowering challenges that are thwarted and enabled in the context of this part-state, part-feminist program. I build on the analysis presented in chapter 2 to unravel the paradoxes that arise when empowerment is mobilized, with state endorsement and involvement, as a category of governance (Chatterjee 2004). I shed further light on (a) the gender and discursive construction of the state and (b) the governmentalization of society through empowerment techniques.

I argue that government participation in grassroots women's empowerment is a double-edged sword. It has the potential to deradicalize empowerment by turning it into a bureaucratic, professional governmental intervention.[1] But if empowerment, at its very core, is about power relations, as I argued in chapter 1, then even its most bureaucratic renderings are inherently political although they might appear in apolitical garb. Empowerment programs undertaken by states, GONGOs, or NGOs do not depoliticize struggle as much as they open up new vistas and forms of political action. These programs "[structure] a field of possible actions rather than determine outcomes"

(Cruikshank 1999, 23). I show how MS engenders unintended effects (Ferguson 1994) that end up empowering women, but perhaps not in accordance with hegemonic statist scripts. Regardless of what the official line on women's empowerment is or the competing agendas of various state actors on that issue (see chapter 2), officials are, to an extent, unable to rein in the unexpected excess that programs such as MS unleash.

MS and Its Employees

In this section I examine how the MS program's crossbred GONGO nature manifests itself in the daily work lives of its employees and how it impacts MS workers' employment terms and perceptions of their work identities and practices. I use this analysis to illustrate popular imaginations of the state and nonstate entities and to shed further light on the discursive and gendered nature of the state.

Almost all MS staff members are women, except for drivers, accountants, and some office assistants (which reveals a gender typing of work). An important consequence of the program's semiautonomous GONGO structure is that MS functionaries are positioned by the government as NGO employees. At one level, this sat well with many program personnel whom I interviewed. Although they complained about the program's marginalization within the governmental hierarchy, as it is a women's program that employs mostly women, they were also thankful for this distancing from the state. They looked on MS as different from other government programs in terms of its approach, ethic, and mode of operation and took pride in distinguishing themselves from government employees. For example, Seema Batra, a mid-level employee, explained that

> More than 80 percent of the people who work for MS do not treat it like government service . . . or a job. They are . . . here because they have some experience and they want to do something with that experience. . . . The salaries people get in MS are not enough for survival. So the people who work in MS do so only because they have a certain devotion toward their work. You don't see that in government departments [where] people only come for the sake of their salaries.

Whereas "government service" implies stability and status, criticisms about the "nine to five–job" mentality, lack of motivation, and low productivity of government employees abound in Indian public cultural discourses. MS employees' efforts to dissociate themselves from this state-related negativity partook in this widely prevalent critique of the state. Their careful self-positioning as NGO workers reproduced an image of the state as an entity that fosters sloth and apathy and employs inefficient people who treat their work as merely a job. They implicitly constructed the nonstate sector as a distinct space characterized by creativity, hard work, enthusiasm, and innovation. This sector, unfortunately, was also associated with job insecurity and lower salaries.

Even though MS employees were proud of their nongovernmental identity and manner of working, they nonetheless lamented their lower earnings. Comparisons with government employees, who did less work and earned more money, were inevitable. Because MS functionaries are not considered part of the state's bureaucratic apparatus but as employees of a GONGO, they are denied the privileges and benefits that come with government employment. Thus, they are hired on temporary performance-based *anubandh* [annual contracts], and their compensation takes the form of *maandey* [honoraria], which are less than the salaries for comparable government jobs and do not include the health or pension benefits that state employees receive.[2] In 1998 full-time MS sahyoginis [field-level workers], for example, drew honoraria that were not much more than the state-stipulated minimum daily skilled wage.[3]

Categorizing MS personnel as nongovernmental is not only financially convenient for the government but it also gives the impression of a more streamlined state in the form of a smaller and more flexible workforce. Meanwhile, the program's staff suffers from job uncertainty, low earnings, and a lack of benefits, even though a significant portion of this workforce consists of women, many of whom have no alternative means of support. As one employee put it: "[MS] is famous for attracting 'abandoned' women—women whose husbands kick them out, who are divorcées or widows. [They] need this job for survival." MS has been a refuge for women who are actual or effective heads of their households and whose salaries are a critical source of income for their families. And yet the program's employment practices suggest that its planners viewed workers' earnings as supplementary, as indicated by their low pay packages and relative lack of benefits. Ironically, the ability to "stand on one's own feet" was a common refrain I heard from government officials, NGO activists, MS personnel, and clients when I asked them to define women's empowerment. They told me that unless women are economically independent, they will not be able to make decisions within the family or make strategic personal choices, which are the key pillars of empowerment. Despite the critical link that people in the government and in MS made between economic self-reliance and women's empowerment, the survival needs of the women who worked for the program tended to be overlooked.

This lack of attention might itself reflect the feminization of empowerment work as "unskilled" and "voluntary" (chapter 2). Seema Batra recounted an occasion where a bureaucrat in charge of program finances refused a request by some mid- and lower-level MS workers for a salary increase. He allegedly told them that they should be grateful for employment in MS because, with their inferior skills and education levels, they would not even be considered for government jobs.[4] He at once challenged MS personnel's denigration of state work as dead-end and slothful and suggested that empowerment work was less skilled and more expendable than employment in the formal structures of the state. His comments hinted at a neoliberal logic of government that marginalizes empowerment and poverty-alleviation work as "social" work, shifts it from state agencies to social institutions, and redefines proper state work as facilitating productive economic growth (through reduced government intervention). Such representations carve out the state as a zone of "serious" and "real" economic development efforts requiring a higher degree of skill and thus help reinstate its vertical authoritativeness.

These examples of MS employment practices shed further light on the ways in which gendered and classist ideologies are woven into the program. Designating empowerment labor as altruistic social work, as I explained in chapter 2, implies that it is extra-economic, un- or underskilled, and feminized. The work that the MS program's predominantly female employees do is conceptualized as a natural extension of the reproductive labour they perform at home and in their communities; empowerment labor is therefore seen as deserving lower remuneration. Paying women supplemental honoraria for "feminized reproductive work" and denying them state-associated benefits ensure MS women's economic dependency. The program's employment practices, quite like its construction of its ideal target population (see chapter 2), reinforce patriarchal notions about women's roles and identities and help normalize a middle-class and caste-based, male-headed family in which women's work is marginal. MS's employment arrangements, yet again, perpetuate some of the very classist and gendered hierarchies that its empowerment goals seek to unravel.

These normative ideologies and the material consequences they wrought, however, were not unquestioningly accepted by program staffers. Although they cherished their NGO-like work ethic, MS employees often criticized the official slights and material disadvantages they bore because of their NGO linkage and challenged official portrayals of their work as altruistic. For example, field-level MS workers, or sahyoginis, proudly told me that their work never ended. "This is not a job, *didi* [sister], where you come in at nine, sit at your desk, and leave at five. We work all the time," one sahyogini claimed. They also saw their MS-related work as *qualitatively* different from what they did at home, and not as an extension of the latter (Gupta and Sharma 2006). Many sahyoginis told me that working with the program enabled them to "emerge from their houses" [*ghar se bahar nikala hai*]. It gave them newfound access to public spaces and helped them develop skills in report writing, speaking in public with men and women, leading workshops, interacting with bureaucrats and understanding state procedures, and even riding a bicycle (women riding bicycles in this part of U.P. were an uncommon sight). As far as they were concerned, their program-related tasks were distinct from the work they did at home as wives, mothers, sisters, and daughters-in-law. Furthermore, MS functionaries saw their mobilization work as absolutely necessary for equitable national development. Their empowering interventions were not only important in and of themselves, but also crucial to the success of other government projects. It was through their efforts that marginalized rural women became aware of their rights and entitlements (rationed food and subsidized housing, for example), developed the ability to access state-provided resources, and learned how to hold officials accountable. MS workers refused to let their selfless devotion to their empowerment tasks be mistaken for normative feminine altruism. Their work was not ancillary "women's work," but a critical part of development and therefore deserved better remuneration (see also Gupta and Sharma 2006). They openly complained about their heavy workloads, low pay, and the class, educational, and gender hierarchies associated with the program.

In two of the three states in which MS was first initiated, field-level staff members contested the material and ideological inequalities perpetuated by the program by attempting to unionize and demanding a regularization of their jobs. However, their mobilizations were squashed, and in one state, many of the workers who took up the unionization fight were fired. One of my informants explained that such a step was taken because had MS workers' jobs been regularized and their salaries and benefits brought up to government levels, women working on time-bound contracts in other state-initated development projects (such as ICDS) would have probably demanded similar benefits. This would have had serious financial implications for the government. Moreover, she stated, once unionized, MS women would have likely treated their work like a government job and the work quality and quantity would have consequently suffered. Neither of these potential outcomes was desirable. Increasing financial outlays for MS and other redistributive development programs would connote "big" government and a welfare state, which is exactly what states want to avoid in the neoliberal era; decreasing work-related productivity and dedication among workers would hamper the MS program, which relies precisely on these factors for its success.

Regardless of these justifications, however, the fact that some female functionaries of a women's empowerment program were fired when they dared to collectively organize and demand their economic rights as workers sheds stark light on the contrary logic of state-involved women's empowerment and on the gendered nature of state power. The threat of destitution wielded by officials to curb dissent among workers reaffirmed the state's vertical authority and effectively countered MS women's resistance against the material and social hierarchies at play in MS.[5] These incidents also hinted at the kinds of empowerment state agents considered legitimate and the extent to which they were willing to let MS women, both employees and participants, empower themselves.

Mahila Samakhya's Two Hats: The Program as a Moving Target

In addition to mystifying its workers' identities and negatively affecting their job security and pay packages, MS's hybrid GONGO form and the state's participation in the program raised a second dilemma for its workers: they had to figure out how to position the program in different situations in front of varied groups of people. Although they readily explained the program's crossbred nature to me, I did not observe program personnel identifying MS as a GONGO in field-level interactions. Instead, they shifted the program's identity between its government and nongovernment labels or, according to Prabha Kishore, its "two hats." She told me that MS personnel put both these hats to good use. For instance, she kept two letterheads in stock. "When we write to NGOs, we use the . . . letterhead that states that Mahila Samakhya is a voluntary organization registered under the 1860 Societies Act and gives our registration number. We open [the letter] with 'Dear Colleague or Dear Friend, Namaste,'" she said in a sweet, nonthreatening voice. A different audience and situation, however, required a different kind of letter. "When we need to put pressure . . . [we use] the letterhead bearing the words 'Ministry of Human Resource Development.'" Prabha Kishore enunciated the last phrase slowly, emphasizing each word. "This letterhead evokes the reaction," she now lowered her voice and mimicked what would be the (fearful) response: "Oh God, this is a government program!" She then added, "We even stamp our seal on these letters and sign them—we write them exactly like government letters are written." She conveyed the sense of power that properly written, formatted, and worded official letters carried and the wariness that they instilled in people. To express authority, MS employees used "official" labels, styles, languages, and tones of voice.

I observed them enact this official style when introducing the program to state administrators. Meena Rani, for example, identified MS as a government program to Nizabad block office administrators in order to garner the support of officials who might otherwise be hostile toward NGOs that implement women's empowerment projects (see chapter 2). She also made sure to mention to these local government functionaries that MS was a program started by the Government of India, which sat above them, in New Delhi. In so doing, she attempted to work the bureaucratic hierarchy to her advantage: the program's association with a vertically higher branch of the government was meant to give it more authority. However, these efforts were not always successful, as I demonstrated in the last chapter. Officials at varied bureaucratic levels did not necessarily give MS the kind of importance it deserved despite its state linkage.

MS workers also wore the government label in front of rural audiences when they wanted to exercise statist authority. For instance, Leela Vati, a field-level employee, used the government tag to intimidate her clients. She, along with two of her colleagues, visited some villages from which the MS program was being phased out and told the participating women that they had to return the few things that their collectives had received from the program, such as water pails, rugs, and storage trunks (she did not have any explicit mandate from her superiors to demand these things from her clients). Program participants in the village of Bilaspur told me later that Leela Vati had threatened them when they refused to follow her orders: "If you don't return the things, the government jeep will come tomorrow, forcibly take everything, and dishonor you in front of everyone!" She also pressured the leader of the Bilaspur MS collective to sign a blank paper. Residents alleged that she had done so in order to cover her tracks—she could easily write a note on that piece of paper stating that the village women had voluntarily returned the things to her and thus avoid any accusations of wrongdoing. When I asked the collective leader why she had signed on the blank piece of paper, she shrugged her shoulders, stating that Leela Vati had threatened the local women with punitive action from higher authorities if they refused to comply. Leela Vati thus effectively used statist symbols and practices, such as the jeep and written documentation, to perform official authority and exploit her clients' fear of the repressive state-as-taker.

Not all MS functionaries were as successful in deploying the state label as a symbol of power in front of rural subaltern actors. Rani Kumari, for instance, donned the government hat when she wanted to conduct a preliminary household survey in Banipur village. Although MS is not a target-driven program but a "process-oriented" one (as several program documents describe), which focuses on qualitative assessments of empowerment strategies, quantitative tools such as participatory rural appraisals and surveys are used by program personnel (see also Gupta and Sharma 2006).[6] I observed one such quantitative encounter where Rani Kumari positioned MS as a government program. On a winter morning in December 1998, I set out with an MS survey team, in the usual blue MS jeep, for the village of Banipur, which had been identified as a potential program site. The driver parked the jeep at the edge of the village, and the team walked to the center of the Dalit hamlet, which proved deserted. As we stood there, wondering what to do, a woman, wielding a sickle, appeared from around the corner. Rani walked up to her and, without introducing herself, asked her where everyone was. The woman told us that the residents of the hamlet were working in the fields. Rani took out her pen and questionnaire and asked the woman her name. The woman eyed her suspiciously and said, "First you tell me why you are here and then I will tell you my name." Bindu, a teacher at an MS preschool in the area, walked up to her and said, "Sister, we are here to start a school for your children. We have come here to listen to your problems." The woman looked at Bindu, unconvinced, and replied, "Are you here for votes?" Now Rani shook her head and said that they wanted to conduct a survey of the village and write down the residents' names. The woman paused for a moment and then said, "It is your job to write our names down. You will write our names for the purpose of your job and leave. Meanwhile we will continue to live our lives of drudgery and servitude." At this Rani said, "All right, I will tell you my name." But the woman interrupted Rani: "What will I do with your name? Go and tell your name to the government!" As an afterthought she added, "Are you writing our names in order to give us money?" Rani said no and introduced herself as a representative of the MS program. She explained that it was a government program that worked with poor women and gave them information on their rights. After listening to Rani, the woman said, "If you want to write my name down then give me a piece of paper with your name on it." Purba, another MS team member, chuckled softly and remarked, "This one knows about her rights!" The village woman ignored Purba's comment and continued, "You can write my name down only if you give me money." Rani seemed a bit irritated. "All right, then," she stated, "we will leave. It was nice meeting you. Let us shake hands." But the village woman had caught the sarcasm in Rani's voice and refused to shake hands with her. "Why should I shake your hand? I will do it only if you offer it with love," she said defiantly. Everyone said, "Yes, of course, with love," and shook hands. The MS representatives still had not learned the woman's name.

As the team walked back toward the jeep, we ran into a group of women and men. Upon finding out that they were residents of Banipur's Dalit hamlet, Rani told them that her team represented MS, a government program, and wanted to conduct a survey. One woman commented, "Sure, write down the names of all eleven member of my family—maybe we will get some food in return for telling you our names." But a man, who was part of this group, declined to answer any questions, stating that "People have come here before and taken our names, and then nothing happens." Other residents agreed to be surveyed, but only after they had condemned the failed development initiatives in the village and sought MS functionaries' help in obtaining cash, food, and water facilities available through government programs. After recording the answers of these residents, the MS team walked back to the jeep. As we boarded the vehicle, we were approached by four men. "This jeep is from the Department of Education," one man remarked. He had obviously read the official license plate. He then looked at us and loudly declared, "All development programs have failed in this village" and walked on.[7]

Banipur's inhabitants clearly associated Rani and her team with the state. First, the MS jeep, with government markings, stood in plain sight of the residents. Second, MS functionaries were in the village to gather census data and record it in written form, practices that are generally linked with the state and help produce its vertical authority (Gupta and Sharma 2006). Third, Rani had introduced the program as a government initiative, which prompted some residents to demand development assistance from her in exchange for providing information about their households. The villagers clearly saw the state as a provider of resources necessary for survival. The Banipur incident revealed the extent to which subaltern imaginations of the state are bound up with both material need and powerfulness (see chapter 5). Despite the authority associated with the state, however, some residents refused to participate in the survey. They questioned the legitimacy of the state-as-taker, which took information from poor villagers without giving anything in return. Rani Kumari's use of the government label in this instance clearly did not guarantee her unquestioned authority and compliance.[8]

When it was not authority but legitimacy that MS staff members desired or when they needed to justify the program's lack of resources, they rejected the government hat and took on the NGO label instead. I saw them don the NGO hat on several occasions. On an unusually cold and overcast day in January 1999, for instance, I joined district- and field-level MS staff members for their monthly staff meeting in their new block office in Nizabad. The office was located on the second floor of a private home. After climbing a set of steep and narrow stairs, the meeting participants and I entered the one-room office. The room was barren except for a low wooden bed, strewn with cooking utensils and posters in one corner. The walls were painted a bright aqua green and the cement floor was covered with red and black striped cotton dhurries. There was a small storage closet on one end of the room. Outside of the room was a narrow balcony facing Nizabad's main road.

We shut the door and windows in the room to keep out the cold and street noise and sat on the floor, huddled close together for warmth. The lone forty-watt bulb in the room provided barely enough light for us to write. After distributing some stationery items among themselves, the staff members began discussing whether they should close down some of the MS-run alternative preschools because other government-run schools had opened up in the area. As these deliberations proceeded, someone knocked at the door. Danu Bai got up and opened the door to find a stocky man standing before her. He was dressed in a white cotton *kurta* [long shirt] with a wool vest and sported a cap and gold-frame sunglasses. Danu bent her head and greeted him. She introduced the man as Yogender Maurya, a local *neta* [literally a leader but this word often connotes a political party worker] from the Dalit Sena Party. We exchanged greetings, and Danu cleared the bed and offered him a seat. Meanwhile, the MS women and I sat on the floor, facing him. Maurya remarked that he had dropped in to wish us all a happy New

Year. He proceeded to show us a card that he had received from one of the cabinet ministers in New Delhi and also some pictures of himself taken with the same minister. He was obviously establishing his credentials and legitimacy as a member of the local power elite—a greeting card from the office of a national minister was a clear marker of Maurya's privileged status.

Danu informed the rest of us that Maurya had helped her secure the office in Nizabad. She thanked him but complained that the landlady was not only charging a higher rent than she had originally quoted but also threatening further increases. Maurya tried to ease her worries. "I know the woman; she will not increase your rent. . . . You people are working here like government workers. The landlady must have thought that since this is a government program, she would be able to get more money [*maal*] out of you. I will talk with her." With that assurance, Maurya departed. Nirmala Devi, another staffer and local resident, notified Danu of an alternative office location and the rest of the team decided to inquire about it.

We all piled into the blue MS jeep and proceeded towards the prospective office. It was already getting dark by the time we pulled up in front of a fairly large brick house. Two men, seated on a cot outside of the house, recognized Nirmala Devi and exchanged greetings with her. Nirmala introduced us as MS workers and told the men that we were interested in the office space on their compound. The older man walked us to a building next door and turned the light on. We stood in a large room, surrounded by neatly stacked sacks of grain. He informed us that this "office" was previously used by a bank and promised to clear out the stored grain in no time. When Danu Bai inquired about the rent, he quoted a figure of Rs 740, which was what the bank had paid. Danu pleaded with him to lower the rent. MS was an NGO [*sanstha*], she explained, and could not afford market rents: "Even Rs 500 is too much for us." But the landlord was unwilling to negotiate. As the MS team was leaving his house, Sushil, the MS driver, commented in a low tone that the landlord had demanded a higher rent because he saw us arrive in a government jeep. The MS jeep had "Department of Education, Government of India" printed on it in prominent white letters; the license plate also had government markings. MS was perceived as a government program, and government officials were obviously expected to pay higher rents.

These instances are indicative of how people imagine the state, and how MS personnel have to therefore carefully reposition the program to circumvent their expectations. Two landlords allegedly inflated office rents because they saw MS as a government program that could thus be "milked" for money. The staff members positioned MS as an NGO in these situations in order to negotiate a lower rent, but their efforts at challenging the landlords' perceptions of who they were proved unsuccessful.

Like these landlords, the women that MS staff members wanted to recruit as program participants also construed the state as an entity flush with resources and as a giver. These women often asked what they would receive from MS for participating. In their experience, most development programs distributed tangible resources to their clients, and they expected MS to do the same. MS, however, is not a service-delivery program, and its functionaries had to identify it as an NGO in such situations to establish legitimacy in the eyes of potential clients. Because it was an NGO, they explained to village women, MS was a trustworthy entity that would support and stand by them, even though it did not have anything material to offer. In positioning MS as an NGO on such occasions, program personnel implicitly distinguished between the ways in which state and nonstate organizations operated, played on the apparent association of the state with material resources, and strengthened the image of the state as a provider.

Identifying MS as an NGO in front of rural women proved beneficial for program functionaries in other situations as well. Two days before the botched-up rent negotiations described earlier, I witnessed Danu Bai interacting with a group of program clients from Seelampur block, where the program was being phased out. The women were upset that MS was leaving their area. "You are leaving us alone," they accused, "now who will support us!" "This is not a government program that will go on forever," Danu explained. She reminded the women that MS was an NGO, a time-bound project, and therefore had to end. In fact, some MS field-level workers in Seelampur block, whose employment was being terminated because of program phase out, used the same NGO explanation to reconcile with their own loss.

MS functionaries' shifting positioning of the program in different contexts and in front of diverse audiences both catered to and shaped their interlocutors' ideas of the state and NGOs. People's perceptions of these entities are based on their social locations, previous interactions with bureaucrats and NGO workers, and public cultural discourses (Gupta 1995; Sharma and Gupta 2006). For example, the subaltern actors I encountered envisioned the ideal state as a caring provider. This state-as-caretaker was supposed to ensure their means of survival. In practice, however, officials were dishonest, untrustworthy, and uncaring (see chapter 5). What subalterns encountered more often, therefore, was the authoritative face of the state-as-taker, which took away information, possessions, and even fertility.[9] Such experiences compromised the legitimacy they attributed to the state-as-caretaker. MS representatives had to navigate around these sedimented understandings of the state when pitching the program to differently positioned audiences. They played the divide between the two sides of the program's GONGO identity, constructing NGOs as legitimate, trustworthy, and time-bound entities with no resources and the state as an authoritative, perpetual entity flush with resources but questionable in terms of its legitimacy and the dedication of its workforce. Through their practice of mobile identification, MS staffers discursively constructed the boundary between state and nonstate spheres.

The fact that their strategy of donning different hats was not always successful in its objectives also illustrates the tense nature of performative moves (which enact and make real "the state," authority, and identities, among other things). Such moves involve straddling a fine line between positioning and being positioned, between self-definition and being defined in certain ways by relations of power; MS staffers were not always able to negotiate this line in the manner in which they intended or desired.

Although they wore different hats in different situations as a programmatic strategy, most MS functionaries saw themselves as allied with a just and compassionate NGO world. This self-identification proved financially expedient for state officials, as I discussed earlier, who positioned MS employees as NGO workers in order to justify low compensation and benefits. But in matters relating to antistate mobilizations, officials treated MS personnel as government workers. Like other government employees, MS representatives were forbidden from participating in or spearheading rallies against the state. Ironically, most issues that MS women took up in their projects for empowerment and social change involved government agencies. Whether it was the issuance of land titles, dealing with police matters or legal issues, or fulfillment of basic needs, most problems that program clients sought to resolve were connected with specific branches of the state system. But the women working for MS, positioned as quasistate employees, were not allowed to take part in the antistate struggles of subaltern women.

Seema Singh, a mid-level MS staffer, explained this Catch-22 in the following manner:

> All the issues that we take up are, in some way, connected to the government. So if we come within the ambit of the government and

> succumb to governmental pressure, we will not be able to take up any issues. For example, the government issues licenses for *thekas* [liquor shops]. In our district we took up a big fight on this issue. In one village the police beat up women with wooden sticks as they were trying to bust the local theka. Many women had broken bones but we did not back off and surrender to the government. A few days later, the theka closed down. . . . If we had caved into governmental pressure, we would have never been able to take up this fight.

Singh told me that the presence of a government-licensed liquor store in the main market of her program area had increased incidents of harassment and gendered violence against women and girls.[10] The local MS office took up this matter under Singh's leadership. "We got a written notice that we could not participate in any *aandolan* [protest or struggle]," she explained. "[But] we devised ways of participating; we strategized. Can't participate? Hah! We spearheaded a big antialcohol campaign and shouted so many slogans against the government. During the protest, when government officials asked us who we were, we simply pretended to be village women!" Singh's team members filed properly worded leave applications at the office, took the day off, and protested as ordinary citizens. The creative self-positioning of MS workers as local residents and their careful adherence to bureaucratic procedures, such as filing written records, assisted them in working around the state's disciplinary strategies and in carrying out the empowerment work they aspired to do.

Renu Rawat, a former mid-level MS staffer, used similar tactics but was not as successful as Seema Singh in countering bureaucratic surveillance. Rawat and I met in her motel room in Delhi on a hot and humid July afternoon in 1999. It so happened that the motel was experiencing a power outage, not an unusual occurrence during Delhi summers. We spoke for about an hour and a half, alternatively sweating and fanning ourselves with old newspapers, and drinking warm soda. Rawat, a small-framed, bespectacled woman, had spent many years working as a grassroots activist, especially on the issue of violence against women. She was soft-spoken but firm in her manner and speech. She exuded a clarity and strength, which I had noticed among many MS functionaries. She narrated an incident in which she had been unable to participate openly in village women's protests against the government's liquor licensing laws; however, she figured out other ways of backing their struggle.

"One of the NGOs in our area had launched a big campaign against alcohol," began Renu. "We were a government program and, as representatives of a government program, we were not allowed to participate in any protests. The DM [District Magistrate] called me and ordered me to stop working with this NGO on the antialcohol issue. He told me, 'Just give it to me in writing that this NGO is not working properly, and I will force the NGO to close down.' He really harassed me. . . . But I did not say a word against this NGO. . . . Our MS women participated in the protest meetings organized by the NGO. There was a government-licensed liquor store in the middle of town and women wanted it removed. . . . We were supporting the NGO and these women [in their struggle]. The dharnas [sit-ins] went on for two months and our MS sangha [village collective] women took turns at participating. I also [participated] initially when the issue was not yet 'hot.' I even gave a speech at one of these rallies. But when things started heating up and officials began suspecting our involvement, I stopped going to the protests. Then I began helping [the protestors] by writing letters on their behalf, preparing press briefs, and garnering other people's support. I . . . remained in the background. At one of the protest rallies, women decided to stop traffic. A lot of MS women were present. . . . I had instructed the sahyoginis to put leave applications on file, take off for the day, and participate in the rally. MS clients are, of course, free to do what they want—sangha women do not come under any such government-imposed conditions [that prohibit them to participate in anti-government rallies]. I, on the other hand, was affected by these stipulated conditions—I could not go. I stayed in the office that day. The SDM's [Sub-District Magistrate] vehicle was continuously driving by our office and keeping a close watch on me. [The officials] knew that I was involved, and even leading this protest, but they were unable to catch me red-handed. They were constantly watching me and so I remained in the office the whole time. The police resorted to *lathi*-charge [using wooden batons on protestors] at the rally. Many of our women were badly beaten up and had to be admitted to the local hospital. I dispatched our program jeep, which was a government vehicle, to bring the MS women back. Many of the [MS] sangha women returned to the office and yelled at me. 'We got beaten up over there and here you are comfortable in your office!' I sat them down and provided them with tea and food—they had not eaten all day. That is the role I played. I had already informed our state-level program director that the DM was harassing me. I told her that if the DM called [and questioned] her [about the program's or my participation in the antialcohol rally], she was to tell him that I was not involved in any way. And as far as [the other program] functionaries were concerned, they were technically on leave for the day and we did not keep tabs on what they did when they were on leave! My superior reassured me and told me not to worry."

Here was an instance of direct state repression. Renu Rawat was prohibited from joining an antialcohol rally. Government officials in the area knew that she headed the local MS office, kept tabs on her movements, harassed her, and prevented her from protesting the government's liquor-licensing policies. Forced to remain in her office the entire day, she assisted the protesters in other, less obvious, ways—by writing press briefs for the campaign, for example, and by allowing her field-level functionaries to take the day off to join in the rally. Whereas her efforts succeeded in insulating her from direct state repression, Rawat bore the ire of her clients who accused her of escaping the police beatings they received; that was the price she paid for occupying the ambiguous position of a government-program representative.

Sunita Mathur, another mid-level MS employee, used a combination of statist proceduralism and shifting positioning of herself and the program to get her work done. Sunita had been working for MS for a few years when I met her in the city of Lucknow. She was a slight woman with a thick mane of black hair hanging in a long braid down her back. She almost always dressed in *khadi*—hand-spun cotton promoted by Gandhi. Her most prominent facial features were her large black eyes that gazed directly and unflinchingly at people. Sunita rarely smiled. She made people uncomfortable, as I had often observed and had been told by others, not only by her demeanor but also because she raised tough questions in staff meetings. She was intensely committed to her mobilizing work in one of the toughest regions of U.P. known for its stone quarries. Most MS clients in her program area were Dalits and poor tribal women, who worked in these quarries as daily wage laborers. The quarries and the land in the area were owned by upper castes. Poverty, wage labor, control over land, and violence against Dalits and tribals were the primary issues confronting MS women living in Mathur's district, and these issues were intimately interconnected.

> Our main issue here is land. MS sangha women are not strong enough yet to be able to fight the administration alone. They can fight with local officials [and] surround [*gherao*] a local police station in protest. But at the district level, unless they have my support, my backing, they will get killed or defeated [*maari jayengi*]. . . . I and

> other members of my staff have had to face a lot of threats. . . . We have successfully dealt with several cases of violence and land which has made us infamous, especially among rich upper-caste people.

The first such case Sunita Mathur described was in the village of Ganna, where she worked with women belonging to the *Kol* tribe, who lived in a very small hamlet of the village. Kol women complained to Sunita about the lack of water and sanitation facilities, and of space in their hamlet—it was too small to accommodate all the residents and their animals. As a result, people were suffering from infectious diseases. "We called the *pradhan* [chief] of the village," narrated Mathur, "and organized a meeting with all the residents. The pradhan told us about a piece of land bordering the canal; this was common land that belonged to the entire *gram sabha* [village community]. He said that Kol residents could go and live on that piece of land. So, many Kol women built huts and started living there. The upper-caste people were now upset [because] they had lost an important piece of land, which was located right on the road and had a good supply of water; so [they retaliated by] razing the Kol huts. . . . The Kol women called me on the phone. I advised them to go the SDM's office and hand in an application. I dictated the content of the application and asked them to get in touch with me if the SDM's office refused to receive their application. I also asked them to send me a copy of the application so that I could follow up at my end. . . . The SDM's office did refuse to accept their application initially but the women forced the SDM to receive their letter [and] they brought a copy [for me] . . . The SDM had indeed stamped 'Received' on the letter and signed it, but he was not taking any action on the matter. So I called him and asked why he was not taking action. He gave me some excuses, [but] I reminded him that he was bound by government rules to [do something]. He ultimately did take action, and the Kol women got the piece of land. In the meantime, however, some upper-caste people had built their own huts on that land, [which] were [then] forcibly removed. This was a very positive result for us," Sunita concluded proudly. However, the upper-caste men in the area had become aware of the MS program and of Mathur and saw them as a threatening presence.

Sunita Mathur's first victory over the upper-caste men in Ganna was simultaneously an instance of successful negotiation of the local state machinery where she used statist languages and governmental methods to ensure accountability and response from the administration. She also instructed the village women in proper grievance procedures: they were to bypass the local block-level administration and file two copies of a written complaint directly with the SDM. In addition, they had to ensure that the SDM signed and stamped both copies, one of which they retained for their records. Sunita knew that once a written complaint was submitted and recorded, the administration had to address it, and she used this mechanism of redress to good use.

Although successful in this case, the use of such administrative strategies may have contradictory implications for empowerment. These strategies governmentalize women's everyday lives and tie them to networks of bureaucratic power and disciplinary rule. They can also construct problematic hierarchies between MS functionaries and participants; the former are "in the know" and sometimes, as in the case of Leela Vati discussed earlier, use bureaucratic languages and methods to demand compliance from the very women they are meant to empower. These hierarchies might ultimately subvert, or at the very least hamper, the equality-oriented agenda of the MS program. However, encountering officials, gaining information about how bureaucracies work, and learning statist methods can also enable subaltern women to mobilize and demand accountability and entitlements from ignorant and uncaring state agencies (see chapters 4 and 5). MS field staff members also use these procedures to their benefit. The empowerment work that they do can sometimes be dangerous, and MS women who work in the field face threats of violence from those in power. Their adherence to proceduralism and careful self-positioning allow them to circumvent repressive power.

"When you contacted the SDM did you say that you were calling from MS, which is a Government of India program?" I asked Sunita. "No," she replied. "I simply said that women from such and such village have filed a report with you: what are you doing about it? [The SDM] asked me where I was calling from. I stated that I was calling from the city of Mirzabad; that I work with MS which is a women's collective, and it is in that capacity that I was calling [him]" "So you never said that MS is a Government of India program," I clarified. "No, because that would cause problems," she replied and proceeded to relate the following incident.

In the village of Naudia, Mathur's team helped MS women to fight against upper-caste control over land. With Sunita's help, MS clients called a meeting of the entire village to discuss land-related matters. Sunita asked the village chief to include a meeting announcement in the panchayat [village council] register that was circulated among all residents. When upper-caste men saw the meeting notice, they threatened to attack MS women. They also (mis)informed the senior superintendent of police (SSP) of the area that MS had mobilized a large group of people who were planning to surround the police station in protest. On the day of the meeting, the forces of five local police stations, including policewomen, surrounded the meeting participants. The SSP, the SDM, and other local officials were also present and summoned Sunita to a place some distance away from the gathering. She was unwilling to meet them alone because she considered it risky, but the officials refused to walk over to where Sunita was standing with MS clients. In the end, a few village women accompanied Sunita to the spot designated by the officials, acting as chaperones and witnesses to the exchange that ensued. Here is how Sunita Mathur described it:

> The circle officer [a police officer] asked us a lot of questions—as a harassment tactic. He pointed to the MS jeep and asked me whose vehicle that was. I just shrugged my shoulders. "Where did you get this vehicle?" he questioned. The jeep had Government of India written on it. I avoided answering the question directly and simply stated that we got it from whoever gave it to us. . . . He asked me for my name. I said, "You can write it down—my name is Sunita and I work for Mahila Samakhya." "Is this a government program?" he asked. "Well, if the board on the jeep says Government of India, then maybe [it is] a government program. I, however, am not from the government," I answered. Then he told me that he . . . had received information that we were going to surround the local police station. "You have put a Government of India board on your vehicle and you dare to work against the Government of India! You are going against the administration!" he accused. "We are not doing anything against the administration," I replied, "and this meeting has not been called by MS. Here is the meeting announcement written by the village chief." I showed him the village council register with the recorded announcement. "The issue . . . was put forward by village women. MS staff members are not involved in this. Just like you are here to provide security, we . . . are here [as] representatives of a women's group to support the village women's cause."

The circle officer flaunted his official status to intimidate MS women. His self-positioning as a faithful male officer defending the interests of the state and society also constructed the state as a masculinist superstructure that secures the existing social order (Mitchell 1999). Police representatives and bureaucrats were present in Naudia to protect the entrenched interests of landowning upper-caste men, to defend state institutions from being challenged by subaltern women, and to safeguard their own positions as powerful state officials. Their display of prestige and authority enacted the prerogative dimension of state power, which, according to Wendy Brown (1995), rests on the state's monopoly over legitimate violence. Their use of "security" issues to threaten MS women reveals how violence underpins governmental concerns about the care and protection of society (Dean 2001; Sunder Rajan 2003); here it was being deployed to ensure the welfare of some members of society over others. Indeed, as Sunder Rajan posits, "the masculinity of the state must always be in evidence for its authority to stick. It figures not only in the state's militaristic displays . . . but also in the paternalism of its justice and welfare functions, in the professed objectivity and neutrality of its functioning, in the institutional supremacy and authority it represents" (2003, 226-7).

Caught in this performance of state authority and masculinism, Sunita Mathur had to avoid becoming implicated for instigating an antigovernment protest and endangering the social order. At the same time, she had to forestall imminent violence from government functionaries and powerful landowning men. She employed a number of tactics to these ends, including being vague about the MS program's GONGO identity, identifying herself as an NGO activist, and using the written meeting announcement sent out by the village chief. She explained

> I felt that if I really had been a government representative, then I would not have been able to accomplish anything [or] . . . do anything against the government. You see, the local mafia is supported by the administration. And we have to fight against the mafia because otherwise the issues of land and violence will never get solved and economic self-reliance will never happen. . . . That is why I have strategically decided not to use the government label.

Mathur chose the word *mafia* to describe the nexus of the powerful, which includes landowning elite, local government functionaries, and organized corruption and crime. Upper-caste landowners acquire common lands as personal property with the help of local administrators who authorize land titles. They threaten low-caste women who challenge them, hiring goons to beat or rape the women, burn their fields, or tear down their houses. The area police and officials collude with the landowners by not preventing land encroachment and violence and by not assisting low-caste women in filing cases against powerful men.

The Naudia incident vividly illustrates the entanglement of state officials in the issues that concern disenfranchised women (who are MS clients). The struggles that MS takes up in the interest of undoing social inequalities and challenging entrenched power hierarchies are simultaneously struggles against government officials, who are a part of the local mafia. This view from the "bottom" also underscores the untenability of drawing a clear boundary between state and nonstate arenas and actors. The embeddedness of local officials in relations of power reveals that the state is sometimes imagined not so much as a distinct entity but as a key node in a network of power relations through which social inequalities (such as those of class, caste, and gender) are channeled and reproduced (see Ferguson 1994). In this context, power and authority are messy and not neatly contained within the conventional boundaries of the state. MS participants' activism is not always directed against a distinct or an abstract state, but against entrenched webs of power in which state functionaries are key players. This blurring of state boundaries gives officials all the more reason to re-create the state locally as the (masculinist) defender of law and protector of order through periodic exhibitions of power and prestige. Whereas such repressive encounters with the local police and administration play a critical role in shaping subaltern ideas about the authoritative local state-as-taker, they might also produce images of a spatially separate translocal state writ large—a "just" body consisting of higher-level government officials who can perhaps be called upon to discipline lower-level functionaries and intervene on behalf of the downtrodden.

Mathur's, Rawat's, and Singh's stories also demonstrate the particular dangers and dilemmas that MS personnel face in their daily work of empowerment because of the program's linkage with the state. Field-level staff members must cautiously navigate official dictates, threats, and violence while also tackling local gender-, class-, and caste-based power hierarchies in which state functionaries are implicated. This often requires that they distance themselves from state affiliation. As Seema Singh explained, "The police belong to the government, the courts belong to the government . . . Everything belongs to the government, after all. When we take up a fight, we have to fight at all these levels. If we start believing that we are working for a government project and that we are government workers, then how will we fight . . . [other] government people? Then there is no point in working at all."

Seema made this statement while describing a rape case she handled. A teenage village girl in her program area was gang-raped by a group of four upper-class men from the same village. The police, however, put the wrong man in jail. The real perpetrators had the right connections in the government and were thus able to avoid indictment. Seema described the pains that she and her team had to go through in order to reopen the case and bring the four men to justice. The local police were uncooperative, despite the fact that the main police officer in that area was a woman, a point Seema emphasized. At first they refused to reconsider the case; so Seema mobilized her contacts with higher officials, and with the help of senior MS managers, she was able to get one of the highest ranking police officers in the state, also a woman, to put pressure on the local police. They were forced to reopen the case file because of an order from above, but began harassing a woman who had witnessed the crime but who had not come forward initially. Then the rape victim refused to give her testimony. "If you sit in front of the victim, dressed in a police uniform, with a thick wooden baton in your hand, who would want to tell you anything!" exclaimed Seema. The victim was later forced by the police to state that her testimony had been "coached" by Seema Singh. This was only the beginning of a long and arduous struggle for Seema against the police and court system.

When describing this case, Seema also reminded me of the Bhanwari rape incident that had received national attention in 1992. Bhanwari, a lower-caste village woman and volunteer functionary of the Rajasthan state–sponsored WDP, was gang-raped by five upper-caste men in front of her husband. The rapists were punishing her for trying to stop a child marriage. Bhanwari, as a representative of a government-initiated women's empowerment program, was simply doing what her superiors had told her to do—that is, upholding the law that prohibits child marriages. State functionaries, however, did nothing to assist her struggles for justice. The police delayed Bhanwari's medical examination for over two days and forced her to give her statement several times. The investigating officers dragged their feet throughout the inquiry. The perpetrators were not arrested until seventeen months after the incident took place. Once the trial began, the presiding judge was changed several times. Finally in 1995, three years after the gang-rape, the district court acquitted all five men. For many women this case came to symbolize the violent and patriarchal nature of state institutions. State agencies and representatives had failed to protect and do justice to a woman who represented a government program and who was violated while doing her job of upholding the law.[11]

Seema once again disaggregated the state and pointed to its different arms (such as the police and the courts), which exert repression even when they do not intentionally or overtly collude with each other. Seema therefore reiterated the need for MS functionaries to maintain their distance from such state structures. "So the perception that MS is separate from the government has been very important?" I asked. "Absolutely," answered Seema. "It is definitely separate from the government. [Our attitude is that] *if we* need the administration's help, we will take their help; and we will help them, *if we* feel the need. We will not ask for or offer help based on their demands. It is because of this attitude that we were able to establish independence [from the state] in terms of our work. Otherwise we would be considered like other government workers and the district magistrates would . . . make us dance to their tunes just as they are able to do with other government workers."

Predicaments and Paradoxes

The key impetus behind the MS program's crossbred organizational form was to conjoin the advantages of state resources and wider reach with the flexibility and grassroots orientation of NGOs and simultaneously avoid the pitfalls of a bureaucratic approach to and governmental co-optation of women's empowerment. Interestingly, however, the GONGO structure has not prevented either a bureaucratization of empowerment or official intervention into the MS program. State participation in MS puts constraints on the work of program functionaries and raises serious personal and professional challenges for them that have material and symbolic consequences. However, the dualistic GONGO structure of MS also affords staff members some maneuverability, allowing them to dodge some restrictions and facilitate empowerment in unexpected, if dangerous, ways.

My purpose in this chapter was to show how the MS program's part-state, part-nonstate identity impacts its employees on a daily basis. I did this through examining the program's employment arrangements and the work practices of its staff. MS personnel have to figure out how to identify themselves and the program in different situations. In so doing, they have to consider their own survival needs, their interlocutors' perceptions of state and nonstate actors, local power relations, and the different faces of state power. Analyzing the occasions when MS functionaries were identified by state officials and village residents as either government or NGO workers, and those in which they chose to don different hats, reveals much about how the state materializes—as either a distinctive or a blurry, masculinist entity—through everyday MS program dynamics, and about the kinds of empowerment that are thwarted and enabled in the context of this program.

Government officials identified MS personnel as nongovernmental when it came to determining their employment contracts and terms. The operative assumption was that empowerment labor is altruistic, feminized, and underskilled social work, which is qualitatively different from economically productive and state work; it therefore deserves lower salaries and status. The logic underpinning this designation is gendered, classist, and casteist, and it results in strengthening the very social hierarchies that the program opposes through its consciousness raising work. MS personnel, as I demonstrated, criticized such trivialization of their labor. Some also attempted to collectively unionize, but their efforts aimed at self-empowerment and recognition as workers were stymied by officials. This yet again underscores the contradictory logic of state-initiated women's empowerment—it simultaneously exalts women's economic independence and prevents MS workers from achieving this autonomy.

The paradoxes engendered by state participation in the MS program play a critical role in shaping its workforce's strategies of mobile positioning in varied contests and for different audiences. In front of rural subalterns the staff members take on either the government label or the NGO label depending on whether they want to portray themselves as benefactors who must be feared or as committed supporters who have nothing tangible to give away. In so doing they respond to and reinforce the Janus-faced state of subaltern and popular imagination—that is, the authoritative state-as-taker and the idealized resource-rich state-as-caretaker. With powerful interlocutors, such as upper-caste landowning men or government administrators, MS functionaries wear the state hat when they need to affirm the authority of MS and obtain the cooperation of local bureaucrats. In situations of direct confrontation with dominant actors, they position themselves as NGO activists or as village residents, so as to protest state policies or corruption without being constrained by their positions as "state employees" (who are disallowed from participating in antigovernment struggles). The dual identity of the program enables MS staff members to partially prevent a state-hijacking of empowerment and to retain some semblance of work-related independence from local officials, who tend to be individuals with entrenched interests in maintaining the status quo.

The incidents of direct government intervention into MS women's activities starkly reveal the gendered, classed, and casteist nature of the state, and the paradoxes inherent in state-involved women's empowerment. They also highlight the kinds of empowerment that state officials consider legitimate and the extent to which they will allow marginalized women to empower themselves. One can see how empowerment programs might serve as disciplinary vehicles for creating manageable female subjects who obey governmental dictates. State power, moreover, goes beyond discipline. Wendy Brown argues that state power "is real but largely intangible except for the occasions when it is expressed as violence, physical coercion, or outright discrimination" (1995, 179). As I illustrated above, struggles involving land, alcohol, and violence against women, which directly threaten the status-quo and implicate state institutions and actors, bring the coercive aspects of the state to the fore—whether it is through administrative red tape (the police and courts dragging their feet over rape cases), surveillance over women, or harassment. These instances of repression and the iteration of statist masculinism show that state power is not simply disciplinary but also repressive and deductive (Foucault 1990), and that "the state" can sometimes operate as a coherent "vehicle of massive domination" (Brown 1995, 174) even in the absence of any singular intention to that effect. The incidents recounted above also reveal the illiberal underside of neoliberal governmentality (Dean 2001; Hindess 2004), which MS staffers often encounter in their work as empowerment facilitators. The state's prerogative power to wield violence is deployed to uphold relations of domination, to protect the institution of private property and the gendered interests of propertied classes, and to enact violence on subaltern classes and deny them justice. Such enactments entrench the verticality, authority, and the hypermasculinity of state institutions. Even though MS employees try to negotiate the coercive, masculinist face of power through mobile-positioning strategies, their success is not ensured.

Whereas the aforementioned counterproductive effects are connected with state participation in the MS program specifically, I would argue that these uneven consequences are an outcome of the wider implementation of empowerment as a technology of neoliberal governance. In other words, the danger that MS faces is not simply one of governmental intervention in and subversion of empowerment, but indeed of the neoliberal *governmentalization* of grassroots empowerment. As I explained in chapter 1 alternative envisionings of empowerment—as a transformative political praxis leading to self-liberation and social change—sit awkwardly with and have been partially recuperated by neoliberal strategies of self-actualization and freedom enacted through the market (see Rose 1999). Empowerment today comes prepackaged as a mainstream development strategy sponsored and funded by dominant development institutions and state agencies. Despite its commitment to radical pedagogy and feminist goals, MS articulates with and unwittingly becomes implicated in the neoliberal reworking of society.

The contemporary governmentalization of empowerment entails its professionalization as an expert intervention and its objectification as a measurable variable. In fact, MS staff members often lamented the fact that program's affiliation with the Department of Education meant that literacy indicators were increasingly being used to quantify women's empowerment and to measure the success of the program. Some education department bureaucrats desired "hard" evidence on the effects of the program's literacy efforts with adult women and adolescent girls. Even though program representatives understood the importance of numbers for the government and donors, they were uncomfortable with the reductive and superficial enumeration of a more comprehensive and complex process of empowering education. Such measurement, according to them, did not capture the variety of meaningful and, to an extent, unquantifiable changes that had happened in the clients' lives through the program. Moreover, it subverted the flexible, contextual, and processual nature of empowerment emphasized by radical thinkers, such as Gandhi and Freire, and by GAD feminists (whose ideas influenced the MS program).

Rendering empowerment into a development program also requires setting up appropriate hierarchical structures and bureaucratic procedures for its implementation, which are evident in the MS program. The spatial organization of the program into national-, state-, district-, and block-level offices, for example, reflects the scalar structure of the Indian bureaucratic setup. The women staffing different program levels belong to different social strata, and thus have unequal access to educational and cultural capital. For instance, field-level employees tend to come from rural, lower/middle class and lower caste backgrounds. In contrast, most of the managerial staff is drawn from urban and relatively privileged backgrounds in terms of caste, class, and education. MS consciously attempts to address and rectify hierarchies between its staff members through encouraging their educational endeavors and vertical moves within the organization. A few employees who started at lower rungs have progressed up the organizational ladder through education and experience. Others, however, have faced a glass ceiling of sorts. Some complained that they could not rise beyond a certain level in the program because they were unable to compete with the English-speaking urban women with a masters degrees education who staffed the managerial ranks. These criticisms called attention to the hierarchicalism in MS, which is a reflection of the governmental professionalization and bureaucratization of empowerment that threatens the very spirit of change and equality that empowerment is supposed to connote and promote (see also Nagar and Raju 2003).

The MS program's institutional structure and practices show how it becomes implicated in the spread of bureaucratic power throughout society (Ferguson 1994). Even though the program's carefully worked-out GONGO structure was intended to prevent a bureaucratic takeover of the program, in practice, bureaucratic proceduralism has become a crucial thread of the program's fabric. Staff members deploy statist acts and procedures in their daily work to handle both state officials and "errant" program participants. Their use of administrative techniques highlights the dangerous slippage between tactics of subversion and strategies of domination. Governmental methods are mired within the logic of disciplinary bureaucratic power; their proliferation through the program institutes hierarchies that are counterproductive to MS's goal of equality.

Thus it is not surprising that several people associated with MS, who were extremely supportive of the program and its goals, also expressed some skepticism. As Anil Bordia iterated, "The state, by definition, can only be . . . status-quoist. [In] every program [such as MS], there are seeds of destruction—because the people who control the resources, who have all the say, would not . . . easily allow these things to happen." The wariness and concerns expressed by my MS informants about the deradicalization potential of state-sponsored women's empowerment are clearly well founded, as the incidents retold in this chapter show.

However, my ethnography also demonstrates that there is another side to the story. Does bureaucratization necessarily imply only a depoliticization of struggles and/or a deradicalization of politics? While the governmental use of empowerment bureaucratizes the daily lives of MS women, I contend that it also educates them in the ways with which to "manage" the government.[12] MS representatives learn how the state works and transfer these skills to their clients. It is especially crucial for disenfranchised subjects in India to learn about statist techniques and strategic tactics for encountering bureaucracies; even though its faces and modalities might be changing at the present moment, the state remains a ubiquitous presence in people's everyday lives. Acquiring knowledge about bureaucracy and proceduralism helps MS women to devise ways with which to confront and circumvent state surveillance and repression and to demand that officials work in a lawful and accountable manner. They use the very languages and techniques, which are intended to discipline them, to this end. In so doing, MS women empower themselves in ways that are unanticipated. Even though state administrators and donors may have their own agendas with respect to women's empowerment, a different kind of women's "empowerment" ends up happening through the program. Empowerment, then, is a "moving target," whose meaning continually changes through its ground-level deployments; and it does more than just regulate. Government-sponsored women's empowerment does not suffocate activist politics as much as it generates particular kinds of women's struggles against local power networks (mafias, which include state agents) and for recognition, resources, and justice. Thus, along with the risks of state-partnered empowerment projects, come promises; along with the perils of governmentalization, come interesting political possibilities. In the chapters that follow and in the conclusion to this book, I further unravel the complexities and unpredictability of state and feminist partnered women's empowerment and development in the neoliberal era.

4

Staging Development

A Drama in North India

Curtain Raiser

In February 1999 I joined a team of MS functionaries for a program introduction event in Jhabua, a village located in eastern U.P. The staff had planned an elaborate *jatha* [a band of people]—to gain visibility for the program. The jatha began with a procession through the village. Members of the MS team and I held placards, shouted slogans, sang songs about women's rights, and invited women and girls to join us at the local primary school. Once a sizable group of people gathered at the school, the remaining program unfolded. There were games for children and educational activities for teenage girls. MS functionaries held a separate meeting with adult female residents, asking them questions about their lives, development problems, and local government institutions, and giving them information about the MS program. This meeting was followed by the grand finale—a theatrical performance.

MS staffers organized this performance as an illustrated story scroll-cum-drama. As Meena Rani and Usha Kumari unfurled a painted scroll, frame by frame, Rajni Bala and Gayatri Singh enacted the scenes displayed on each frame. This story scroll-cum-drama was set up as a discussion between two women, one belonging to a village with a good chief and the other belonging to a village with a bad chief. The first scene on the scroll depicted the village with a bad chief: it was dirty and lacking in basic facilities. The resident of this village complained about the many problems she and others faced. The audience learned that the chief had misused development funds allocated to him and had amassed personal wealth. Whereas the residents lived in dilapidated houses and had no access to water, the chief lived in a large house with amenities such as a hand-operated water pump and a television. Instead of using development funds for fulfilling the resident's needs, he spent them on such unnecessary projects as erecting an ostentatious gateway at the edge of the village. The next scene showed a "model" village with a good chief, whose house was like any other in the village. The village was clean. It had a playground for children and a well that was used by all residents, regardless of caste differences. The chief's wife regularly met with village women to discuss their problems and then represented these issues at village council meetings. The final frame and act detailed what the residents of the village with the bad chief could do to improve their situation. It gave the audience information on topics such as the duties of a village chief and residents and the schedule and nature of village council meetings. The onlookers nodded their approval of the performance. One woman remarked that the chief of Jhabua village was just like the bad chief in the story and asked MS functionaries to tell their chief to solve village problems. Meena Rani, a program staff member, however, prodded the residents to take the lead in this matter—"it is your right to talk with [the chief] . . . about your needs."

Performance techniques and spectacles, as the one described above, are regular features of development work but are understudied by scholars working on development. As I conducted fieldwork on the MS program in rural north India, I observed that MS functionaries often used street theater, story scrolls, and songs to give information about the program to potential clients; to raise awareness about political, civic, and economic rights; to spread social messages; and to mobilize subaltern women to take action on specific issues. Performance, however, is not simply a development *tool*; rather, I argue here that development itself is performative and a "performed practice" (Sivaramakrishnan and Agrawal 2003, 6).

In this chapter I examine two common and interrelated development practices—program monitoring and evaluation—and elaborate on the theatricality and performativity of development discourse. Using anthropological and feminist lenses of performance and performativity to study discreet but oft-repeated development encounters, I contend, reveals much about the dynamics, ruptures, and effects of the mimetic, realist logic that frames the social world of development. In what follows I illustrate how development encounters operate as social dramas in which development identities, hierarchies, and norms are shaped and challenged, actors are fashioned, and different visions of development and modernity are articulated. I pay attention to the meanings that these space- and time-bound dramas convey and to the effects that they produce. My purpose is to unmoor developmentalism from its monolithic and static connotations and to revisit questions of agency.

To do so, I reenact the staging of a development encounter between rural clients of the MS program, MS staffers, Indian government officials, and a team of international experts in Nimani village in eastern U.P. The international team was led by World Bank representatives and included dignitaries from Ghana, the Ivory Coast, Mexico, El Salvador, and Morocco. The team visited South Asia in 1999 to observe and assess innovative education initiatives. MS was a part of this itinerary not only because it is a flagship program of the Indian government's education department but also because its unique and inclusive approach to gender, education, and empowerment issues complements the World Bank's current social development agenda. As discussed in chapter 1 the World Bank has promoted and funded development initiatives focused on women and gender, empowerment, education, and microenterprise since the mid-1990s (Bergeron 2003; Elyachar 2002). In 1998–1999 when I conducted my primary fieldwork, the MS program received World Bank monies. As a partner in India's "Education for All" initiative, the World Bank funded two projects in U.P.—the District Primary Education Project and the Uttar Pradesh Basic Education Project (World Bank 2001)—and the MS program in turn received funds from these projects. The World Bank's position as an indirect donor to the MS program and as a major lender and important player in India's liberalizing regime,[1] and its reputation for conducting frequent and exhaustive project assessments and audits meant that both MS representatives and Indian government functionaries saw this trip as a monitoring and evaluation of the MS program and of the government's broader gender-focused development efforts.

Monitoring and evaluation are commonplace development practices. Their goal is to enable program planners, staff, and funders to observe ground-level program facts and client realities first-hand, design appropriate interventions, ensure proper implementation of plans and usage of funds, problem solve, and judge program performance against stated goals. The data generated through these exercises is compiled, assessed, and abstracted into reports that serve different audiences (such as program managers and donors) and varied purposes (such as evaluating the state of the program and making necessary changes). These practices are considered indispensable by development experts because they presumably facilitate program success and, ultimately, real development.

Monitoring and evaluation events are particularly amenable to analysis as social dramas because they involve public stagings of development realities by program functionaries and clients and judgment by experts. In this chapter

I narrate the World Bank tour of Nimani through a two-act play. My use of performance tropes plays on the machinations that went into producing this stage show and is meant to highlight the various scripts, subjects, enactments, differences, and antagonistic reality effects this show produced and displayed.

Positioning the Nimani event as a social drama, I posit, helps accomplish two important objectives: first, to ethnographically substantiate how development functions as a "regime of representation" (Escobar 1995) that creates identities and hierarchies and exerts power and, second, to illustrate how development operates not as a closed and totalizing discourse but as a morphing and possibly transformative realist theater. I build on insights gleaned from anthropological studies of performance (Goffman 1973; Moore 1977; Schechner 1988; Turner 1988), feminist studies of performativity (Butler 1999; Kondo 1997), and postcolonial theory (Bhabha 1997; Chakrabarty 2000; Mitchell 1988, 2000).[2] Applying the analytics of performance and performativity to development studies allows me to revisit questions about agency and subjectivity and to delineate the nature, workings, and effects of the transnational development regime.

I begin by contextualizing recent studies of development and elaborating on the frames of performance and performativity. This is followed by a two-act play set in Nimani. In the final section I elaborate on the positivist, mimetic logic at work in this drama, analyze its resultant reality effects, and discuss issues of subaltern agency. Before I proceed forward, however, a brief word about my role and representational strategies. I was conducting research on the MS program's functioning and effects in Nimani village when the World Bank visit took place, and was invited to take part in this event by senior MS functionaries.[3] I participated in this performance neither as an MS representative nor as a monitor and evaluator. I was seen both as an Indian (native but not local) and as a researcher trained and located in the West. The role scripted for me was that of a mediator and informant on the MS program's operations in Nimani. I was also a part of the audience. As an "über spectator" of sorts, my goal was neither to judge the quality of the MS program performance in Nimani nor to analyze the recorded results of the World Bank evaluation (to which I was not privy); rather, I desired to delve into what this time- and space-bound event revealed about the logics, dynamics, and consequences of development.

I script this development encounter as a drama with two caveats in mind. First, the symbolic and material effects of social dramas cannot be fully accessed or known (Moore and Myerhoff 1977, 13). Second, embodied and ephemeral live performances resist fixation by written words (Kondo 1997, 20–21). Writing about the "undocumentable event of performance . . . [means invoking] the rules of the written document" (Phelan 1993, 148), not to mention disciplinary conventions, which change the event itself. What follows, therefore, is not a definitive or an exhaustive account of what happened in and around Nimani village, but a partial fashioning and analysis of a development drama, which heeds Kondo's call for performative ethnography with a political purpose (Kondo 1997, 20). I aim to unravel development as a protean script that is at once regulative and productive and that speaks with many voices.

Interregnum: Development, Representation, Performance, and Performativity

In considering development through the performance lens, I participate in interdisciplinary debates about the nature and effects of development. In the 1960s and 1970s scholars writing from a political economy perspective (Cardoso and Faletto 1979; Frank 1969) challenged mainstream models of capitalist modernization that posited that underdeveloped nations could progress by following the industrialization trajectory of developed Western nations (cf. Rostow 1971). In contrast, dependency critics argued that proper development could not occur in the peripheries because of their unequal structural relations with capitalist centers (Cardoso and Faletto 1979; Frank 1969). Even though they shed critical light on the historical inequalities of the world capitalist system that resulted in a relationship of dependency between peripheries and centers, political economy theorists also emphasized the necessity of nondependent, autonomous, industrial development in the peripheries.

In the 1990s a group of scholars, writing from an anthropological perspective, shifted the terms of the debate and critiqued the very idea of development. These scholars posited that development operated as a regime of representation and a depoliticized discourse of power and control. This discourse conferred lopsided identities onto developing "others" (such as passive, poor, and uninformed people and communities) and exerted power over these constructed objects of development (Crush 1995; Escobar 1995; Ferguson 1994; Gardner and Lewis 1996; Mitchell 1991). Some critical development theorists called for an end to this violent discourse and argued for the urgent need to imagine and instate alternatives to development (Escobar 1995; Rahnema 1997; Shrestha 1995). Sachs (1992, 1), for example, wrote that the "epoch [of development] is coming to an end. The time is ripe to write its obituary." These critics advocated for an antimodern, postdevelopment political praxis that rejected Western modernity without necessarily invoking a fixed tradition and pristine past. However, did they perhaps construct too monolithic a picture of development as solely destructive? Did they unwittingly position marginalized people of the global South as deluded and wretched victims of development thinking and practices, whose "real" agency, therefore, lay in rejecting development and in embracing antimodernism? What indeed are the ethical and practical implications of announcing development's death (as Corbridge (2007) and Ferguson (2002b) also ask) especially during an era of neoliberalism when many people's hopes of meaningful improvements in their life conditions have been dashed?

In this chapter I take up these questions in an attempt to scrutinize development and trouble its singularity, without losing sight of misery and abjection (Ferguson 2002b) wrought by development interventions. I argue against one-sided depictions of development and subaltern subjectivity and agency and complicate the putative antimodernism/antidevelopmentalism of struggles at the margins. In so doing I participate in projects aimed at ethnographically thickening development. The textual focus of certain critical development theorists, as a few scholars have recently argued, leaves little room for thinking about how human beings interact with development.[4] Those writing from this perspective have reemphasized actor-oriented approaches to development (Grillo 1997) that recognize "the 'multiple realities' and diverse social practices of various actors" (Long 1992, 5). These studies show how different actors' understandings of development relate to their social positions (Walley 2003) and highlight development's multivocality. I build on this body of work and attempt to reopen the "development discourse" monolith to anthropological inquiry, empty it of an essentialized and definitive quality by showing its instability and heterogeneity, and analyze subaltern agency and political action in the context of development encounters.

I enter these ongoing anthropological dialogues by framing development encounters as social dramas; doing so, I suggest, opens up much-needed space for asking questions about the enactment of power, agency, developmentalist identities, and conflict. Performance, as scholars of cultural and secular rituals have demonstrated, operates as a mode of communication and metacommunication that tells us something about social structure, relationships, norms, order, and change (Gluckman 1958). Using the analytic of performance lays bare the worldviews and hierarchies that make up particular social contexts and also reveals how people enact, reflect upon, and contest these worldviews and hierarchies; it helps us to pay attention to the dramatic and agentive aspects of daily life and encounters (Goffman 1973) and everyday practices (de Certeau 1988), and to the staging of social inequalities and conflicts in rituals (Turner 1982, 1988) and play (Geertz 1973). Performances operate not only as mechanisms for the reproduction of social worlds, but also as liminal and "subjunctive" spaces (Turner 1988) for "deep play" (Geertz 1973)—that is, performance is an arena with the potential for social transformation and rearticulation. Social dramas, unlike precisely scripted aesthetic dramas, are mutable and less certain in their outcomes (Schechner 1988). Whereas ritual performances are supposed to mitigate social chaos and reinstate the "natural" order of things, they also signal the constructedness and shakiness of the social order and thus open up room for contestation and reinterpretation (Moore and Myerhoff 1977).

Despite Norman Long's (1992, 6) call to analyze development interactions as social dramas or "'interface' situations where the different lifeworlds interact and interpenetrate," the performance lens, which has long been applied by anthropologists studying social and political rituals and everyday practices, remains underutilized in development studies.[5] I argue that performance is a productive way to examine what constitutes the social world of development, how it works, and how different actors negotiate and transform this world. Actors do not, however, enter the development stage as already formed subjects; rather, as I demonstrate below, they become subjects through enacting and improvising on scripted roles. Here I reference Judith Butler's (1999) idea of performativity.[6] Performativity troubles voluntarist and humanist notions of agency, which theater-based performance studies sometimes tend to take for a given (Schechner 1988). Rather than viewing actors as intentional subjects who precede the script and action, performativity reverses the unidirectional actor–action equation and embeds subjectivity and agency in the workings of discourse (Butler 1999).[7] Using this lens allows us to see how performances of developmentalist identities are not willful acts of autonomous subjects but instead are contextually defined, discursively constrained, sometimes slippery enactments of development-defined ideal types through which subjects emerge. These acts are performative in that "they bring to life that to which they refer, rather than merely naming something already present" (Kondo 1997, 8). Thus developmentalist identities (and indeed development itself) are not static essences but are continuously shifting products of encounters and practices.

Performativity also questions the idea that performances constitute an onstage enactment of backstage realities. Viewing performances as staged representations of prior scripts or preexisting realities (Schechner 1988) tends to maintain a problematic distinction between onstage shows and backstage realities and thus paints an essentialized picture of reality as something that comes before its representation (Beeman 1993).[8] Goffman (1973, 65), for example, posits that a performance is an idealized impression of a prior reality. His formulation signals an ontological truth underlying a contrived (if idealized) act. Performativity destabilizes the notion of original and foundational realities and allows us to see agency and subversion in a new light. If performance can be described as a singular and originary act, performativity emphasizes repetitiveness and the lack of an origin. Where performance enacts backstage realities on stage as a symbolic representation of a signified real, performativity delineates how realities are not anterior to stagings but are products or resultant *effects* of repeated stagings. Performative acts are mimetic gestures that (re)enact social norms, not real essences; they thus hold open the possibility of subversion. The act of copying idealized images is a slippery one because the danger of imperfect mimicry and mockery is ever present (Bhabha 1997; Chakrabarty 2000; Mitchell 2000). In this chapter I build on these ideas to argue that development dramas are mimetic and realist performative acts that fashion actors, shape resistance, create differences, produce multiple and hierarchical reality scripts, proliferate modernities, and undermine any original and definitive meaning of development.[9]

The World Bank Comes to Nimani: A Two-Act Play

Stage Sites: Nimani Village and Begumpur City in the eastern part of U.P.
Key Actors, Crew Members, and Spectators: 1. *Nimani Village Residents*—MS collective members (Kevla Rani, Dayawati Kumari, and others), and Bhagwan Das and Shankar Dev (male residents); 2. *Mahila Samakhya Program Functionaries*—Diya Verma (district-level head of MS in Begumpur), Seema Singh (district-level MS employee), Arti Trivedi and Mallika Mehta (state-level senior MS representatives), and preschoolteachers and field staff; 3. *The performing anthropologist*—Aradhana Sharma; 4. *Government Representatives*—Ram Kumar (block development officer or BDO), CDO (chief development officer), and Kamala Shukla and Avinash Kapoor (state-level bureaucrats); and 5. *International Visitors*—World Bank representatives and foreign dignitaries from El Salvador, Ghana, the Ivory Coast, Mexico, and Morocco.

Act I

As I made my way over to the MS program office in Begumpur City on a hot March morning in 1999, I noticed traces of fuchsia, yellow, orange, and green on the streets, telltale signs of the recently concluded Hindu spring festival of *Holi*. The rhythmic rattle of generators and the smell of kerosene fumes told me that power was out in the neighborhood. I entered the MS building at around 9:30 AM and headed straight for Diya Verma's office. Diya, a tall, thin woman with a perpetual smile on her face and loads of energy, managed the MS program in Begumpur district. She hailed from a farming family and had many years of experience in both rural- and urban-based grassroots development work. I found Diya seated at her desk, working by the dim light of an oil lantern. The aqua green walls of her office and the green glass panes of the only window in the room did nothing to cheer up her surroundings, and Diya's face reflected the general gloominess. I had not seen Diya for nearly two weeks and asked after her health, remarking that she looked tired and pale. She managed a weak smile and complained of being under a lot of pressure. She had recently received news from her superiors at the state-level MS office in Lucknow that a World Bank team was scheduled to visit her program area, and she barely had two weeks to prepare for this visit. The team wanted to see a village-level MS women's collective in operation and an MS-run alternative preschool for village children. Unfortunately, however, the MS program was being phased out of Seelampur block, the area that the team wanted to visit. MS had been working in Seelampur for over nine years and its formal structures were now being dismantled. Hence, some of the village-level MS collectives had ceased holding weekly meetings and only two MS preschools still operated in the area. Diya wondered out loud how she was going to show a properly functioning program. She had asked the state officials coordinating this visit to shift the event venue to a neighboring block where the MS program was fully operational. But her request was turned down. The World Bank team was scheduled to see other programs in Seelampur and would not be able to visit the neighboring program area because of the distance and time involved. Diya frowned. She was clearly unhappy with this decision and worried that clients living in the program-phase-out area might not appreciate this additional intrusion into their lives; but she had no alternative options. Diya had to put on a good show. The World Bank was certainly not an entity to trifle with.

Because of the high-profile nature of the visitors, two senior MS staff members, Arti Trivedi and Mallika Mehta, came down to the Begumpur office to assist with the preparations. Arti informed Diya that she wanted a "perfect presentation" of the program. Diya told me that she was planning to cast some "good, vocal" MS participants from across the program area, gather them in one village, and showcase that constructed locale for the visitors. "We will tell [these MS women] to say that they are from that [particular] village." "But what if it comes out that these MS participants are not residents of the village you are showcasing?" I queried. Diya shrugged and remarked that there was no deception or sham involved in such a representation: as long as the actors were MS clients, the specific village to which they belonged did not matter. Moreover, she was simply heeding Arti's call for a "perfect presentation." Meanwhile Mallika Mehta, the other MS functionary, had different ideas about what to show and how. She shared with me her impressions about the changing vision and desires of donors, relaying that they "want to see the reality" and not a "perfect, decorated, and cleaned up [village and program]." Mallika and Arti had divergent takes on the program presentation, but they jointly conducted a location search and auditioned over one hundred MS clients. They proposed to show the women's component of the program in Daipur village and children's component in Nimani.

The final decision about the staging location, however, rested with Kamala Shukla, a state-level bureaucrat in charge of coordinating this international visit. She told Diya that she wanted to prescreen the locations and actors. Diya dutifully collected some MS women in Daipur and schoolchildren in Nimani on the appointed day, but Shukla failed to show up. Meanwhile, the MS participants and other village residents who had gathered in anticipation of the bureaucrat's visit and forfeited a day's work and wages, took out their ire on Diya. Diya sympathized with the villagers. "Will [Shukla] pay their lost wages?" she asked rhetorically. Diya had to put her anger aside, however, because Shukla's office asked her to reorganize the meetings in both villages in two days' time.

Kamala Shukla did keep the second appointment, arriving at the MS office in Begumpur several hours late. Diya told me later that Shukla was rushed and reluctant to spend time in the chosen villages. She only wanted to peek at the two locations from her vehicle. But Diya knew that local residents would view such an action as an official slight. So she convinced Shukla to "show her face in Daipur" and to spend a few minutes with the MS clients who had gathered for the second time in two days for Shukla's benefit. Nimani, however, was not fated to receive Shukla. She refused to enter Nimani because of time constraints, choosing to view the village from her car instead. She decided that both the women's and children's components of the MS program would be showcased in Nimani, because it was a shorter ride from the city hotel where the visitors would stay.

Why Nimani, I wondered. Nimani was one of my key fieldsites, and I was not sure if it was the ideal stage location for Arti's perfect presentation. There were three potential issues. First, Nimani no longer had a functioning MS preschool. The MS team would have to *simulate* a school for the visitors. But would the visitors know that this was only a simulation? Second, Shukla's repeated no-shows had infuriated some men in the village. A visit from an important and senior state bureaucrat was not an everyday occurrence and thus was something that village residents looked forward to. Nimani's women, men, and children had waited excitedly for Shukla on two occasions and felt let down by her cancellations; they had also lost work and wages. Some of Nimani's male residents were now bribing their children to either stay away from the mock school or tell the truth about their stand-in school to the visitors. Finally, Nimani's soon-to-be-showcased MS collective was rife with tensions.[10]

Diya was aware of these goings-on and realized that they could hamper the perfect program performance that her superior, Arti, desired; hence, she and Mallika decided to conduct a stage rehearsal in Nimani a few days before the actual event. I reached the village on the appointed day, ahead of schedule, carrying photographs of Nimani's MS clients, which they had earlier requested me to take. Some liked how their pictures turned out and others did not. "I am wearing such a dirty sari," bemoaned Dayawati Kumari. "[You] should have given me more time to comb my hair," cried Kevla Rani. Laughter, teasing, compliments, and complaints ensued. Soon Diya, Mallika, and a handful of field-level MS functionaries arrived for the rehearsal. After greeting them I excused myself because Shankar Dev, a male resident who had been instrumental in initiating MS in Nimani, wanted to speak with me. Shankar stood in the doorway of his house, watching all the MS-related commotion. As we walked into his courtyard, he turned to me and stated in a puzzled tone, "I don't understand the goal of the MS program." "But you helped start the program [here], didn't you?" I responded. Shankar immediately clarified his statement. "I mean who is running this program? Is it the government or the World Bank?" He obviously knew about the upcoming monitoring visit and was curious about the role of the World Bank in MS. I explained the program funding structure to him and we continued conversing for forty-five minutes. As soon as we were finished, I walked over to where the MS women were seated and found them engaged in a heated argument.

This argument had started as staff members went over the script and the dos and don'ts for the final show. Some MS collective members accused others of not supporting their previous bid for a village council house, or *panchayat bhavan*, in Nimani (see chapter 6). They claimed that a few members were secretly against getting a village council house. The allegedly uncooperative collective members retaliated with accusations of their own. As the pitch of voices rose, Mallika stepped in to ease the tension. "We should not blame each other in this manner," she scolded, nervously adding, "Please don't do this in front of the World Bank team." Diya and Mallika reminded the village women to remember their instructions for the final performance and called the meeting to an end.

Bhagwan Das, a male resident of Nimani, had watched this preparatory rehearsal and was visibly perturbed by what he believed was an unreal staging of the village and the MS program. After MS staff members had left, he shook his head in disgust and exclaimed, "[Development functionaries] showcase the program whenever outside monitors come and tell the villagers not to badmouth the program. They clean up and decorate everything so that you would think that this is *the* most developed village." "But you tell me," he asked, looking me straight in the eye, "who is *really* getting developed here? The village, the nation, or these functionaries!"

A day later at the MS office in Begumpur, I found Diya and her colleague, Seema Singh, putting together a program report for the purpose of the impending visit. Diya complained that preparations for this visit were wasting her time. Instead of doing real development work, she was forced to heed commands from above. Seema nodded in sympathy and stated that the World Bank's entry into MS as a donor had bureaucratized the program. "MS used to have flexibility in designing and implementing programs," said Seema. "Directives were never thrust upon us. . . . Now it is all about orders from above [and] dancing to the government's tune. . . . Since a World Bank team is supposed to visit, a government official shows up and tells you how to plan for the visit. Do this and do that. Bring something from one village and something from another village. . . . Bring children from villages ten kilometers away. . . . And the program is ready to show. . . . What is all this! These things are not genuine." Seema disliked the idea of simulating a school in Nimani and remarked that she believed in showing the program "as is" rather than arranging "something extraordinary."

Meanwhile, the local bureaucratic machinery was also revving up for the visit. A few days before the Nimani event, I met a senior state-level bureaucrat,

Avinash Kapoor, in Begumpur. As we conversed about the MS program and women's empowerment, I happened to mention the upcoming World Bank visit. Kapoor's eyebrows shot up. He was obviously caught unawares. He asked me for more information and I told him what little I knew—that this was a fairly large team interested in observing innovative educational programs in the area. "We had better pull up our socks," he remarked, but added, with a smile, "It is easy to handle large groups but harder to handle one person because he or she will ask questions." He then picked up one of several phones lying on his desk and called the CDO who worked under him. He learned that the CDO was coordinating the details of this visit with the Department of Education in New Delhi as well as with state-, district-, and block-level administrators. The CDO had delegated the stage management work in Nimani to his subordinate, Ram Kumar, the BDO of Seelampur block. Several officials were scheduled to accompany the monitors on their visit.

Act II

The day of the Nimani performance finally dawned—it was a national holiday but MS and state functionaries in Begumpur were on high alert. When I reached the local MS office, Diya and her team members were getting ready to leave for Nimani to take care of arrangements. We all commented on how "smart" we looked for the occasion. Diya was dressed in an orange-and-red starched cotton sari and had her long hair tied in a bun. I had chosen to wear my best *salwar-kameez* [billowy pants and long shirt] outfit. Diya asked me to accompany her superior, Arti Trivedi, to the five-star hotel where the international team was to stay. Arti briefed me on the day's events. The team was slated to arrive at 11:30 AM and visit a government-run primary school in the area before heading for Nimani.

When we reached the visitors' hotel, I noticed a fleet of government cars and jeeps lined up in front. The inside lobby was full of government officials, including Kamala Shukla, the CDO, and other district- and state-level functionaries. The twenty-one-member international team arrived an hour and a half late because of a flight delay. They were welcomed with marigold garlands and vermillion powder by the officials present. After the formalities and a quick round of introductions, Arti and I were asked to board an air-conditioned bus along with the visitors and some senior bureaucrats, and all of us were given boxed lunches. Other government representatives accompanied us in jeeps and cars bearing official license plates and the characteristic red lights atop their roofs. A police jeep led our entourage. It felt surreal to me to head out on a development tour in a protected caravan, munch on finger sandwiches, and gaze at a familiar landscape through tinted window panes—a colored reality indeed.

After making a brief stop at a government primary school in the town of Sitapur, our caravan finally reached Nimani. We were over two hours late. I noticed that the path leading from the main road to the Dalit hamlet of the village had been swept and decorated with powdered chalk and red sand. A makeshift stage had been erected at the entrance to the hamlet and chairs placed in front of it; these arrangements, the local MS women informed me later, were made by the BDO, Ram Kumar. Kumar had landed in Nimani earlier in the day, for his first ever visit in his sixteen-month tenure. There was work to be done—the village had to be swept, potholes filled with fresh dirt, a stage constructed, chairs rented, and local residents made presentable. As his staff took care of the setting and the props, the BDO tried to familiarize Nimani's Dalit women with their acting routine. He told them to avoid mentioning development problems or needs in front of the visitors. "[M]ake sure you embellish the development wrongs that have happened in your village," he instructed. The irony was that Nimani's MS clients had previously approached the BDO several times with development-related requests but were unsuccessful in obtaining any resources, thanks to his foot-dragging; today he wanted them to cover up his failures.

Kumar now welcomed the visitors to Nimani and the final performance unfolded. A group of neatly dressed children of pre- and primary-school ages, sitting next to the makeshift stage, opened the show with a song. They were followed by MS teachers, who spoke about their preschools and answered the visitors' questions. Arti began translating the teachers' words into English but was interrupted by a government official who alleged that she was embellishing the teachers' words; this official took over the translation herself. Once the children's and teachers' acts were over, the visitors were asked to walk around the corner to the center of the hamlet. Seated in the clearing near the well were roughly sixty women—MS clients from Nimani and three surrounding villages—dressed in their best saris, heads covered.

The women's act began with an MS participant explaining the vision and approach of the MS program. Another client chimed in about the activities of Nimani's women's collective. This was followed by a song in the local dialect describing gender inequalities that the women had learned from MS representatives. In the middle of the song a government functionary approached the World Bank team leader, who happened to be sitting near me and to whom I had been informally introduced. The official was concerned that the visiting team was behind schedule and wanted them to leave right away for their next engagement. The team leader turned to me and remarked that she did not think it was appropriate for them to leave in the middle of a song. I nodded in agreement and we stayed for another song.

After the songs, someone asked the women if they had any questions for the visitors. Some laughter and nudging ensued, and then four MS participants from Nimani rose and walked over to the CDO. Kevla described their development needs to him: these included a village council house, a proper road, water facilities, and houses [*avaas*].[11] She referred to the CDO as their *mai-baap* [mother-father] and asked him to take care of their needs. Dayawati presented him with two copies of an application requesting these facilities and had him write "Received" and sign one copy of the application, which the women kept for their records. They openly contradicted the BDO's orders by publicly speaking about their development needs and slighted him further by directly approaching his boss with their request. The CDO smiled at the four women and agreed to look into the matter.

And so the Nimani event ended. I walked with a group of MS clients to where the vehicles were parked. The women were in a festive mood. It was fun, they claimed, to have had such "big" people in their hamlet, and they were happy and relieved to have finally handed in a written list of their development demands to higher-ups in the government. We said our good-byes and the entourage began to roll back to the city. During the bus ride, Arti formally introduced me to the World Bank team as a researcher from the United States conducting fieldwork on the workings of the MS program in Nimani and invited the visitors to ask me questions. I stood at the front of the moving bus and fielded questions about the local social landscape, economic situations, gendered division of labor, and MS-related activities. After the question-and-answer session, the World Bank team leader sought me out and asked me about my research. I explained that I was examining how women's identities, lives, and struggles were changing within the context of this state-initiated empowerment program. The team leader gave me knowing look and smile and asked, "So, what is the *real* story?"

Performance Review

The development monitoring event at Nimani had all the makings of a social drama (Gluckman 1958; Schechner 1988; Turner 1988). It was a public, participatory drama where the lines between the audience and performers shifted as various groups of actors watched and judged one another. It combined "mundane-practical-technical activities" with "special occasion-ceremonial-representational activities" (Moore 1977, 152). For the World Bank experts, the practical goal was to observe the activities of the MS program and to evaluate its results. For Nimani's residents, however, the drama was exciting and special. Even though MS workers were a familiar presence in Nimani, the village had not been visited by a BDO in years, let alone by senior officials or foreign experts. This performance gave the residents the rare opportunity to share the stage with people whom they considered powerful. Although the Nimani drama was a discreet occasion with a beginning and an end, it represented a particular *type* of development event—a monitoring and evaluation ritual—that is repeated across time and space. The formulaic form and repetitive occurrence of such events helps to naturalize developmentalist ideologies, as I argue below (see Moore 1977). Furthermore, these bounded, yet routine, dramas lay bare the disciplinary and productive dynamic of development and the mimetic, realist logic that frames it.

Development discourse works by creating differences and hierarchies through a process of mimesis. The project of development rests upon and reproduces a spatial and temporal binary between the West and the Rest (Escobar 1995). The West possesses the essential qualities of development and modernity, whereas the Rest is represented as lacking in them. The West, according to this logic, is, and will always remain, ahead of the Rest and can thus track and evaluate the latter's progress. To develop and cultivate proper modernity, the Rest must mimic Western modernization. Developmental mimesis, therefore, positions the West as the original and real modern, of which the Rest can only be an imitation. Whereas mimesis assumes a truthful relationship between the original and its copy, it is also haunted by the possibility of difference between the two (Bhabha 1997; Diamond 1987). In the context of development this means that the Rest can become *like* the West but cannot become Western. Third World mimic copies are characterized by a lack and lag, a difference that makes them discrepantly modern (Rofel 1999), a point to which I will return later (see also Chakrabarty 2000; Gupta 1997; Mitchell 2000).

Development's mimetic logic also dictates that whereas the original cannot be exactly replicated, the copies are endlessly reproducible (Mitchell 2000). Premised on this is the very idea of modular development, which entails building models of programs that have succeeded in a particular Third World location and transferring these models to other Third World settings.[12]

The composition of the international team visiting Nimani, for instance, alluded to modular development. World Bank experts led a group of dignitaries from developing countries in Africa and Latin America to South Asia and it was entirely possible that these dignitaries were expected to replicate innovative South Asian programs, such as MS, in their own countries.

Centering the West as the ideal and original modern, and naming Western modernization as a classic, universal template that all other nations and people must follow, allow development to function as a transnational regime of governance and discipline. The Nimani drama instantiated how development's mimetic logic normalizes Western modernity and proliferates differences and hierarchies. This event became an occasion for villagers, MS staff members, state officials, and international experts to find their place along the translocal development–modernity ladder.[13] The international donor-experts from the World Bank sat atop this ladder. They were the unambiguous and stable referents of modernity, in relation to whom the status of other actors was judged and named. These development experts came to Nimani as representatives of one of the most powerful organizations in the world, with the institutionally linked authority, skill, and mandate to observe and assess the MS program. They delegated the work of coordinating this visit to Indian officials, thus positioning state actors below themselves but above nonstate actors on the development–modernity ladder.[14]

Thus, on the one hand, the Nimani visit helped the Indian state to secure its status as a vertically authoritative national body (Ferguson and Gupta 2002) and a mediator in international development interactions. On the other hand, this event also brought Indian officials under the governmental scrutiny of international funders and monitors. State actors' agenda for this visit was simultaneously shaped by their compromised identity as a borrower government (in relation to the World Bank) and their authoritative role as legitimate representatives of the nation. For them the Nimani drama was an occasion to portray India as a developing nation worthy of continued World Bank support. This visit also symbolized a test of the officials' self-positioning as modern individuals capable of governing and leading the nation toward development. This meant displaying professional capability and efficiency and exhibiting skill at designing programs that fit within the hegemonic development script authored by the World Bank. This neoliberal script includes policies such as structural adjustment, fiscal discipline, empowerment, participation, and decentralized governance (see chapter 1). The MS program, which prepares subaltern women to develop themselves and participate in local governance but does not give them material resources, was used by government officials as an appropriate example of the convergence between the Indian state's and World Bank's goals of lower government spending and grassroots empowerment.[15] Government actors needed a good performance of the MS program in Nimani. They were under the donor gaze and were understandably concerned about the consequences that a poorly staged performance might entail (such as reduced funding, increased scrutiny, and job insecurity). To circumvent these potentially negative effects, bureaucrats who otherwise sidelined this low-budgeted "women's" program now appropriated MS as a model initiative and an illustration of their development innovation. They also made MS women dance to their own tune, as Seema Singh noted. Even though MS is formally structured as a GONGO, it virtually became a state entity for the purpose of the World Bank visit. Bureaucrats dictated where and how to organize the MS show, conducted reconnaissance trips, and even overrode the translation that an MS representative provided at Nimani.

Perhaps these official tactics also redressed the partial sidelining of the state in the World Bank's currently dominant proparticipation script. Even as the World Bank continues to work primarily with national governments, it also positions the "local" as the authentic site of development and promotes direct partnerships between itself and civil-society actors; thus, in bypassing the government on occasion, it partially displaces the Indian state's self-defined centrality in development (see also Fox and Brown 1998). In this context, the government actors' move to position themselves as translators between the World Bank and localized entities such as MS staffers and clients can be viewed as a way of renegotiating the vertically authoritative place of the state in development matters.

MS staff members ranked below international experts and state actors in the transnational development–modernity schema. They had to perform in accordance with their scripted roles as dedicated and efficient "NGO" workers and showcase a thriving, deserving program to two entities that supported MS—the Indian state and the World Bank. MS functionaries had to prove that the donors' monies were well spent and that their efforts to collectively mobilize subaltern women for social change had shown positive results. They knew that the visitors had a special interest in the MS program, given the Bank's gender- and empowerment-based social agenda.[16] Their jobs, their institutional identities as more developed subjects than their clients, and their future relationship with state agencies and donors rested on a good performance.

MS program clients in Nimani were placed on the lower rungs of the development–modernity ladder, and yet they had an important responsibility. These women had to act out ambivalent roles. The World Bank's gender script positioned women like them as vulnerable and marginalized actors who were capable of being empowered and becoming reliable "engines of development" (Bergeron 2003, 162; see chapter 1). MS clients had to perform both as underdeveloped actors and as subjects of a nine-year empowerment effort. They had to simultaneously exhibit neediness, in order to make continued claims on development programs, and show raised awareness levels and an improved potential for self-development, in order to depict a flourishing and much needed MS program.

MS clients successfully accomplished this tightrope act. They displayed their agency by enacting the development-discourse–scripted underdeveloped role to demand entitlements from the CDO and by going beyond this role. Underdevelopment, however, was not a material essence that the women possessed; rather, it was a status that they made real through their act. MS women's mimicry of the underdeveloped norm, moreover, was tinged with subversive play and mockery (Bhabha 1997; Butler 1999; Diamond 1987). Through performing their MS-scripted roles as women undergoing empowerment, they contested and exceeded the narrowness of the underdeveloped norm. Although they might be poor and needy, they were neither passive nor unaware. The MS program had informed them about the resources they were entitled to through various government schemes (see chapter 5), and they used proper written petitions to demand development goods. They openly challenged the BDO's script, according to which they were supposed to hide their development needs. In so doing, MS clients challenged statist discipline and positioned lower-level state functionaries as unfit administrators who fail to enact their role as harbingers of development and whose orders can therefore be disobeyed.

By petitioning the state for development resources and endorsing a more state-centric view of development, MS clients also contested neoliberal definitions of the state as a catalyst, which encourages self-development efforts but does not dole out dependency-inducing "handouts" (see also chapter 5). They asked for their entitlements, which the state owed them, in an idiom that government actors understood. They used the presence of donor-experts to lodge a protest against state inaction and lower-level corruption, to forward their demands to a senior bureaucrat (the CDO), and to hold him accountable. By referencing discourses of corruption and accountability, these women implicitly invoked ideas about rights and citizenship (see Gupta 1995 and chapter 5). Their improvisational act allowed subaltern women to construct themselves as wards-cum-citizens of the state whose right to development had been infringed upon by a venal and unresponsive local administration, but who needed to be protected by a more benevolent and caretaking translocal state. In so doing, they not only ratified the authority of higher-ups (Moore 1977) but also tied these officials' legitimacy and status to development acts that benefited the poor.

It was through their role-play that MS participants became particular kinds of subjects of development—empowered, yet needy, citizens. MS clients' mockery of powerful scripts was an aspect of developmental mimicry (Bhabha 1997). Their improvisational performance was not free play but a creative act that both instantiated and subverted hegemonic and constrictive development scripts; that relied upon development categories and also resignified them (Kondo 1997). Subversion, however, as Judith Butler avers, "is . . . an incalculable act" (1994, 38) whose consequences cannot be predicted in advance. Nimani women's performance probably satisfied MS workers who had taught them to act in exactly these ways. How their act was perceived by the World Bank experts, however, was less clear. On the one hand, there was something about the drama that did not fully convince the leader of the visiting team, who questioned me about the veracity of what she had witnessed. On the other hand, some aspects of the women's performance likely pleased the international team members, who presumably came to Nimani to observe how downtrodden, yet empowered, women can collectively make the government more efficient and transparent. The participatory agenda of the World Bank, after all, called for precisely such civic acts.

The women's play did not, however, easily pander to the accountable governance idea endorsed by the World Bank. Rather, it demonstrated a layered understanding of proper government. On the one hand, MS clients used long-established terms, such as mai-baap, to address officials, which referenced a different time and moral universe where just rulers, like good parents, were ethically bound to look after their wards. On the other hand, they also used modern developmentalist categories and bureaucratic procedures to demand resources as rights. Mixing codes allowed subaltern women to enact their ambivalent location. They might be behind on the development scale, as they used older, historical terms of address, yet they were acutely aware of modern development hierarchies and bureaucratic rationality. These women embodied a discrepant modernity (Rofel 1999) that was contextual and had a not-yet quality to it (Chakrabarty 2000)—it was a modernity defined through lack, lag, and difference and that referenced the West but was not Western (Gupta 1997).

Discrepant modernities, as I mentioned earlier, are a result of development's mimetic logic, which posits that the original can be imitated but not exactly replicated and which, therefore, proliferates differences (Bhabha 1997; Mitchell 2000). In the context of development this logic implies that while the stated goal of modernization is to transform developing nations and peoples in the image of the modern West, what it ends up producing are mimic copies whose modernity is "almost the same but not quite" (Bhabha 1997, 153). Development practices and events, such as the monitoring and evaluation drama in Nimani, reproduce an irreducible difference between the West and the Rest. This difference is necessary for reifying the West as the modern norm and for justifying the continued need for development. But difference is also threatening in that it references the specters of failure and subversion that haunt development: that is, the Rest cannot (will not?) cultivate perfect Western modernity or churn out disciplined modern subjects.[17]

The Nimani event dramatized the social world of development, exposing its mimetic logic and the resultant matrix of transnational hierarchies. The encounter enabled actors—experts, officials, activists, and clients—to locate themselves relative to one other and thus materially realize abstract identity categories. These actors became subjects through acting out, and sometimes improvising on, institutionally and discursively prescribed and proscribed roles. They did not enter the stage as already constituted subjects but were conjunctural actors/agents who played out roles made available to them in the context of the drama. In sometimes outperforming these roles, however, subaltern actors also revised the available scripts and subject positions.

The Nimani drama also staged conflicts within and between groups of actors. Different sets of key players functioned more as "contested arenas" (Fox and Brown 1998, 16) than as unified collectives with singular agendas for the performance. For example, MS staff members, who I had the opportunity to observe closely, disagreed about the mechanics of the staging in Nimani: some desired a perfect performance whereas others wanted a realist presentation. However, the social and institutional locations of these various groups of actors, the demands of the drama at hand, and its possible material repercussions helped to cover up the dissensions within groups and lent them a veneer of cohesion (Moore 1977). The institutional and social masks worn by the actors, and their related levels of authority and social capital, made the tensions *across* different actor groups more readily apparent. These groups had varied visions for and expectations from the drama. For instance, although MS functionaries were interested in presenting a good program so that they would have continued funds and jobs in the future, state actors wanted to show a properly developing, liberalizing nation and an efficient bureaucracy.

The at-times agonistic interaction of varied actor-groups with one another in the Nimani drama, however, was not a clash of inherently different worldviews. Arce and Long (1993) propose that different sets of development actors, such as bureaucrats, program clients, and researchers, inhabit separate social worlds, which explains the tensions between them. In contrast, I contend that the apparent incompatibility between the perspectives of the different actor groups in Nimani was a product of the drama (and its underlying development script) rather than a reflection of their a priori disjunctive worlds. These actors' identities, positions, and roles on the development stage were defined as distinct. The international experts, for instance, were positioned on top because they were developed, whereas MS clients on the bottom were not. The presumed separateness of these two positions underscored the need for mediators who could act as bridges between the developed and the developing. I was cast in one of these mediating roles. As both Indian and from the West, and as an anthropologist, I was positioned as an expert who traveled between contexts (Grillo 1997, 25). I was a link between the purportedly distinct worlds of those who *have* and *do* development and those who *lack* it. My mediating presence in effect helped to produce the separateness between different actors' worlds.

In fact, however, all actors in the Nimani drama were a part of the interconnected, translocal development world. Development was as much a part of the social imaginaries of MS clients as of experts and officials (Pigg 1997). The distinctly defined positions and roles of the actor-groups, and the apparent antagonisms between them, in other words, were sutured by the logic of developmentalism. This meant that although different actors had disagreements, they also had shared concerns. One common preoccupation centered on the issues of reality and artifice. The villagers, the BDO, MS workers, and the World Bank team leader were all anxious about the nature of reality that was represented on stage. Their shared concern sheds light on another aspect of development's logic—positivist realism.

Development is driven by the desire for success, which purportedly rests upon accessing and grasping truths about people's needs and programs.

Development realism, quite like photographic (Lutz and Collins 1993) and theatrical realism (Diamond 1987), assumes that a preexisting reality (either the preprogram condition of people or the real effects of a program) can be known and should be represented truthfully; this reality can then be intervened in and molded into something more desirable. Monitoring and evaluation procedures play a critical role in this endeavor. These development practices are structured as reality tours that facilitate first-hand searches for backstage truths. The emphasis put on "being there and seeing that" reveals development's positivist epistemology that privileges presence and visibility, such that reality is "reduced to appearance" (Morris 1995, 569). This revelation, of course, begs questions about how one sees, how categories of seeing anticipate certain realities (Butler 1999), and how power and visibility are interconnected.[18]

Development monitors define the village as the site of authenticity and go there to see realist dramas that depict things as they are. They evaluate the true effects of programs and also judge how realistically program functionaries and participants represent themselves and the program during the course of the performance. In other words, they assess both the *stage* or phase of development that the program clients are in and the accuracy of the *staging* of development. Rural actors have to appear recognizably different and developing—their authenticity is yoked to imperfection and lack. Program funding can be threatened if rural actors are represented in an idealized manner or if they show too much development. To be convincing, these dramas have to present the reality that the monitors expect to see (Goffman 1973) but simultaneously deny their staged character.

Developmental realism was at play in the Nimani drama. This event, after all, ended with the question, "So, what is the real story?" By asking this question the World Bank team leader alluded to artifice and indicated that the Nimani performance might not have been a convincing reality show; that there were "really real" program effects masked by the representation she observed. Her question expressed a commonplace suspicion and success-related anxiety in the development industry that projects might be "faking it"—the countertrickery lies in being able to see through contrived performances to the actual (singular) reality on the ground. The World Bank team leader knew that I was a researcher from the United States who had been working on the MS program in Nimani. In asking me about the real MS story, she positioned me as someone who had privileged access to a truer behind-the-scenes picture of the program and the village that was presumably hidden from her.

MS staffers echoed this expert's preoccupation with reality. Arti Trivedi wanted a perfect program presentation, whereas Mallika Mehta desired to show the rural reality with all its imperfections. Diya Verma, taking cues from both Arti and Mallika, did not think that inviting "good" MS clients from across the Seelampur block area to Nimani for the purpose of the show and simulating a preschool in the village were unreal or deceptive tactics. Seema Singh, however, disagreed and criticized the fakeness of the MS school in Nimani. She wanted the visitors to see the MS program "as is." Reality, for Seema, was unmediated; it was natural, not naturalized. Meanwhile, the BDO wanted to depict a sanitized version of reality that consisted of a clean and organized village free of all development problems.

Nimani residents also had different conceptions of their own and the MS program's reality. MS clients, such as Kevla Rani and Dayawati Kumari, who gave the CDO a list of their development demands, referenced their material realities. Some male residents opposed the simulated school in their village. And Bhagwan Das was displeased because the engineered performance in his village was unrealistic. "[Development functionaries] showcase the program whenever outside monitors come. . . . [Y]ou tell me, who is *really* getting developed here? The village, the nation, or these functionaries!" Bhagwan disaggregated the different spatial levels of the development machine—the nation, the state, the program, and the village—and inverted it to claim a morally superior status for the village. According to him the entire edifice of rural development was a deceptive show, which had little to do with the real needs of poor people. Development failed because of corrupt intermediaries and misrepresentations. He thus alluded to the backstage rural realities that monitors and donors did not view; if only they could see through the artifice staged for them, real development would happen.

By questioning and judging how reality was being staged, the different performers in Nimani constructed institutionally and socially specific, hierarchically arranged versions of development realities. There was no singular, preexisting, natural, backstage reality that the Nimani drama represented on stage; rather, this drama brought into being multiple and uneven realities as shifting effects. Performances do not simply *represent* social realities but *fabricate* them. Theatrical realism "is more than an interpretation of reality passing as reality; it *produces* 'reality' by positioning its spectator to recognize and verify its truths" (Diamond 1987, 60). Members of the World Bank–led team, who sat atop the development–modernity ladder, were in a position to either verify or reject the truth-value of reality scripts authored by other actors. They would probably record what they saw in Nimani in a written document, making their observations fit the World Bank's institutional ethos, rules, and categories.[19] This translated and partial version of reality would be the authoritative script, given its organizational signature (Bergeron 2003). Such a text would reorganize multiple, often agonistic, understandings of ground realities into a singular, seamless narrative and thus help recreate development discourse's monolithic quality.

The reaction, "So, what is the real story?" from the World Bank team leader, did not seem like a promising judgment on the Nimani drama. This query hinted at the possibility that the appearance management efforts of some performers had not worked (Goffman 1973). They had either misjudged the reality that the monitors wanted to see or failed to persuade the monitors to accept a different account of reality. Or perhaps this realist drama was not entirely persuasive because different groups of actors were performing for varied audiences with diverse agendas. The World Bank's goal was to observe and evaluate, whereas state officials wanted to display an efficient bureaucracy and a properly developing nation for donors. MS employees sought to portray a good program for both the donors and state officials. And Nimani's MS clients wanted to access state resources and used the international monitors as witnesses who might help to ensure official accountability. This drama was a composite of reality scripts, enacted for different groups of audiences with varied expectations. The discrepancies opened up by the plurality of narratives, goals, and audiences may have resulted in a reality show that was less than convincing for the visiting experts. But these very discrepancies may have also provided Nimani's MS clients with the space for subverting and negotiating hegemonic and disciplinary scripts.

Curtains Down

Development monitoring and evaluation events, I argue, are always staged and their veracity, therefore, is perpetually under question; in other words, the performed nature of development dramas, and the distortion of reality performance supposedly connotes, make them suspect. Because an element of failure is written into the scripts for such development events, the international team's leader question, "So what is the real story?" at the end of the Nimani drama, was unsurprising. No kind of staging, regardless of its supposed realism, would have persuaded the monitors given the organization of monitoring and evaluation events as reality-excavation exercises and their underlying presumption that what monitors view is an always-already unreal or stylized staging of the truth. The Nimani drama, then, was coded as a partially unconvincing reality show from the start; it could not be otherwise.

Instead of speculating further about the possible failure of this performance, I want to shift focus to what it in fact achieved: the Nimani event successfully depicted the logic, dynamics, and antagonisms that constitute the social world of development. At one level, this performance, like other social dramas, helped lend coherence and stability to developmentalism, and indeed reinforced the need for development. At another level, however, it also ended up highlighting the instability and made-upness of the development world (see Moore 1977). And herein lies the danger of social dramas for those in power—"the possibility that we will encounter ourselves making up our conceptions of the world, society, our very selves" (Moore and Myerhoff 1977, 18). While the form and purpose of these dramas might serve to legitimize things as they are, they carry the lurking threat that the fabricatedness of purportedly natural realities will be revealed. The World Bank team leader's query about the real story and Bhagwan Das's criticism of how development works through misrepresentations spoke to this danger and also pointed to the impossibility of ever fully knowing the underlying reality. The Nimani drama showed that such a singular, backstage reality does not precede performances but is a negotiated and shifting effect of everyday development dramas. The very danger that these dramas will reveal how a given order is naturalized also signals their transformative potential. By exposing the constructedness of realities and subjectivities, they sometimes enable actors to challenge accepted scripts and to remake themselves and their worlds.

Examining development encounters as iterative performances illustrates how identities are fashioned within discourse and how subaltern subjects, in particular, interpret and negotiate powerful, disciplinary scripts. Identity formation, as Stuart Hall (1989) suggests, involves an interplay between "being positioned" (by powerful discourses) and repositioning. The Nimani drama highlights this dialectical and ambivalent process by which subjects are made; it reveals how subaltern actors are at once positioned and normalized as "underdeveloped" and how they tweak this identity and role scripted for them through improvisation and parody. They use developmentalist and other languages to demand material benefits and contest essentialized notions of what it means to be underdeveloped. Marginalized actors desire and demand development even as they critique how development is set up to benefit the rich and ignore the poor. Indeed, their ambivalence may well be a product of development's logic that rests on a binary between real development and the fake theater of development. Subaltern actors express their demands in an idiom that is at once modern and traditional, bureaucratic, and moralistic (I will elaborate on its moral aspects in chapter 5). In so doing they contaminate the technicality of development with ethical questions about justice and accountability. Their struggles over development cannot be regarded as "purely" antimodern. By mixing codes marginalized subjects enact a discrepant and conjunctural modernity.

Additionally, subaltern struggles may not be aimed against development per se but against dominant meanings of development; they enact a politics of resignification, transformation, and inclusion. Development thus needs to be seen as more than just a singular and totalizing discourse that exerts power over marginalized Third World people by scripting underdeveloped identities for them. This assertion made by antidevelopment critics and their related calls to declare the end of development (see Escobar 1995; Esteva 1992; Sachs 1992; Shrestha 1995) are important scholarly interventions and political moves, but they paint a one-sided picture of development as solely destructive. There is little doubt that development has proved "to be simply a myth for the millions it was destined to serve" (Rahnema 1997, 378); yet development, in its variously appropriated forms and meanings, has also provided dispossessed actors with a mechanism to position themselves as *visible* subjects with urgent survival needs and to talk back to the powerful. The current era of neoliberal globalization threatens this visibility and legitimacy of marginalized people by either naturalizing poverty or by blaming the poor for their own abjection. "If nothing else, 'development' put the problem of global inequality on the table and named it as a problem; with the development story now declared 'out of date,' global inequality increasingly comes to appear not as a problem at all" (Ferguson 2002b, 146).

Neoliberal attacks on redistributive-style development and radical obituaries of development discourse are strangely coeval and represent an example of what Evelina Dagnino (2005, 158), in a different context, has termed a "perverse confluence" between hegemonic and counterhegemonic ideas. Even though neoliberal and radical critics of development are firmly rooted in divergent ideological frameworks and take opposing views on modernity, "the end of development as we knew it" rhetoric promulgated by neoliberal institutions curiously and dangerously converges with "the death of development" talk of antidevelopment scholars.

These scholars invoke Gandhi's antimodernism to argue that true independence means liberation from the institutions and ideas of Western modernity (see chapter 1). For today's antidevelopment advocates, development is one such modern discourse and apparatus that needs to be dismantled. True freedom from development requires that Third World people decolonize their minds (Rahnema 1997; Shrestha 1995). These critics assert that the desire for development on the part of subalterns represents ideological mystification and pathetic enslavement—that if "Third-World people have themselves sought development . . . they have been misguided" (Ferguson 2002b, 144). Those arguing against development thus raise the specter of subaltern false consciousness, which needs to be vanquished along with the development machinery so that the populations targeted by development can realize "their true needs and aspirations" (Rahnema 1997, 379).

Even though they provide a powerful critique of development discourse, radical antimodern scholars also appear to partake in development's realism; this too is an awkward conjuncture. I want to highlight two aspects of the realist assumptions apparent in antidevelopment critiques. First, they assume that the true needs of subalterns lie suppressed under layers of purportedly false needs and aspirations generated by the dazzling imagery of development and modernity. My analysis, in fact, shows that the determination of "true" needs and desires is both a site and stake of struggle, which forces us to contend with how these needs may be defined, by whom, and through what procedures; these questions are not adequately addressed by antidevelopment critics. Second, antidevelopment advocates assume that the true agency of the oppressed is suffocated by the development industry and that real subaltern agency lies in agitating against development, not for it. Subaltern subjects, therefore, are implicitly projected as either victims of development or active participants in their own ideological colonization. In the first case, they do not have agency; in the second case, they have the wrong kind of agency, because they have bought into the development myth. Accordingly, the ideal agency of the oppressed lies in rejecting development and in following an antimodernist praxis of liberation. Radical critics further contend that the margins (variously described as communities, barrios or grassroots social movements) constitute ideal spaces for formulating an antimodernist project and alternatives to development. The marginalization of subaltern subjects is thus a cause for rejoicing in the radical narrative. It hardly needs to be reiterated that those being cast aside and disempowered by the current forces of globalization may not view their situations as worthy of celebration, but as dismal experiences of invisibilization, abjection, and tenuous survival (see also Ferguson 2002b).

In my view, the challenge for academics and activists, in the face of the stark and growing inequalities spawned by neoliberal political-economic processes, is to not overlook the onstage workings of development for the "truly real" backstage or prestage ideals. The imminent task at hand is to respond to subaltern political mobilizations around development (including struggles that demand certain kinds of development and those that seek to stop particular development projects) without falling into the traps of false consciousness and easy antimodernism (see also Ferguson 2002b). Paying careful attention to the ways in which marginalized subjects use development talk as a way to critique inequality and demand redress, and indeed the way in which they talk against dominant understandings of development shows how development functions simultaneously as a discourse of control and of entitlement (Cooper and Packard 1997, 4). The disadvantaged actors in this script work to improvise and negotiate constraints. They empty development of an essentialized core and instead signal the heterogeneity congealed therein. Subaltern struggles reveal that development is not an original and unchanging discourse but a fluid and contradictory script whose trajectory and end are not given. Development, then, is a morphing effect of everyday performances. While it presents itself as an ensemble that hinges upon unearthing realities, development, in fact, produces realities. Slippery stagings and engineerings, interruptions and reimagings: this messy theater is the reality of the development world, with no single *really* real story to start with or to go back to. And so the show goes on. . . .

5

(Cross)Talking Development

State and Citizen Acts

One of the first interviews I conducted in Nimani was with the elected village chief, or *pradhan*, a Dalit male named Gyan Ram, who sketched an outline of the social, political, and economic landscape of the village. He informed me of the various caste groups residing in the village, the agricultural and other income-generation activities the residents were engaged in, and the eleven village council [panchayat] members, six of whom were women. When I asked him about the development-related situation of Nimani, he told me that they had recently started a new primary school in the village with the support of the World Bank. A government-run Primary Healthcare Center (PHC) was operating near the village, but most residents did not go there because of the poor quality of care provided. Adult education–related initiatives were also being implemented. Champa Vati, a local resident who had accompanied me to Gyan Ram's house, chimed in, "the literacy work is only happening on paper. And our village has only been sanctioned one avaas [house] in the last three years even though SC's [Scheduled Castes][1] constitute 50 percent of the village population." Champa was referring to houses built under a government-run subsidized housing program for poor, lower-caste people, which had not benefited the Dalit residents of Nimani. Instead of either denying or affirming Champa's allegation, Gyan Ram proceeded to tell me that income-generating work was going on in the village but not on a very large scale. He paused again. "We have not gotten much help from the government for village development," he remarked. "They did assist us in building a 6 kilometer road under the *Jawahar Rozgar Yojana* [JRY, a government-sponsored employment scheme]. But government officials rarely come here. . . . We don't get justice. People who are able, strong, and economically secure—upper-caste Thakurs—create obstacles in the path to justice. . . . Rich people do not want the entire village to develop and they have political backing." When I asked him what Dalits in his village needed, he recounted a list, which included literacy programs for women and children, income-generation activities, a proper road, a good health clinic, and, interestingly, unity and good behavior in the community. He added, "We need the government's support in all these things—the people of the village cannot do this on their own." Ram Prasad, a Dalit resident of Nimani, seconded the chief's opinions about development and greed. "Development programs do exist," he stated, "but work only for those who have money. Poor people do not get anything because of corruption and commission taking."

The interaction just described was one of several such development-related conversations I had with the Dalit residents of Seelampur block, who were supposed to receive a variety of development benefits from the government. The most common terms subaltern subjects used when talking about development were *failure* and *rights*. Development had failed to reach them because of morally corrupt government officials and elected representatives, powerful upper castes, and self-interested individuals within their own communities; but reach it must, because development was their *haq* [right] as citizens. Narratives of development as a right and as a failure are mutually imbricated in that laments about failure implicitly reference ideas about rights and entitlements. For the poor and disenfranchised, the failure of development as a material entitlement was not something to be lauded but bemoaned (see chapter 4).

The state officials I spoke with, who were the supposed repositories and dispersers of development, also invoked the trope of failure, but in a different manner. Although they did not portray national development as a complete failure, they derided welfare-based rural-development initiatives targeted at the poorest as unproductive; such programs were bound to be unsuccessful because of the dependency they encouraged. Officials also blamed the failure of poverty alleviation programs on the destitute and marginalized, who were lacking in moral character and self-reliance.

In this chapter I ask what these conversations or stories (Sivaramakrishnan and Agrawal 2003) about the failure of development enable (Ferguson 1994). For rural Dalits as well as government officials, failed development was a matter of concern. Moreover, both the state and "the people" had central roles to play in these stories about development, but the interpretation of these roles was a contested matter between my two sets of interlocutors. Although subaltern and statist stories about development showed some convergences, they also represented a cross talk of sorts.

My purpose in this chapter is to put subaltern and statist narratives in dialogue with each other. I do not assume that the stories told by these two groups are internally homogenous and mutually exclusive; they do, after all, share the common discursive framework of development. Juxtaposing the stories, however, illustrates interesting antinomies. I emphasize the disjunctures between subaltern and statist stories to chalk out a complex picture of the meanings and function of development in the lives of these actors.

I argue that narratives of failed development function as a form of morality talk that marks and attempts to resolve the tensions between socioeconomic inequalities, the ideology of legal equality based in bourgeois, possessive individualism (Macpherson 1964), and locally relevant notions of moral citizenship grounded in ideas of *collective* good, not individual self-interest. Morality talk, in other words, references rights, justice, the state, and subjectivity. Development operates as a means to both entrench and critically examine social distinctions and political fiefdoms, to articulate different meanings of justice and moral personhood, and to shape alternative kinds of citizens, states, and communities.

I begin by laying out how subaltern subjects frequently referenced development in terms of state-distributed material entitlements and as a right that must be guaranteed by the state. Then I recount official stories about development as self-help and the role of the state and of people in it. I analyze these actors' respective explanations for the breakdown of development, teasing out how official and subaltern actors use and engage with neoliberal ideas about proper state and citizen identities, and elaborating on the connections between development, redistribution, empowered self-help, corruption, and information. In the concluding section I unravel the complexities of contemporary neoliberal development discourse. I argue that development is a contradictory and fertile arena that at once informs and forms the state, personhood, and communities. Whereas development operates as a key mode of social distinction and economic advancement within and across caste and class communities, and between subaltern and state actors, it also provides an important ground for the disenfranchised to critique inequalities and reimagine themselves. And the idiom they most commonly deploy is that of rights-inflected, justice-imbued morality talk.

Wishful Development: Resources, Entitlements, Rights

"Yahan koi vikas nahin hua" [No development has happened here]: Gauzpur's Story

In November 1998 Damyanti Rani and Nirmala Devi, MS staff members, and I set out in the government-issued blue MS jeep for Gauzpur, a village in Nizabad block, with the intention of introducing the program to local residents.[2] Nizabad is an agricultural area in the eastern part of U.P., a region colloquially referred to as the Hindi-speaking "cow belt." It was just past harvesting time and most of the rice crop had been cut and stacked in neat mounds in the fields. We passed several women carrying bundles of paddy on their heads, winding their way briskly through the chaotic traffic. The driver parked the jeep at the edge of Gauzpur, where two men stood, untangling some fuschia-colored yarn. Damyanti approached them: "We are from Mahila Samakhya and would like to talk with the residents. Is there a place here where we can sit and talk?" The men looked at us and then at the jeep and nodded. One of them led us through the narrow village lanes, calling out to people along the way, to a large clearing in the center of the village. This clearing was bordered, on one side, by a shallow ditch, which had a profusion of lotuses and water hyacinths, and by mud and bamboo huts on the other. A few women, their heads covered with one end of their saris and feet bare and muddied, stood conversing in front of one of the huts. They glanced at us as we approached. Our local guide told them that we wanted to speak with the residents. One woman gave us a pointed look and stated, "You have raised the prices of everything—have you come here to decrease them now?" They all laughed.

The women were referring to the skyrocketing prices of essential commodities, particularly oil, salt, and onions. *Rotis* [flat breads] and rice with onions and salt form the staple food for the poor in the region. The rise in the prices of these staples had caused much hardship and public debate. People overwhelmingly blamed the New Delhi government (then led by the Bharatiya Janata Party) for the spiraling inflation and for starving the poor. The woman who accused the MS staffers and me for causing the price hike obviously saw us as state representatives, who were responsible for her misery and who, therefore, needed to find a resolution.

As I contemplated this woman's reaction, a man brought us a cot to sit on; the men sat on similar cots to our left and the women squatted on their haunches to our right. This seating arrangement was usual practice, as I had figured out by now. Damyanti Rani began her presentation.

> The Government of India has a program called Mahila Samakhya, which works with women and children. This is a program about education and awareness-raising. We give all kinds of information. We are not like other programs that operate only on paper and then leave. We work with people from backward castes and classes [*pichhade*

> *jati aur varg*][3] . . . who do not have any information on government programs. We will give you information on women's rights.

After briefly introducing her colleague and me, Damyanti asked her audience members the name of their village chief. "Rajinder," came a reply. "He lives in the neighboring hamlet." Damyanti queried whether Rajinder or his wife was the chief. "His wife," yelled someone. Damyanti's request for the female chief's name was followed by silence. She persisted. "I know the name of your pradhan. I am just testing you to see whether you know who your pradhan is." "The pradhan never visits our hamlet so why would we know her name?" a woman scoffed. Damyanti did not provide the residents the name of their chief; instead she asked them for some basic population statistics. We gathered that there were eighty-five houses in the hamlet and its approximately 225 residents were Dalits. As Nirmala Devi recorded this information, the woman who had complained about inflation spoke up. "The *sarkar* [government] should give us some work," she said emphatically.[4] Damyanti retorted, "The sarkar did not ask you to produce six children. You produced them. Now it is your duty to bring them up. It is not the responsibility of the sarkar to bring up your children and provide you with employment."

Damyanti now turned to the others and asked if there were any government programs operating in the village. The villagers unanimously said no. "There must be a health nurse who visits and gives free inoculations to pregnant women and children," stated Damyanti. A woman responded that a nurse did visit their village periodically but did not provide free inoculation. "She charges Rs 5 or 10 for the shots. . . . " "What about the water situation?" asked Damyanti. A man answered that the water board had installed some taps but none of them worked. Then an elderly man, Kishen Kumar, spoke up. He criticized the government for not helping physically disabled people and widows (who were not receiving the government-stipulated widows' pension). Damyanti listened patiently to Kishen. "The village chief is the primary sarkar of the village," she explained, "and if you had chosen the right chief, then things would have been much better. . . . We can make demands and ask for things only when we have information about programs and rules and attend village council meetings." She pointedly alluded to the villagers' lack of awareness, which had led them to make bad choices, which in turn explained their lack of development. Kishen, however, was not convinced by this explanation. "The rules and laws of the government are one thing, but these officials, they are another matter altogether," he said skeptically. He conjectured that corrupt local officials, who did not follow stipulated rules, caused development to fail. Damyanti agreed that there was indeed a discrepancy between what the government said on paper and what local officials actually did on the ground. "The sarkar is not at fault—it is the people who implement the [widow] pension programs who are at fault," she remarked, distinguishing between an abstract state, or sarkar, that was beneficent and its local representatives who were dishonest. Kishen nodded and stated, emphatically, that the only way that their hamlet would develop was if they separated themselves from the chief's hamlet; development had only occurred in the latter because its residents were upper castes.

This conversation proceeded for a few more minutes after which Damyanti asked the villagers for contact names. "We will not give you anything in exchange for taking down your names. We only want to keep in touch with you. . . . We will not do anything with your names, so do not be afraid. This is a matter of trust and we are here to build a [meaningful] relationship with you." And yet nobody volunteered their names.

The Gauzpur interaction was one of several program introduction exercises I attended, and it was a fairly typical one. MS staff members (and I) arrived in a clearly marked government jeep, which had "Mahila Samakhya" painted in white letters and sported Government of India [*Bharat Sarkar*] license plates. The two men we met initially in Gauzpur likely viewed us as state functionaries. They saw us disembark from a jeep. Jeeps, even unmarked ones, were associated with authority figures and official business (Gupta and Sharma 2006). The group of women we ran into next also viewed us as government representatives and held us responsible for their inflation-related misery; moreover, they asked us to find a solution to their immediate problems. Perhaps our manner of dress (associated with "modern" urban fashions), authoritative manner of engagement, and the notebooks and bags we carried, lent us a governmental air.

Damyanti's introduction of the program did not clarify our status, as she simultaneously collapsed MS into the state and demarcated it. On the one hand, she introduced MS as a government program and used standard bureaucratic practices such as asking questions and recording data. Her style of communication was also statist. She belittled the residents on occasion, chiding them for not knowing who their real village chief was. She defined subaltern subjects as unaware, informing them that MS worked with people from "backward" castes and classes, who "do not have any information on government programs." These statements and practices, quite similar to ones deployed by state officials, gave the MS program and Damyanti an "official" status.

On the other hand, Damayanti communicated to the villagers that MS was not government-as-usual. First, MS was unlike state programs that run "only on paper and then leave;" Damyanti even sympathized with the villagers' complaints about the corrupt local administration. Second, she told the residents that MS, (implicitly) unlike government programs, would not give them any money or goods (see chapter 3). And finally, she informed the residents that they need not be afraid of her because she, presumably in contrast to state representatives, was trustworthy and dependable, and would not misuse the information that villagers provided. Because of Damyanti's ambiguous positioning of the MS program and our manner of interaction, the residents were unable to distinguish between the state and MS, and no one came forward willingly with their names at the end of the meeting.

That the villagers associated us with the state also became apparent when Damyanti questioned them about the development situation of the village. They alleged that no development had happened in their village [*yahan koi vikas nahin hua*]; however, the neighboring hamlet, where upper-caste people and the village chief resided, had indeed developed. They blamed the unevenness of development on local social hierarchies (which determined people's differential access to government programs and resources) and on corrupt state officials. For those at the bottom of the socioeconomic ladder, development remained a pipe dream. A woman specifically asked us to give them jobs and to lower the prices of staples. She saw us as state agents who were duty bound to listen to and appropriately address the woes of the poor; at the very least, we had the wherewithal to relay her message to the concerned authorities.

The villagers spoke about the state and development in the same breath, and regarded development as the responsibility of the state. This was neither unusual, nor surprising; the people of Gauzpur were simply echoing the populist rhetoric of the postcolonial state. Upon independence, the national(ist) state had assumed the mantle of equitable national development (Chatterjee 1993; Gupta 1997; Ludden 1992) and the various governments in power and political parties reiterated this state responsibility, especially during election sloganeering. Just because the state had failed in its duty of social provisioning did not mean that people's expectations for redistributive assistance and justice had evaporated. The villagers associated development with state allocation of material resources, and described it in terms of health initiatives (like inoculation programs), social support systems (like widow's pension and employment), and infrastructural and basic needs (like water and food).[5]

The Dalit residents of Gauzpur further coded basic needs and entitlements as rights. The integral connection between state-provided benefits and rights in the popular imaginary was vividly illustrated by Shyama Lata.

"That [house] was my right!": Shyama's Story

Shyama Lata, a petite, middle-aged Dalit woman, was employed with MS as a sahyogini when I met her. Shyama was widowed when she was eighteen and pregnant with twin boys. She recounted the hardships she faced, as a young, Dalit widow. Ostracized by her husband's family, she struggled to support herself and her sons by performing daily labor on upper-caste farms, cutting and selling grass as cattle fodder, and occasionally begging for food. When two MS representatives came to her village in 1991 to recruit literate Dalit women as field-level staff, Shyama's erstwhile village chief, an upper-caste Brahmin man she called Dubeyji, recommended her name. Once she began working with MS, Shyama learnt about a government subsidized housing scheme [*Indira Avaas Yojna*] for poor, lower-caste rural people. Under this program, eligible candidates receive funds from the government, in two cash installments, for construction materials and labor. Shyama needed Dubeyji's approval for accessing this scheme and he agreed to help her. Once the construction of her house began, however, Dubeyji reversed his position. "He became jealous, *didi* [sister]," explained Shyama. "He wanted to keep some of the funds, intended for my house, for himself. So he only gave me half the materials—some very bad quality bricks and stones for the roof. He did not give me any beams. And later he had the construction stopped." Dubeyji warned Shyama that unless she paid Rs 1000 and signed over the second housing installment check to him her house would remain incomplete.

Shyama spoke with a colleague at MS about her housing situation and together they confronted Dubeyji. This angered him even more and he threatened to have Shyama killed. But instead of cowering in fear, Shyama replied that he would do her a favor by killing her—death at the hands of a high-caste Brahmin, according to Hindu belief, would free her from the cycle of rebirth. Shyama persisted in her efforts and sought the assistance of the chief of a neighboring village, an upper-caste Thakur man. This man reminded Dubeyji that it was election time, and that if Shyama's house was not built in a timely manner, Dubeyji would lose all the Dalit votes in the village. Sure enough, Shyama's house was completed soon after. As Shyama explained,

> The pradhan of my village wanted me to be grateful to him and remain servile. . . . And I had dared to answer him back. But I felt that he had only given me my haq. He had not given me anything from his own pocket. That [house] was my right! I had received the appropriate information from MS and I had questioned the pradhan which he did not like. . . . There is another government-house in my village that never got completed. I spoke out [and] that is why things got done.

Shyama built her house by outwitting her village chief. Her timing was perfect; that local elections were around the corner probably worked in her favor. In Shyama's retelling, however, timing was only incidental. There was, after all, another government house in her village that remained unfinished. Shyama was the agent in her story, who not only took credit for her success, but also refused to see her subsidized house as an act of charity on the part of the village chief or the state. Rather, the house was an entitlement, which she, as an aware and worthy citizen, rightfully demanded.

Shyama's story underscores how disenfranchised subjects think of development in terms of material entitlements that are rightfully theirs and that must be guaranteed by the state. As a critical interface between state officials and subaltern actors, development serves as a site on which marginalized groups elaborate rights talk (Merry 2003; Osanloo 2006), rights consciousness, and citizenship.[6] However, they do not necessarily imagine citizenship in individuated, autonomous, neutral, and generically equal terms.[7] Their rights consciousness is deeply shaped by their position of subordination, experiences of oppression, and by ideas of proper moral personhood that might be individually enacted but is collectively imagined, as I explain later in this chapter.

Shyama's story also highlights the problematic nature of assumptions that officials make about subaltern women's alleged passivity and lack of agency. Even the MS program sometimes engages in such stereotyping (chapter 2). A program document, for instance, states that "[Women] are socially and physically oppressed. They do not have access to information beyond their immediate present. . . . [T]hey relate to Government's schemes and programmes as passive recipients. They do not have any information about their rights" (Government of India 1988, 2). This logic was apparent in Damyanti's interactions with the residents of Gauzpur as well: she marked their ignorance as an obstacle in their development, which the MS program could help them overcome. Although Shyama did not see herself as a passive individual, and indeed highlighted her survival struggles and labor prior to joining MS, she also readily admitted that being part of MS gave her access to information on a government-housing program. What was equally important in Shyama's story was how she *used* that knowledge to her advantage. Bracketing for now the links between information control, development, and state power, what I want to underscore here is that Shyama took credit for strategically using information and successfully negotiating with powerful men to access development in the form of a government-sanctioned house. Empowerment, as a means to obtain development resources, in Shyama's story, meant understanding local caste and class hierarchies and power networks, political processes, and state practices well enough to be able to demand and get material entitlements. Shyama enacted precisely the kind of empowered citizenship, combining knowledge and an attitude of defiance, which the MS program strives to achieve.

Shyama's story can be read as an affirmation of the MS program, but it can also be read as a challenge to the antiwelfarist logic that the program seems to embody. Unlike welfare programs, MS is not "involved in the delivery of services and resources" (Government of India 1997, 9). Yet Shyama, like the residents of Gauzpur, equated these very resources with development, and saw them as rights, not charity. In so doing, she and others used development as a way to gain recognition as legitimate citizens of the nation.

Subaltern understandings of development as tangible entitlements and rights offer a powerful challenge to official discourses on what proper development entails and who should be responsible for it. The dominant language of development policymaking, building on neoliberal ideas, has shifted from welfare-oriented development in which the state is a key player, to empowerment-based self-development for which individuals, communities, and civil-society organizations must assume responsibility. It is to these statist narratives that I now turn.

Arrested Development: Official Talk

"It is really about self-development"

Subhash Mishra, a senior civil servant, met me in his Begumpur office. He knew that I was conducting research on the MS program, and in the context of discussing what rural women's empowerment might mean or involve, he specifically brought up a recent shift in MS strategy. Mishra lauded the fact that the program had discontinued its earlier policy of paying sakhis [village-level MS collective leaders] a nominal monthly honorarium of Rs 200: "You cannot pay somebody to become a leader. The next thing they will want is minimum wages! Leadership should emerge by itself, and the moment you start paying, you kill the process."[8] Mishra's notion of empowerment as self-actualization ignored the relationships of structural and economic inequality within which rural Dalit women exist. He contended that paying people to take on leadership roles and to work for village development was the equivalent of handing out welfare, and that social change cannot come about through this kind of state charity. He also declared that the government should stop welfare-type programs, such as minimum wage, which were basically counterproductive.[9]

Vivek Rai, a New Delhi-based civil servant, endorsed Mishra's negative, and indeed gendered, opinion about welfare dependency. Rai labeled government development initiatives as the state's "dole system," which, he argued, countered the spirit of self-help and, instead, encouraged the "mai-baap syndrome" set in motion by India's erstwhile Mughal and British rulers. He complained that poor people looked upon the state as their mai-baap, or mother-father, and expected the government to take care of them. Rai further iterated that the success and sustainability of development rested on society, and that the state could only serve as "a catalyst, a facilitator." Here was a classic example of the reimagined neoliberal official rhetoric on development and the roles that the state and civil society ought to play in it.

A middle-level government administrator took these sentiments a step further. Vishnu Pandit, using both neoliberal and Gandhian doctrines (see chapter 1), opined that development should not be about dependence but about building moral character and self-reliance. I met Pandit, by rank a district development officer (DDO), at his 4th floor office in Begumpur in March 1999. I was ushered into Pandit's room at the sound of a bell. The office space, like that of most government functionaries I had met, was dominated by a large desk and several audience chairs, one of which I occupied. The walls were lined with metal cupboards that had inventory markings on them. Pandit, a graying, bespectacled man, was seated at his desk and pouring over some files. Once he was done, he looked up and greeted me. He then rang a bell and asked his assistant, who appeared instantly, for some tea. During our conversation Pandit spoke about the overall development status of his district and gave me some bound statistical records. He elaborated on the primary reason why welfare-driven development programs targeted at the poorest failed, stating matter-of-factly,

> Village people should be taught about *duty*. Everyone thinks that the sarkar will do things for them. This attitude . . . has negative results. They forget that they are responsible for their own development—it is really about self-development. For example, they produce five kids and then expect the government to take care of them. That is not right! You have produced them and you cannot leave it up to the government to bring them up. Giving free things to people is not good—it does not have positive results. We need to change this thinking.

Pandit argued that welfarism subverted self-reliance. What the poor needed were not handouts, which encouraged free-ridership, but moral lessons in fertility control, personal responsibility, and self-reliance; only then could development take place. Interestingly, Damyanti from MS had used a similar explanation in Gauzpur when she informed local residents that "It is not the responsibility of the sarkar to bring up your children and provide you with employment."

In contrast to such statist understandings, Phoola Devi, a Dalit resident of Nimani stated, "We need development in this village. By development I mean this—we have produced children; now they need a proper place to sleep. . . . And this is the responsibility of the sarkar. By sarkar I mean those who are supposed to serve and assist the 'public.'" Phoola Devi specifically used the English word *public*. She not only asserted the value of children for economically marginalized people like herself (which statist discourses denied), but also stressed that it was the state's responsibility to work for the welfare and interests of the public, of which she was a part. The Indian state, through its self-appointed duty of developing the nation and its populist slogans, like *garibi hatao* [remove poverty] and *roti, kapra, aur makaan* [food, clothing, and housing] (coined during the 1970s), promises to provide for the basic needs of the poor. These promises are deeply enmeshed in electoral politics in India and are also outcomes of demands from below that are articulated powerfully enough so as to compel the state to respond. Once the immediate need for such rhetoric fades, however, those in power tend to ignore their basic needs- and redistribution-oriented pledges. However, as Phoola Devi's comments indicate, shifts in policy language and practices do not erase from popular memory the promises of welfare made by state representatives.[10]

Instead of commenting on their failed pledges, my official interlocutors blamed the failure of development on two interrelated factors, both of which referenced prevalent neoliberal ideologies. First, they labeled basic needs as charity and criticized welfare-based policies for discouraging self-reliance among the poor. Reiterating neoliberal attacks on the dole served a critical purpose for state actors. Economic liberalization and austerity measures call for streamlining the social sector budgets of states by decreasing spending on health, education, and the like. In this context denouncing welfare "handouts" as dependency-creating and immoral, helped government representatives to explain why redistributive programs were problematic and to justify why the state had to step back from fulfilling the basic needs of the poorest.[11] Second, officials accused subaltern subjects for failed development. Thus, not only were poor people spoilt by over-reliance on welfare charity, they were also inherently irresponsible and inept. State agents' explanations for the breakdown of development relied upon the neoliberal distinction between "rights-bearing citizens," who were aware and self-reliant, and "undeveloped dependents," who were ignorant and incapable of enacting proper civic citizenship; this distinction was also caste, class, and gender-based, as I explain below.[12]

Good States and Subjects, Good Husbands and Wives: A BDO's Story

I was introduced to Ram Kumar, the BDO of Seelampur block, in September 1998 and had the opportunity to converse with him on several occasions during the course of my fieldwork. Ram Kumar, a stocky, middle-aged man, who rode his motorcycle to work, believed in "plain-speak." During our very first meeting, he complained about the poor state of development in his block and blamed this on the reservation policy of the government. According to this policy, a certain percentage of local elected positions in village- and block-level governance bodies are reserved for people belonging to lower-caste groups and for women. "No [development] happens now, because of reservation," Kumar declared. He revealed that the former elected block chief of Seelampur, an upper-caste man, had taken care of all development work. "The BDO did not have to do anything!" Seelampur used to be one of the most developed blocks in the district, Kumar told me, proudly displaying the trophy that Seelampur received for this honor. However, the new chief, a man belonging to a *backward caste* (a commonly used governmental category), was inept. "Now [the] BDO has to do all the work and also guide the block chief," bickered Kumar. Unprepared and incompetent lower-caste people elected into positions of power, therefore, prevented progress.

When I queried Kumar about the state's role in development, he explained that the government was responsible for making laws, designing programs, and ensuring funding for development programs. The responsibility of program implementation and success lay with NGOs and the people. Development, he posited, included the "basic things" that people "need in order to live—good air, water, food, transportation, educational facilities." So far his understanding of the materiality of development and its relationship to basic needs was not all that different from that of subaltern subjects; however, the critical distinction lay in his conception of the roles that the state and the people ought to play in the development endeavor. Kumar declared that an "ideal village is one that can make good use of the various development facilities provided for it." He used the following example to illustrate his point. "I buy vegetables and spices and bring them home to my wife. If I have a good housewife, she will make optimal use of these ingredients and prepare a delicious meal for me." He clearly demarcated the state's gendered role in development—the government, like male providers, could design programs and provide basic infrastructural and programmatic ingredients. Like good housewives, villagers were supposed to make appropriate use of the programs and develop themselves. There was no mention of the fact that often the basic ingredients of development were either not provided or were inaccessible for the most disadvantaged sections of the population; or that there could be possible contradictions in the very definition of the basic ingredients of development. In the BDO's blatantly paternalistic and casteist script, the state was idealized as male provider and benefactor, and the lower-caste beneficiaries of development were feminized, domesticated, and pathologized for being improper subjects.[13]

The statist narrative on the failure of development illustrates two important things. First, it shows how government functionaries absolved themselves of the responsibility for arrested development by accusing subaltern actors; governmental ineptitude and inefficiency found no place in officials' stories. Second, it demonstrates the extent to which officials' thinking and practices were shaped by caste and gender biases (see also chapter 2). Accordingly, lower caste people and women wanted everything handed to them on a platter. State agents did not see development as a right or perceive the dispossessed as fit and deserving citizens.

Interestingly, an interaction that I observed between Kumar and his assistant, a few days after the abovementioned interview, contradicted his thoughts on program implementation and state responsibility, and revealed a different aspect of failed development. One morning I decided to stop by the Seelampur block office in order to collect some statistical reports. Upon reaching the office compound, I found the BDO standing on the steps outside the building instructing the sweeper to clean the grounds and place some new potted plants. Kumar informed me that he was preparing for the visit of a state-level minister and also getting ready to conduct a separate weekly meeting with village chiefs during which they would resolve local development problems. "Actually," Kumar grumbled as we walked to his office, "my workers do not do their jobs well. They do not visit the villages regularly, like they are supposed to. Otherwise they would be able to solve many of the village-level problems right then and there, and there would be fewer issues [for me] to deal with every Friday."

Once in his office, Kumar rang for some tea and asked his assistant to purchase sweets, marigold garlands, and cigarettes for the minister's visit. He then turned toward a sheaf of papers and discussed some numbers with another assistant. "Shall we make up numbers on this project?" Kumar queried, pointing to something in particular. "The target was supposed to be 70 and we only have 7 to show. What will I say to the minister tomorrow?" he asked his assistant. "Just tell him that the bank did not give us sufficient funds," was the reply. Kumar, however, was not satisfied with that answer. He asked his assistant to show 27 instead of 7 of item X; if questioned, he was to say that the target of 70, which was not set locally but rather at the district level, reached them late. Clearly my presence did not deter the men from fudging numbers. The BDO's assistant then brought up a hand-operated water pump project and asked how many hand pumps he should report as installed. Not all the pumps that had arrived at the Seelampur block office had been fitted. Kumar told his colleague to include the uninstalled water pumps in the report. "They have arrived and will be installed, eventually. Just put the total number down." Kumar then turned to me and gave me the statistics on Seelampur block that I had asked for. I rose to leave, but before I could thank him, the BDO launched into an unprovoked story about thefts in his office. "The cashier here is a *daaku* [robber]" and had stolen Rs 3000 from the office. Former BDOs had appropriated the good quality cups, plates, and flower vases issued by the government. "You tell me, what I am supposed to do!" Kumar asked incredulously. Perhaps he was looking for sympathy from me, or maybe he wanted to clarify that he was not personally responsible for any wrong doings and failures at the block office during his tenure.

My interaction with Ram Kumar provided an example of government inaction, inefficiency, and corruption, which often went unmentioned in statist stories about failed development. Block administrators were expected to meet unrealistic development targets that were set by district officials, who were several steps removed from the grassroots level. The administrators were also expected to redistribute the development resources they received from higher-ups in the government to villages, and to resolve local development issues. However, this did not happen because of corrupt block-level functionaries. Some stole things and money from the office; others did not implement the planned programs in a timely manner, and wrote reports in a way that indicated that targets were being met when perhaps they were not. It was not clear to me whether the villagers who were supposed to receive things like hand pumps were actually informed about these potential resources or about the eligibility criteria. Interestingly, while Kumar was quite open about fudging numbers and criticizing the dishonesty of his staff, he did not overtly connect the failure of rural development programs with such (mis)happenings. Subaltern explanations for failed development, on the other hand, picked up on precisely these issues as I demonstrate next.

Arrested Development: Subaltern Talk

Rights, Information, Power, and State Corruption: Ajay's Story

Ajay Kumar, a Dalit resident of the village of Gamiya, was an elected member of the Block Development Committee (BDC) of Seelampur Block, when I met him in March 1999. A middle-aged, educated man, Ajay owned a small tailoring shop in a nearby town. I arrived at his house, the only concrete dwelling in the village, at 9 AM on a Sunday morning and found him waiting outside. We sat down on a coir-woven cot and conversed about the politics of rural development over hot cups of sweet, milky tea.

I began the interview by asking Ajay about the composition and purpose of the BDC. He told me that Seelampur block had seventy-nine BDC members (one for every 2000 residents). BDC members, like village chiefs, were elected and reported to the block chief. When I asked him what BDC members were expected to do, he shook his head stating that the local administration had not clarified the duties of BDC members, despite repeated inquiries. Ajay informed me that BDC members were supposed to meet every three months. When I questioned him about the content of these meetings, he replied, "[We are supposed] to discuss village issues and needs, and resolve them. But the meetings do not happen. The BDO and block chief are corrupt. All they want to do is usurp the money that is channeled through various development programs. Take housing for example. Houses are supposed to be constructed for Harijans,[14] but we only receive a portion of the total outlay," he stated, confirming the story Shyama had told me about the problems she faced when having her house constructed. "I know only one thing," Ajay continued. "Nobody gives 'power' to anybody. We have to demand and forcibly get our rights [haq]."

When I questioned him about government development programs operating in his area, he replied, "Government programs are never implemented in our hamlet. Technically we are supposed to have the Integrated Rural Development Program, housing and loan programs, and skills training for women. But low-caste people never get [to participate in] the programs the government plans for them. . . . Village development is the responsibility of the BDO and the block chief. It is also the responsibility of the village chief—however, that depends on whether the village chief receives any development funds or programs from the officials above him. [But they] are all corrupt and eat up the development funds. . . . For example, earlier the entire budget for the Jawahar Rozgar Yojana scheme [a government-initiated rural employment program] was under the control of the BDO. . . . Now the block development committee, of which I am a member, is supposed to directly receive 15 percent of the funds allocated under the scheme and use them for development work. But the BDO and block chief [still] control all the money." "So why don't you go to the district administration and complain?" I asked. Ajay replied that it would be of no use. "They are all in it together—even the district magistrate is part of this. They all get affiliated with the party in power, rather than staying neutral, and play political games. The only reason I know [about all these development initiatives] is because I have contacts with top level officials. . . . I have been to [the state capital] several times and have met senior administrators. That is how I obtained all this information."

I then asked Ajay to describe the needs of the people in his village. "Water, housing, electricity are the things that most people need. . . . They need concrete houses and a road," he responded. I followed this up by inquiring whether his village had progressed in the past few years. "Some development has taken place," he answered. "We have developed as far as education is concerned but we have done it ourselves—it has not happened because of any government program." Ajay pointed to the hand-operated water pump on the side of his house, about twenty feet from where we sat. "I got this pump because of my own 'power'," he proudly claimed. The block office had installed a faulty water pump in his hamlet, which had fallen apart within ten days. So Ajay circumvented the local block-level administration, went straight to a senior district bureaucrat with his request for a new water pump, and got it approved. He also made sure that the junior engineer responsible for installing the pump used proper parts, and not substandard ones, as was usual practice. "I fought with the government for my rights," said Ajay emphatically, "and the government gave us the water pump. It is our right . . . [and] in order to demand and get our rights, we need strength [*taakat*]."

Ajay, like the residents of Gauzpur, and like Shyama, saw development in the following manner: it catered to the survival needs of the people and was symbolized by material markers, like the water pump distributed by the state; accessing it required proper information about programs and procedures, connections with the development administration, and personal initiative and strength to fight local state corruption; and finally, development was a right that had to be safeguarded by the state (but in reality was something that the downtrodden had to constantly fight for).

Ajay iterated the common theme of development as a failed project. Even though the government supposedly implemented many programs for poor people, Dalits were unable to make use of these programs because of local corruption and politics. Government bureaucrats indulged in political wrangling and personal economic gain, thus subverting the purported neutrality and disinterestedness of the state. These officials, in cahoots with elected representatives, political leaders, and other groups with vested interests, fleeced the system.[15] These were the reasons why development programs did not benefit the poor.

Ajay also took credit for the development that had happened in his village. It was only because he had sought help from his higher-level connections in the government, and obtained critical information about development programs and the procedures for accessing them, that he was able to override corrupt local officials and claim what was rightfully his. At first glance, Ajay's narrative of personal success would seem to overlap with neoliberal and statist tales about self-help and self-development that emphasize individual initiative, effort, and awareness as keys to advancement. These dominant narratives take the existence of neutral state institutions, rules, and rights for a given, and view personal drive as the critical factor that allows people to access their rights and make institutions work in their favor. I would argue, however, that Ajay's vision of the state's central role in distributing material entitlements (as rights) and his relationship to the state were at odds with neoliberal and official themes. Ajay's story spoke of an agonistic relationship in which state agencies (that are anything but neutral) must be compelled to play their designated role, and this required a particular kind of practical cunning or intelligence (see Scott 1998). Additionally, personal drive would only be successful within a larger supportive system of governance that provided entitlements and information to those in need in a fair and unencumbered way. By contrast, in neoliberal and statist narratives individual efforts are all that are required for self-development; and these efforts are not supposed to be directed against the state, but toward solving development problems on one's own.

Moreover, Ajay offered a different perspective on the link between information and development from that of state actors. Many officials I spoke with alleged that they distributed information about development programs, but that lower-caste poor people, especially women, did not make proper use of the information and programs because they were illiterate, ignorant, and passive. Ajay, on the other hand, contended that dishonest local administrators did not disseminate the necessary information; rather, they used information as a key instrument of power and actively prevented poor people from gaining access to development resources and rights. For example, the government had instituted BDCs in an effort to make governance and development administration more decentralized and participatory. The idea was to include the supposed beneficiaries in the allocation of development funds and in the implementation of programs. But the government had not given these committees any teeth. Their members were not informed about their duties and local officials, when queried, used standard bureaucratic jargon—"no duties have been stipulated yet"—to mask inaction.

Participatory and decentralized governance is a crucial part of the Indian state's agenda and of the broader neoliberal project. Ajay endorsed this policy, but was frustrated because it was improperly implemented; popular participation and decentralization was spoken about but had not been actualized on the ground. He echoed the criticism made by Kishen in Gauzpur—that there was dissonance between what the state wrote on paper and what state officials actually did. Consequently, even good development legislation failed in practice and development, as a system of patronage, continued to be controlled by and profitable for the powerful.

Shanti, a resident of Seelampur block and an MS employee, explained this issue succinctly:

> One [problem] is that there is a lot of distance between the people for whom development programs are meant and state functionaries — [between] the common people [*aam janata*] and government servants [*sarkari naukar*]. . . . State functionaries do not inform people about the [eligibility] rules of the various programs. If they had proper information, people would use the programs to their benefit. [Government functionaries] . . . keep the most crucial pieces of information to themselves. [They] do not implement programs from the point of view of the people; they implement programs for themselves.

Shanti referred to the symbolic and material gulf between the subject positions of a *government employee* and a *common person*, and used it to explain why development only benefits those who occupy the former category. The differences in economic, cultural, educational, social, and political capital encoded in these identity labels created a chasm in knowledge and understanding. State elites claimed that marginalized people were uninformed, defective subjects.[16] According to Shanti, however, these elites were the ones lacking in knowledge. State representatives did not understand (and perhaps did not even attempt to understand) the social relations or needs within poor communities and were therefore incapable of designing appropriate interventions. Even when they implemented programs meant to assist the marginalized, they withheld critical information from the intended beneficiaries, because complete disclosure would close off the possibilities for misappropriating official development funds ("leakages") for personal use.

Not only did officials end up profiting from development programs meant for the disenfranchised and poor but, as Shanti alleged, these programs may very well have been designed with that in mind. The economic and social status of development administrators is premised on the continued lack of and thus need for development among the poor. If the goals of development programs were met, what would become of the social axes of difference between government employees and rural subalterns? What would happen to the government employees' exclusive claims to being modern and developed? Indeed, what would become of their sources of income, social status, patronage networks, and authority, sustained through selective distribution of state resources?

Information was a vital ingredient in the development recipe. The harbingers of development needed information about villages, villagers, and their needs; and villagers needed information about development entitlements, rights, and their rules of access. Without such information, proper, equitable, and participatory development would remain an ever-receding horizon.[17] Ajay and Shanti understood the interconnectedness of information, power, and the state in the context of development, and used this to indict a venal officialdom which withheld critical information from supposed beneficiaries, had little knowledge about the situations and needs of the latter, and misused development funds for private profit.

The Virtues of the Weak: Remoralized Citizenship Talk

In addition to rampant state corruption, the other reason most commonly cited by subaltern Dalit actors for the failure of development was inter- and intracaste prejudice and power politics in their villages. The residents of Gauzpur, as I delineated earlier in the chapter, suggested that development did not reach them because the husband of their village chief, an upper-caste man, diverted all resources to his hamlet. Similarly, Gyan Ram, the chief of Nimani, commented that poor Dalits in his village did not get development or justice because "people who are able, strong, and economically secure—upper-caste Thakurs—create obstacles. . . . Rich people don't want the entire village to develop and they have political backing." Other Dalit residents of Nimani gave me evidence of such caste-based discrimination. Their hamlet had one nonoperational water pump, while the upper-caste hamlet had between five and eight working hand pumps. When the government distributed fruit-tree saplings, the Dalit residents did not get any because the upper-caste Thakurs took them all. I heard similar stories about upper-caste monopoly over state-sanctioned development resources nearly everywhere I went. Whereas officials blamed the poor Dalits for their lack of self-reliance, moral character, and awareness (and for their resultant failure to develop), the Dalits I spoke with accused locally powerful people—upper castes and state functionaries—for keeping them bereft of development.[18]

In addition my Dalit informants also cited intracaste rivalry as a reason for the unevenness of development. For instance, the chief of Nimani brought up the lack of "unity and good behavior in the community" as matter of concern; village development required that this lack be addressed. Nimani residents who lived in mud huts pointed fingers at those who inhabited government-sanctioned concrete houses. They told me that only those who were "in" with powerful people were able to secure houses and steady employment for themselves. Some residents of Gamiya village accused Ajay, the BDC member, for only taking care of his own family's welfare. They pointed to the water pump, installed right in front of his house, and lamented that Ajay's family regarded the pump as their personal property even though it was supposed to be for communal use. Similarly, Ganga, a female resident of Nimani, alleged that even though her elected village chief was a Dalit man, he did not look out for the interests of his caste community. Instead of assisting poor Dalits in obtaining government-subsidized houses, the chief built one for himself. "[The chief] is responsible for spreading the work of the government. The government gives money for village development to him but he does not do anything," Ganga charged.

Development talk, thus, brought forth stories about communal fractures and disunity (see chapter 6). Self-interested and morally corrupt "big" people, or "mai-baap," who were associated with the state and had social, economic, and political capital, used development resources for personal gain rather than for the progress of the entire village and caste community. As a result, development, if it happened at all, benefitted only a few.

Development thus functioned as a key axis of social differentiation around which moral personhood, communal belonging, and indeed deserving citizenship were defined. Those who were dominant and cunning had development, and subordinate Dalits with no connections, guile, or power, did not. Socioeconomic and political status, from the perspective of the most disenfranchised, correlated negatively with moral standing and the degree of deservedness for development. Those denied development and kept poor positioned themselves as the most innocent, moral, and worthy; these were the virtues of the weak (Scott 1977, 1985). Neediness served as a measure of righteous citizenship. Furthermore, development itself was not morally reprehensible; at issue were the unscrupulous means by which it was amassed by some people at the expense of others. The poor and disempowered conceptualized their personhood and communal belonging in contrast to those who were self-serving and devious enough to have obtained development, and in contrast to official images of their flawed and unruly subjectivity. The subaltern actors in the above-mentioned stories did not connect their lack of development with high fertility rates or ignorance; rather, they saw themselves as agents who were aware of the existence of various programs. Mere awareness, however, did not amount to much, because selfish state representatives and other people, powerful people, stood in the way of general good.

By blaming the "haves"—both within and outside their communities—the "have-nots" linked the state development apparatus (as it existed) with moral depravity. These popular laments point to how the boundaries between the state and civil society are blurred (Gupta 1995). In the subaltern imaginary, "the state" was not represented by a set of easily identified officials; it was, rather, defined through immoral practices and the abuse of power, knowledge, and resources, which helped shape and reproduce inequalities. These were, perhaps, stories about the inherent corruptability of the bad state, *as is*. However, by desiring and demanding development, subaltern actors also communicated a vision of the good state, *as it should be*, which had a moral imperative to improve the lives of the poor.

Subaltern stories about morality and venality, in the context of development talk, function as discourses about justice, rights and citizenship. Narratives of corruption and exploitation serve as a mode by which the subalterns in postcolonial India implicitly represent their rights to themselves (Gupta 1995) and conjure themselves as morally upstanding citizens who demand justice. Yet the image they construct is not one of an abstract and formal rights-bearing citizen, as defined by the liberal legal tradition; rather, subaltern actors use development talk to enunciate and substantiate novel and expansive forms of culturally coded, collectively informed, rights-bearing citizenship, not delimited by liberalism.

Liberalism, as Mouffe contends, "has contributed to the formulation of the notion of universal citizenship, based on the assertion that all individuals are born free and equal, but it has also reduced citizenship to a merely legal status . . . [where ideas of] public-spiritedness, civic activity and political participation in a community of equals are alien" (1992, 377). "Free" and "equal" liberal rights are applicable to "individuals as isolated atoms, acting in their own interests, maximised through exchange in the marketplace" (Hall and Held 1990, 178; see also Collier, Maurer, and Suarez-Navaz 1995). Contemporary neoliberalism builds on these liberal tenets and enunciates empowered citizenship in self-reliant, individuated, entrepreneurial terms (Rose 1999).

Against this definition, subaltern Indian actors articulate an idea of citizenship, perhaps referencing Gandhian notions (see chapter 1), that is ethically grounded, communally embedded, and collective uplift-oriented. This vision directly challenges possessive individualism and privatized interest as the basis for proper personhood and rightful citizenship.[19] The discourse of the disenfranchised is one that "emphasizes the value of . . . the notion of a common good, prior to and independent of individual desires and interests" (Mouffe 1992, 377). In putting forth these alternative imaginings, subaltern subjects denaturalize the legalistic discourse on citizenship that writes out questions of class, caste, and gender inequality and appears to treat all citizens as formally equal. Subaltern morality and rights talk in India reinserts questions of inequality, morality, and community, and imbues abstract legalistic definitions with materiality and contextual morality. Their claims to development as a right, and thus for justice, are based in their socioeconomic oppression; as wronged victims of willful acts by powerful people, they are more deserving of development. Development thus becomes a ground for the enactment of a morally inflected, culturally shaped, and intersubjective citizenship, and this, I argue, is an *empowering excess*, perhaps unintentional, facilitated by struggles over development.

Conclusion

In this chapter I narrated development stories told by various subjects, like government functionaries, MS representatives, and rural Dalit actors, who have unequal social and economic capital and different relationships to the development regime. Failure was a dominant metaphor in the development stories I heard. Rather than treating failure as a point of closure, I used the trope of arrested development as a point of theoretical entry (Ferguson 1994). My ethnography shows that development is more than simply a disciplinary, expert imposition from above and is hardly obsolete. Indeed, the very ubiquity with which officials and subalterns brought up the failure of development programs and how the latter lamented it points to its continued relevance in people's lives. Development functions not as a moribund and depoliticizing discourse, but as a teeming and politically charged space for social commentary and political critique, and as a means for reenvisioning moral "citizen" selves and a just society.

Although development is part of the social imaginary of both officials and subaltern people, a form of cross talk emerges when the stories told by these sets of actors are read against each other. Where state officials increasingly articulate a neoliberalism-derived vision of development that is divorced from welfarism and material redistribution, subaltern subjects define development as material entitlements coded as rights. Where officials contrast welfare and empowerment, subalterns allege that empowerment is meaningless without welfare-oriented redistribution. Where officials conceive of the state's role as a facilitator, not provider, subalterns consider it a moral duty of the state to provide concrete benefits to its most marginalized citizens and to ensure their survival, social betterment, and rights. Finally, where officials primarily blame the moral lack, ignorance, and ineptitude of lower-caste people for the failure of development programs, subaltern subjects explain their casting out of development in terms of degenerate and self-serving powerful people (including state actors).

Above I have described what I term cross talk: development as a right versus (mal)development as charity; development as material improvement and equitable social change versus development as pathological dependence on handouts; development as the ethical task of the state and of the powerful versus self-development as the ethical responsibility of the poor; lack of development as a marker of moral uprightness versus self-development as a means to moral uplift and discipline; lack of development as a way to claim legitimate and expanded citizenship versus lack of development as a signifier of unruly and unworthy personhood and noncitizenship.

Subaltern counternarratives of development are "derivative" (Chatterjee 1986b) in that they are not autonomous but partake in and reinforce development's conceptual force as a dominant interpretive grid of our times (Escobar 1995; Ferguson 1994). Political critique or even revolt, by dissident groups, as Immanuel Wallerstein reminds us "does not necessarily mean that they do not subscribe, if only subconsciously, to the fundamental values [and] cosmology" of what they contest; rather, it "may just mean that they feel these values are not being implemented fairly" (1995, 1163). The "small acts" (Gilroy 1993) of subaltern challenge are especially significant in a context where statist discourse positions the downtrodden as *problems*—namely, passive, needy, ignorant, disempowered, overly fertile, and irresponsible—and thus undeserving of state help. By articulating counternarratives of development and positioning themselves as victims of moral corruption among the powerful, subaltern actors resignify what development ought to be and who should be responsible for it; they redefine their identities as they struggle for power, status, and recognition as legitimate citizens.

Subaltern struggles and stories vigorously contest official and neoliberal scripts of development, the postwelfare state, and ideal personhood. They provide a compelling example of neoliberalism's troubled travels, illustrating that it does not displace existing histories and ethicopolitical worldviews but articulates with them, resulting in unpredictable, politicizing consequences (see also Ong 2006).

The neoliberal doctrine defines development in terms of market-driven, entrepreneurial self-improvement by empowered subjects, and sees it as a civil society–based participatory project where the state plays a capacity-building, and not redistributive, role. Even as Indian state agents, in keeping with these ideas, try to avoid covering people's basic needs (coded as bad state welfare), marginalized actors view these material resources as a fundamental right that must be provided and protected by a good state. Although the neoliberal doctrine contrasts welfare and empowerment, subaltern actors effectively connect the two. Thus, women's practical interests of survival and access to basic needs and their strategic interests of shaping a gender equal society, also go hand in hand (Molyneux 1985; see chapter 1). Even as the focus of policymakers moves away from resource provisioning, they cannot ignore the ineluctable coupling of empowerment and material entitlement on the ground. Empowerment programs, I emphasize, cannot just focus on delivering power in the abstract. The state simultaneously needs to ensure that the poor are allowed fair access to government programs and that their everyday practical needs are met. It is only through these tasks that the broader strategic goal of just and equitable social change, which lies at the heart of MS, can be attained.

Development, as I have demonstrated, functions as an arena for the elaboration of morality-cum-rights-cum-citizenship talk in postliberalization India. Officials code self-development and self-reliance as the moral responsibility of the poor and in so doing resurrect a liberal subject of rights. Poor people, in statist scripts, are not rights-bearing subjects because they lack the maturity, knowledge, and discipline needed to demand rights and to shoulder the reciprocal obligations that citizenship demands. Furthermore, officials argue that welfare programs have encouraged passive dependency on the state and have failed to cultivate an active, atomistic citizenship of the neoliberal kind where individuals learn to take responsibility for self-governance and fashion themselves into competitive, and consuming citizen-selves. Where neoliberal reinventions detach citizenship "from its modern roots in institutional reform, in the welfare state and community struggles," (Hall and Held 1990, 174), subalterns rebundle these themes.

Citizenship, as Stuart Hall and David Held (1990) write, is a keyword that has a particular history and has also been made to signify differently by social movements that have applied the concept in new and unusual ways.

Moreover, they suggest, the politics of citizenship is critically important in our era of neoliberal globalization, given the erosion, or threat thereof, of the welfare state, civil rights, and entitlements. I argue that in postcolonial contexts development is one of the most important sites where citizenship struggles are taking place, where rights claims are staked, and where the very meanings of the ideas of citizen, belonging, and the state are fought over.

Contemporary struggles around citizenship have to contend with the paradoxes that the hegemonic liberal definition of the term congeals. First, citizenship is a universal status that presumes sameness. Is it possible, then, to mobilize this status to express claims based in difference, plural identities, and fair representation for the underprivileged (Chatterjee 2004; Hall and Held 1990)? Second, even though citizenship confers equal rights on all individuals (positioned as generic, public units), in effect rights are selectively applied; the formal, legalistic discourse on equal rights thus, ironically, papers over existing hierarchies, and is used to maintain forms of exclusion (see Wallerstein 1995). Finally, citizenship is a *social* identity through which belonging to a (national) community is articulated, but it only guarantees rights to *individuals* (Hall and Held 1990, 177). These contradictions raise serious dilemmas for political movements engaging the question of citizenship.

Contests over development in India today, in fact, point to the significant ways in which marginalized actors are using inequality and morality talk to resolve the apparent paradoxes of citizenship and to increase its scope by articulating inclusive, expansive, ethically inscribed, and social definitions of the term. Subaltern actors speak from a place of difference and inequality, and not as generically equal and similar subjects. They use their experiences of subordination and exclusion from development to demand de facto inclusion into the supposedly universal citizenship status. Their uncorrupted mentality, proven by their deprivation and victimization, lends moral force to their equal rights and justice claims.

Those on the margins of society invoke the legalistic ideal of equality, which is guaranteed by the constitution, to contest the social, political, and economic inequalities in which they are embedded. By bringing inequality talk into the heart of rights talk, subaltern subjects expose the illusory promise of equal rights and reveal the selectiveness with which equality actually works. In mobilizing ethical discourses to talk about unequal and corrupt developments, they imbue formal constitutional equality and abstract rights with materiality and morality. Meaningful equality relies upon just state action and means two things. First, it means an equal "right to process" (Hall and Held 1990, 182), whereby marginalized people are given the proper information and means to access their development entitlements and to, therefore, substantively exert and actualize their rights. And second, it means a state-led reallocation of income and wealth. By demanding a right to information and access, and a right to basic needs and concrete resources, subaltern actors send a powerful message that a meaningful enactment of citizenship and social justice require a different kind of state: not a privatized "minimal" state of neoliberalism, or a "withering" state of classic Marxism, or a "no state" of anarchism, but a redistributive, caretaking, and, indeed, ethical state, that plays an active role in undoing the inequalities spread by capitalism and other dominant social and political forces (see also Hall and Held 1990; Sunder Rajan 2003, 112).

Even though the state is a key point of reference in subaltern commentaries on citizenship, their discourses go further. By criticizing the unfair and disempowering governmental practices of powerful people in general (and not simply of state agents), and by putting forth an alternative picture of a collective-based moral personhood, they extend the idea of citizenship beyond the bounds of the state, the national community, and the atomistic individual. Marginalized actors contest the self-interested, aware, choice-driven, autonomous economic individuality that is idealized as the foundation for rights-bearing citizenship under the neoliberal doctrine. The subaltern notion of a good citizen is already collective and social. This sort of personhood cannot be motivated by selfish concerns but must work for the larger good; real belonging is judged through service to (subordinated) others, and not to the self. These notions of proper social subjectivity also speak against the neoliberal idea that profit-motivated acts of individuals will automatically achieve the greater common good (which is economistically defined as the optimal and efficient distribution of resources). Collective good, in counterhegemonic stories, precedes individual interest; the latter must be derived from the former, and not the other way around. Furthermore, individuals must act for the benefit of, and be accountable to, a larger moral community. In this case, *the community* to which a citizen belongs is imagined as a layered formation of which the nation is but one part. Proper communal belonging needs to be enacted in one's social milieu (be they villages or deprived and oppressed groups or caste collectives) as much as invoked through the constitutional laws of the nation-state; in all cases it must be morally defined.

By using morality talk, marginalized actors articulate a particularistic vision of a substantively equal society that is based in collective principles and not guided by individualistic quests for economic, social, and political power.

In the postcolonial subaltern stories recounted in this chapter, development is neither defunct nor passé. On the contrary, it appears as a powerful ground on which marginalized subjects fight against socioeconomic inequalities, an uncaring state, and neoliberal processes and ideas; they fight for self-definition, citizenship rights, and survival. These, I believe, are empowering fallouts of development, which reveal the cracks in its hegemony. Even as development discourse recuperates grassroots struggles and threatens to depoliticizes them, subaltern actors reappropriate development in unforeseen ways and inject it with a politics of citizenship.

6

Between Women?

The Micropolitics of Community and Collectivism

First Impressions

I first visited Nimani in August 1998, just as the monsoons were ending. The village is situated amid paddy fields, not far off the main road in Seelampur block. The paddy crop, about 4 feet tall and bright green in color, would be harvested in a few weeks' time. Tulsi and Sita, the two MS field-level functionaries who had recommended that I work in Nimani, accompanied me to the village to introduce me to the MS participants and residents.

Our first stop was the house of one of the two sakhis [leaders] of Nimani's MS women's collective.[1] An older woman, with leathery, weathered skin, unkempt gray hair, and a nicotine-stained smile came out of her house upon hearing our voices. She covered her head with one end of her yellow sari and greeted us in a loud, rustic voice. "*Namaste Behenji* [sisters]!" This was Gulabi. Tulsi briefly introduced us and asked Gulabi to gather the MS sangha [collective] members for an impromptu meeting.

Together we walked over to a clearing near a water pump in the village; this hand-operated pump, I would soon discover, was nonfunctional. Several neem trees cast a shade over the area, providing some respite from the August heat and humidity. Gulabi walked through the hamlet announcing our arrival and yelling out women's names. In about ten minutes, eighteen women gathered under the trees. We spread a dhurrie on the ground and sat in a circle. Some men joined us as well but sat on coir-woven cots a few feet away, eyeing me curiously.

The women began by introducing themselves. Then I answered their questions about myself, my family, and my research project and asked them about their local MS collective. The women told me that their collective was formed three years ago. Tulsi, the local program representative, immediately interrupted. She glared at the women, reminding them that their group was formed eight years ago and that they had been taking up village issues for just as long. The savings and loan activity had started three years ago, through which the collective received Rs 200 per month from the government for a maximum of three years. Sangha members contributed small amounts (e.g., Rs 10) to this fund on a monthly basis and were expected to use the money for giving loans and starting microenterprises. Nimani women had incorrectly equated the initiation of their collective with the start of the savings and loan fund. Some women nodded in agreement with Tulsi's chronology, whereas others looked confused. I found out that only sixteen adult female residents of Nimani, including mothers-in-law and daughters-in-law, were members of the MS sangha.[2] Although eighteen women had initially joined, two later pulled out because of conflicts. Other women had chosen to stay out of the sangha, stated Phoola, an MS participant: "What will we get from joining MS!" was how they responded when asked to join.

We spoke for a while about the issues that the local MS collective had taken up. The women told me about their successful struggle to raise their daily, in-kind agricultural wages from 1.5 kilograms to 4 kilograms of paddy. "Earlier the upper-caste Thakurs used to force us to work on their farms, but that does not happen any longer. Now . . . we are sharecroppers!" stated Tapisra proudly.[3] Others spoke about the status and space that joining MS had provided them [*ek jageh di hai*]. In the past they were unable to gather in the open because their husbands, mothers-in-law, and other village elders would scold them for wasting time. Now they collectively and publicly discussed and resolved local problems, shared in their joys and sorrows [*dukh-sukh baant'te hain*], saved and pooled money, and gave low-interest loans to sangha members. They no longer sought out the services of moneylenders, who charged interest rates as high as 15 percent per month. They had even learned to sign their names, Gulabi claimed excitedly, and showed me the sangha register with the members' signatures. These women were obviously proud of this achievement: being able to sign their names instead of using thumbprints was a marker of respect and status for women who were otherwise considered nonliterate.

When Tulsi asked the women to talk about some current issues they were facing, Phoola mentioned government-issued ration cards.[4] She complained that she had to pay Rs 10 to obtain her ration card, even though it cost only Rs 2. Tara, another MS participant, looked surprised and informed us that she had to pay Rs 20. She ran inside her hut and brought out her ration card. The ration card had "Cost—Rs 2" printed on it. Tara claimed that the elected vice-chief [*oup-pradhan*] of the village had made it sound like he was doing her a special favor by asking for only Rs 20. A cost comparison ensued, and it became apparent that ration card payments varied between Rs 5 and Rs 20. Tara, angered by this discrepancy, vowed to find out why people had paid different amounts for the same "below poverty line" ration card. Meanwhile, some women stated that they had been unable to obtain ration cards. Siya, who was among this group, openly accused the successful ones for being sneaky: they had neither informed nor assisted other MS participants in getting ration cards. Chinta, another MS participant, grumbled that the village's vice-chief had refused to issue her a "below poverty line" ration card, notifying her that because her husband ran a small business, she was ineligible. Chinta's husband was a petty cobbler who barely made any money; the government, however, refused to recognize their poverty. She sarcastically commented that they would be better off if her husband were to close his business: they would at least qualify for "below poverty line" benefits from the government. Meera added to this growing list of grievances, telling us that the distribution of rations was discriminatory; upper castes got more and better-quality rations than low-caste, poor people.

The meeting had clearly disintegrated. Everyone was speaking all at once and angrily pointing fingers at one another for paying too little for their ration cards or for obtaining them at all. One woman lamented, "There is no sense of collectivity in this *biraadari* [community]." Tulsi and Sita, the two MS representatives, spoke over the din, instructing the women to take action on the ration card issue and called the meeting to an end. Gulabi, the MS sakhi, came up to me. She smiled and said that she looked forward to seeing me in the future. I expressed my desire to meet with all female residents of the village, both MS participants and nonparticipants. Gulabi promised to introduce me to everyone, especially those who had not attended the first meeting. She then lowered her voice, and warned me about the non-MS women in the village. "Do not believe what they say. [These women] will tell you that [MS participants] don't do anything [and] do not take up any issues except for saving money. The nonsangha women don't trust the sangha women."

Gulabi's warning and the tense interactions of the day's meeting intrigued me and portended things to come. Why did some women refuse to join MS and what were the reasons for the disagreements between members of the MS collective in Nimani? How did the MS program play into these contentions? And how did these antagonisms problematize easy assumptions about "women" as a preconstituted community amenable to feminist collective empowerment?

Whereas chapter 3 discussed the risks that the MS program's GONGO status and women's empowerment goal raised for its functionaries in their everyday dealings with state actors, this chapter analyzes a different set of dangers facing the program. Specifically, I delve into the fractious dynamics among MS women: those among MS participants, between participants and nonparticipants, and between participants and program functionaries. I narrate a story about an issue that Nimani's MS sangha took up, focusing on the conflicts it caused among women and on the tension-ridden process of resolution. The unease and antagonisms, I argue, result from strategies of collective mobilization that are based in naturalized presumptions about women's identities and interests: that is, the implicit belief is that women enter development programs as already formed subjects and that they will naturally cohere in groups because they share common gender identities, interests, and forms of oppression. Women's collectives are, therefore, viewed as relatively easy aggregations of essentially similar individuals. This strategy of empowerment, which privileges *similarity* over *difference*, ironically results in an assertion of differences and power hierarchies between women, in competing claims (based on women's multiple and contradictory social positionings), and in the performance of "dangerous" gendered acts that may subvert an emancipation- and equality-driven, feminist vision of empowerment. My point here is not to dismiss collectivization as a political strategy, but to unravel its contextual complications on the ground.

I elaborate on these themes by discussing a series of events set in motion by a decision taken by some MS collective members in Nimani to construct a women's center in their hamlet. Such a center existed in a neighboring village and was much lauded and coveted by MS women in the area. Nimani's MS clients regarded a women's center as an important symbol of women's empowerment and a concrete accomplishment of the MS program: it would give them visibility and provide them with a specially marked space to meet and carry out program activities. But their village chief did not consider erecting a women's center as part of his mandate. Instead he offered to approve a government-sanctioned *panchayat bhavan*, or a village council house, for Nimani's Dalit hamlet. Some MS participants agreed to this proposition, believing that a council house could be put to multiple uses—as a space for village council meetings, MS-related work, and other rituals and festivals. What seemed like a good idea to certain MS participants, however, turned out to be very difficult to implement in practice. It caused much debate and even a physical altercation in the hamlet—an unusual happening—that led to great anger and reflection among Nimani's female residents. In fact, the panchayat bhavan never got built. In my ethnographic retelling of the panchayat bhavan story, I lay out the struggles and arguments surrounding this outwardly beneficial and benevolent issue and examine the fraught relationships between development, community, subjectivity/agency, and collective political action.

I aim to illustrate how development reshapes women's subjectivities and communities, and the ways in which this troubles naturalized notions of women's identities and complicates the MS program's strategy of collective empowerment. Development, as I argued in chapter 4, does not work on backstage social realities and already formed social actors but constitutes them onstage. In this chapter I take that thread forward. I do not assume that holistic communities preexist development or that development programs act on a tabula rasa.[5] I also do not assume, as both those for and those against development do, that communities are "ideal" actors of one sort or another. The current orthodoxy in the mainstream development industry, following the influential work of Robert Putnam (1993), celebrates communities as depoliticized engines for local self-development. The social networks and civic organizations in communities and their ties of mutual trust are viewed as "social capital"—a resource that can be utilized in the service of development and good governance (see Harriss 2002). Antidevelopment critics, meanwhile, view communities as founts of alternatives to development: these "new commons" (Esteva 1992, 20) or marginal/local/minority cultures (Escobar 1995, 225) are represented as the pristine "other" of development and as the "ideal outside" space, to borrow Stuart Corbridge's (2007, 181) phrase, for antidevelopment resistance. In contrast to these perspectives, I suggest that communities are neither given nor cohesive, but are constantly remade through modern governmental practices, such as development, census, and voting, which provoke multiple, shifting, and antagonistic identifications. In this chapter I analyze how development interventions shape contentious communities and shed light on the workings and frustrations of collective-based empowerment program such as MS.

Not a Women's Center, but a Village Council House for Nimani

The day after my first meeting with the residents of Nimani, I met with Gyan Ram, the village chief. Gulabi, Nimani's MS sakhi, and Champa, a resident who had previously worked with MS as a preschoolteacher, accompanied me to his house. After introducing myself and my research project, I asked Gyan Ram about his impressions of the MS program. He replied that he had not "seen much 'success'. The program has definitely brought women out of their homes, but the village as a whole . . . has not gotten anything from MS. There is no income generation happening and no MS center has been built for women." He was aware of such centers operating in some other MS villages in the area. Champa disagreed vociferously: "If the village has not gotten anything, it is the fault of Nimani's MS leaders who did not ask the chief for space for a women's center. In other villages women have been able to construct such centers, where lots of work goes on. The women in Nimani haven't pressured the village chief." Gulabi did not react publicly to Champa's thinly veiled allegations against her and the chief, but refuted them later, as we walked back to her home. She told me that some years ago the question of building a women's center in Nimani had arisen and MS sangha members, with the help of program functionaries, had requested the support of the former village chief. In the meantime, however, a new chief was elected, and the women's proposal was shelved.

When Gulabi and I returned to her hamlet, a few women gathered around us. She recounted our conversation with the village chief. The women stridently countered his charge that their village had not received anything from MS. "What has the pradhan given us?" exclaimed Dayawati, the other MS sakhi. "MS has given us knowledge, awareness, and information, and shown us the way; it has taught us about cleanliness, given us a small monthly grant, taught us how to sign our names, and helped us in our struggle to raise agricultural wages!" MS was obviously important for some Nimani women who felt empowered by its presence and readily challenged outsiders' dismissive perceptions about the program's success and contributions.

The following Wednesday, I decided to attend the weekly scheduled meeting of the MS collective in Nimani. By the time I reached the Dalit hamlet, some women were already seated on a dhurrie under a big neem tree. Gulabi grumbled about the absence of a few members. "They know that today is the day for our meeting. Why should I run from house to house [collecting women]? . . . No improvement has happened [because of MS] in this village!" She then opened the meeting with a discussion about the cost of ration cards. Some women felt that it was too late to do anything about the premiums that most people had paid; the local power mongers would not return the money. Others wanted to get to the bottom of why they had been charged different premiums. "Let's go and ask [the pradhan]. . . . He is so corrupt! We will demand and get our money back," fumed Meera. She brought up the case of an adjacent village whose *female* chief, she emphasized, had assisted Dalit residents in getting subsidized housing and had even built a women's center. Phulesra intervened. "[This ration card discrepancy] is our own people's fault," she alleged, implying that had Nimani's residents been united in their quest for ration cards, they would not have paid varying premiums. But she agreed with Meera that their chief had not "done anything for the Dalit community," even though he was a Dalit himself. Kevla chimed in, "Let us send a message to the pradhan's wife that we are coming to see him on Monday, and she should keep him at home." She then turned to me and asked me to accompany them. I agreed to go along. "We will do the talking and you take written notes [of the exchange]," instructed Kevla, adding that "If we get beaten up, you will just get beaten up along with us. So what!" That said, the meeting ended.

I arrived in Nimani on Monday morning, expecting to meet the pradhan. However, Dayawati informed me that they met with the chief on Sunday. All but three MS collective members had been present, Dayawati recounted, and Kevla had opened the meeting. "You are our brother," Kevla began, addressing the pradhan, "and you can do something for MS and for us, if you so wish." To underscore their urgency, she added, "You are going to be our pradhan only for one more year." The women raised the ration card issue, but the chief told them that the premiums they paid were justified because they covered the cost of the "running around" [*daud-dhoop*] that the vice-chief had to do to get the cards approved. He did not, however, have any explanation for why some people had to pay more than others.

The discussion then shifted to constructing a women's center in Nimani's Dalit hamlet. The pradhan, although seemingly supportive, claimed that he could not allocate resources for building a women's center. However, he did have the authority to sanction a village council house, which would be built with government funds, not MS money. A panchayat bhavan would be used by everyone and required the consent of all residents and a formal request from the elected village council members of the Dalit hamlet. Two women council members (who were also MS participants) were present at the meeting and seconded the chief's proposal to build a panchayat bhavan, with the understanding that it would double as a women's center. I was confused about this proposal because Nimani already had a panchayat bhavan. "Isn't there supposed to be only one panchayat bhavan per village," I quizzed Dayawati. She clarified that the current council house was a "bhavan for the

Thakurs [upper castes]," who did not allow the Dalits to use it; therefore, a second council house was justified.

The women had identified a piece of land for their bhavan: it bordered Kevla's house and was currently being used by women to dry dung cakes (which are used as cooking fuel). Dayawati informed me that the chief had promised to stop by their hamlet later that day to measure land for the council house. "Let's see if he shows up. [He] is afraid to come to this hamlet because some people say nasty things to him," she added. As Dayawati and I were conversing, Kevla joined us. She told me that the pradhan had agreed to put the Nimani panchayat bhavan proposal in front of land records officer [*lekhpal*] and other local state functionaries at their next monthly meeting; some MS collective members planned on attending this meeting. Kevla also expressed irritation because three members of their collective—Sunehri and her two daughters-in-law, Beena and Chameli—had not joined them at the pradhan's residence. She glanced over to where Beena was sitting, washing dishes, and said pointedly and loudly, "They don't want the panchayat bhavan built." "Just because I didn't go to the meeting doesn't mean that I don't want it!" retorted Beena. Kevla turned to me, lowered her voice, and explained that even though Beena was outwardly pretending to be on board with the request, in reality her family opposed it. "[Yesterday] we asked Chameli to give us a copy of the written application for a women's center that we had submitted to our ex–village chief [some years ago], but she refused to give it to us."

Chameli, who belonged to the alleged "anti–council house" family, was one of the few literate members of the MS collective and had previously worked as a local MS preschoolteacher. She was seeking a job at another MS-funded residential school for girls when I met her. I noticed that her status as a "government" program functionary drawing cash wages caused some envy and resentment among the other female residents who worked as agricultural workers or sharecroppers and received in-kind payments for their labor.[6] Some women had complained to me that Chameli was disrespectful and considered herself better than the rest because of her formal education and cash wages. Kevla now alleged that Chameli did not want to share the old application for a women's center. During a block-level MS meeting that she attended along with Chameli, Kevla raised the panchayat bhavan-cum-women's center issue with Tulsi, the local MS functionary, who had promptly informed her that she had helped Chameli draft an application a few years ago. Moreover, Tulsi had instructed Chameli to hand over the application to MS collective members, so that they could revive their stalled request. Chameli had acquiesced in front of Tulsi, but later refused to help, reproaching Kevla for embarrassing her in front of Tulsi. Kevla saw Chameli's reticence as a serious obstacle in their collective bid for a council house and as proof that Chameli's family was against this project.

The following morning Kevla and Dayawati informed me that the chief had visited their hamlet the previous night. All MS women and some men had met him. The chief had asked Chameli's husband, Bhagwan Das, to measure land for the panchayat bhavan, but he had flatly refused. If that were not enough, Bhagwan's father had publicly taunted the MS women for vying for a council house: "When those with moustaches [men] have not been able to do anything about this issue, what can these [women] do!" He had derogatorily equated women with cows [*poonchwaali*] and openly challenged their ability to take the council house matter forward.[7] Kevla and Dayawati were upset with his remarks and accused him of illegally annexing a part of the village commons for personal agricultural activity. Even though his wife, Sunehri, and daughters-in-law, Beena and Chameli, were members of the MS collective, they sided with their family and opposed the MS collective's bid for land. Dayawati stated that two other families were eyeing the piece of land proposed for the council house as well, even though this land was part of the village commons and slated for use as a playground. Some men from Nimani had met with the village chief later and had warned him against approving land for the council house. Land ownership, thus, posed a serious obstacle to the unanimity that was required for the sanctioning of a council house and impacted the relations between MS collective members; it affected which issues the women could take up as a group and how, rendering the dynamics and outcomes of their struggles unpredictable.

A few days later I attended a block-level MS meeting in which Kevla discussed the panchayat bhavan land issue with Tulsi and Sita. Sita commented that "This seems like a fight among residents over who gets control over which piece of land. . . . You need to sort it out among yourselves. And if the piece of land in question is supposed to be for a children's playground [*khaliyan*], then MS does not want to get involved in it—that land should be left undisturbed." Sita opined that Chameli's family opposed the building of the panchayat bhavan because they had, in all likelihood, gotten that piece of common land titled under their name by bribing the land records officer. She also reminded Kevla, "If a panchayat bhavan already exists in Nimani, then the pradhan cannot authorize another one—he is lying." She related the story of a neighboring village where, after struggling to obtain land for a women's center for four years, MS staff members discovered that the said piece of land had been underhandedly titled under someone else's name and thus MS could not use it. Sita advised Kevla to arrange a meeting between the land records officer, Nimani's chief, and MS participants and staff members so as to resolve the issue.

I did not visit Nimani until four weeks later, during which time the women had been busy harvesting and processing the paddy crop. In Seelampur block paddy processing was not mechanized and women did most of the work: first washing and drying the stalks of paddy, then beating them to separate the grain, and finally dehusking the grain. Mounds of dry paddy, ubiquitous sight in Seelampur during September, had all but disappeared. One could occasionally see clouds of husk rising into the air as women beat bundles of dried paddy against the earth.

Kevla was the first person I ran into upon my return to Nimani. Her hair and skin were covered with the fine sawdustlike material. She had just finished processing a load of paddy and was headed for a bath at the village well. I learned that during my absence, some MS collective members had gone to the local Farmers' Assistance Center to check land records. They found that the land they desired for the panchayat bhavan was not titled under anyone's name and asked the block secretary and land records officer to sanction it for the said purpose. Not only were these officials unhelpful, said Kevla incredulously, they also scolded Nimani's MS participants, reminding them that because they were daughters-in-law of local families, it was inappropriate for them to come to the Center. Visiting the Center was seen as a bold move on the part of these women because women normally did not go there, much less ask for assistance.

When I asked after the well-being of other residents, the usually amicable expression on Kevla's face vanished. "Things are not alright," she whispered. She told me that a fight had taken place in the hamlet while I was away, in which two women had been beaten. At this point Gulabi and Dayawati joined us at the well, and the three of them described what had happened.

The "victims" in this altercation, Meera and Phoola, were MS collective members and related as sisters-in-law (their husbands were brothers). The "perpetrators," Piyari and her daughter-in-law, Nirmala, were nonparticipants in the MS program. The latter had verbally abused and pelted stones at the former, and later along with male family members, had assaulted

Meera. Nirmala, I was told, was a constant source of trouble. Even though she "wears a long *ghunghat* [veil]," which is meant to signify respect toward elders, explained Gulabi, Nirmala often used foul language and acted disrespectfully. "Behind that ghunghat, she is a snake!" Gulabi exclaimed. Kevla elucidated that the main reason for this confrontation was land. Piyari and Nirmala's family blamed Meera and Phoola's family for illegally encroaching upon land they claimed was theirs and for building a house on it. Furthermore, the former were refusing to pay back a loan that they had taken from the latter. This ongoing interfamily dispute had culminated in the recent fight between the women belonging to the two families.

Phoola, one of the victims of the fight, now walked over to where we sat and confirmed Gulabi's and Kevla's version of the incident: "There was 'tension' between the families and we got caught in [it]." The men from Piyari's family who had beaten Meera had since disappeared for fear of police reprisal. Kevla shook her head in sympathy for Meera: "Meera is living alone—she has no 'guardian.'" Meera's husband worked as an auto-rickshaw driver in Mumbai, and Kevla implied that the lack of male presence in Meera's nuclear household made her vulnerable. The other three women agreed.

Phoola informed me that she and Meera had sought the village chief's help in approaching the police. The chief, however, was unavailable, and they had proceeded to the police station on their own. But the policeman on duty refused to record their complaint, stating that this was simply a women's fight and therefore did not merit a First Information Report (FIR). "These policemen do not record complaints on behalf of 'ladies,'" Phoola noted. Instead of filing an FIR, the policeman used a different tactic: he visited Nimani and beat up Piyari and Nirmala, the perpetrators. According to Phoola, the two women deserved what they got.

She and Dayawati further opined that Piyari and Nirmala, who did not participate in the MS program, had an ax to grind with MS collective members. Dayawati told me that she had overheard Nirmala yell, "Let's beat up the women who . . . hold [MS] meetings. These *meetingwaalis* [women who participate in MS meetings] have incited Phoola and Meera to fight with us." Gulabi retorted, "But the meetingwaalis do not preach fighting! We want everybody to live in harmony." These women were especially incensed at the behavior of Heeravati, who was a relative of the perpetrators and also a member of the MS collective. As a meetingwaali, Heeravati could have played a positive role in mitigating the tensions between her female relatives and other MS participants. But instead of acting as a mediator or disputing

Nirmala's ill-conceived notions about MS women, Heeravati had incited the interfamily conflict.

Gulabi lamented that Heeravati's actions were "tarnishing the reputation of . . . meetingwaalis." She raised her index finger and addressed us in a very serious tone. "Make a note of one thing—do not trust anyone in today's environment." Phoola, Kevla, and Dayawati nodded. Dayawati philosophized that disunity and mistrust were destroying the community. "We have lost our *maryada* [respect]. If there is a fire in our village, we will be the ones who will ultimately suffer. The upper castes will not come [to save us]—they will say, 'let these lower castes burn!' " Phoola added, "These men—they are the ones who mislead and instigate women! [Men] push women to the frontline in feuds over land." Gulabi agreed. "Men push women to fight [because] they don't want to dirty their own hands. They think, 'our women are now empowered and brave—let them take on these fights.' "

The conversation continued as Phoola and I rose to go see Meera. We found Meera lying on a cot outside of her hut. She attempted to rise upon seeing us but was unable to do so; she was obviously in pain. She told me that she had been to the local Bengali doctor and had gotten some medication. She needed x-rays and asked me to accompany her to a hospital in Begumpur. She also requested me to go with her to the village chief's house. "I got beaten up because of the chief, the panchayat bhavan, and the MS sangha," Meera claimed, weakly.

I knew that Meera had participated in the panchayat bhavan negotiations with the village chief but did not understand how that was linked to the assault on her. Kevla and the others had just informed me that the cause of the Nimani altercation was an interfamily dispute involving land and loan money. My bafflement must have shown on my face, and it prompted Phoola to explain further. She told me, in a matter-of-fact tone, that the land for the council house was indeed a critical reason for the conflict. Some village women had been using that parcel land, which was a part of the village commons, for drying dung cakes. This, she elaborated, was a known way by which women staked claim on land on behalf of their families. Piyari and Nirmala's family, among others in the hamlet, felt threatened that the proposed panchayat bhavan would result in their losing out on a piece of land that could potentially be theirs. Their ire was directed at MS members; Meera, who was an active participant in MS, became a convenient scapegoat.

Meera told us that she would raise the altercation incident before the MS collective and the village council to seek justice. But she intended to wait for her husband's return before convening a council meeting. I wondered if a man's presence would give Meera's story legitimacy in front of the village council, just as it would in front of the police. After all, women had not participated actively in village councils as members until fairly recently.[8]

Two weeks later, word about the Nimani confrontation reached Tulsi and Siya, the two local MS fieldworkers. They asked me for confirmation, and I retold what I knew. Siya shook her head in disbelief. "We made such a strong sangha in Nimani—what is happening!" They called a meeting with the women in Nimani, and I joined them. Siya began the proceedings by looking pointedly at Heeravati, the MS participant who was implicated for inciting the conflict, and stated, in a shocked voice, "What is going on? This sangha was made with so much effort—you all attended so many training sessions. To what end though? Now you are fighting among yourselves. . . . There were no problems for over eight years, and now when the program is being phased out, all these problems are coming to the fore." Siya was visibly angry and disappointed.

She then dispatched Gulabi to fetch Piyari and Nirmala, the two non-MS perpetrators. Piyari came alone on the condition that everybody would listen to her side of the story "with a cool head." Siya first invited Heeravati to tell us what had happened. But Heeravati refused to speak, so Phoola gave us her version. She was followed by Sitabi, another MS participant, who spoke as an eyewitness. She pointed to a bump on her forehead, claiming that the stones that Heeravati's family had hurled at Meera and Phoola had hit her as well. Heeravati countered Sitabi's proof and began with her account of the incident. But Sitabi kept interrupting and correcting her. The meeting had turned chaotic. Some women whispered among themselves, while others shouted accusations at one another. Tulsi tried to restore order but to no avail.

Siya looked fed up. "If you want us to leave, we will," she addressed the women. "But understand," she continued threateningly, "that you will stop getting the *anudaan* [small grant] from [MS]—nothing for you people." Her use of the government-provided small monthly grant for MS collectives as a stick mechanism succeeded in getting the women's attention. Sitabi asked Tulsi and Siya to dictate a solution; she reasoned that Heeravati, the proposed mediator, would not follow the directives of other MS women in the village but would obey Tulsi and Siya's orders because they were higher-up program representatives. Gulabi glared at Sitabi, stating that all women present at the meeting had equal status and that their advice should carry equal weight. Heeravati, however, did view Siya and Tulsi as powerful people, whose orders had to be followed. She looked at the two MS representatives and said, "Now that you have come, we will certainly go to jail." This comment incensed Siya. "Why do you think that?" she shouted. "We do not have any personal enmity against you! Why do you think we will take a decision that is not in your favor?" Although Siya reiterated her position as an arbitrator, she did not challenge Heeravati's perception of her as an official-like figure with the authority to mete out punishment.

"A fight like this brings dishonor to the whole village," continued Siya in a more conciliatory tone. "Unity among the collective would benefit everyone." Meanwhile Tulsi chided the women for involving the police. "The police are there only for dealing with emergencies like murder," she explained. "Why did you go [to them] for little matters like a village fight?" she questioned Phoola. Phoola nodded and stated, rather apologetically, "If our men had been present . . . they would have explained things to us. But neither Meera's nor my husband lives at home, and so we went to the police station." At this Tulsi retorted, "But why look to men for a solution when we, as women, want to do everything ourselves?" Phoola kept quiet.

Siya took over from Tulsi and asked the women if they had attempted to resolve the conflict within the MS collective. The collective, after all, was supposed to be one of the key forums for sorting out local problems. "Heeravati's family cursed at all [MS members], so why should we bother to get involved?" responded Kevla. Gulabi added "When we try to intervene in a village skirmish, [the adversaries] tell us to go away and mind our own business." Gulabi told us that a week ago, when some MS participants had attempted to address the conflict during a sangha meeting, Heeravati had put her foot down, asserting that "This is not what these MS meetings are for." Siya eyed Heeravati angrily. "Where else will you address village issues if not in MS meetings!"

Siya attempted to get the women to find a resolution to the local quarrel, but her efforts were frustrated as everyone was speaking simultaneously. "No MS grant for your people from now on until you make a decision and solve this issue. Return all the money MS has given you to date," she ordered, once again using the MS monthly grant as her trump card. Piyari, one of the instigators of the fight, muttered, "Yes, put an end to MS." But Phoola overheard her comment: "Why should [Piyari] care about the MS grant—she has no stake in [MS]." But Piyari had a ready justification for her supposed animosity toward MS participants. She pointed her finger directly at them: "They did not let me join the [MS] sangha."

At this point Siya gave up trying to moderate the discussion. Someone suggested that the entire MS collective should beat up the people who instigated the fight. Someone else contended, "When two women fight, their men should [intervene] and put an end to it." There was no unanimous resolution in sight, and Siya had reached the end of her tether. She held her head in both hands and shook it slowly. She turned to me and said bitterly, "Let us leave. [There is] no understanding, no responsibility, and no tolerance among these women; everything is over." She instructed the disputing parties to act responsibly in the future and not fight. The women seemed agreeable. "I will take responsibility for my own actions. Neither I nor my daughter-in-law will instigate any fight with Meera and Phoola," volunteered Piyari. "But," she added defiantly, "if they start a fight, we will return in kind."

Siya and Tulsi then asked Heeravati, as a relative of Piyari's and as an MS participant, to take responsibility for her extended family's behavior. Heeravati responded, sarcastically, "I have given money to the [MS collective], so I will have to take responsibility." She clearly did not want to lose the money she had contributed to the MS savings group. Siya and Tulsi ignored Heeravati's monetary motivation and her thinly veiled criticism of MS staff members' authority that demanded compliance. They appointed Gulabi as the mediator between the two disputing parties and then rose, signaling an end to the meeting. But before they left, Tulsi warned the women—"If this happens again, the program will end."

The confrontation in Nimani effectively dampened MS women's active agitation for a panchayat bhavan for a few months. Their enthusiasm for this project got second wind in March 1999, when they were informed that a World Bank team and some Indian government officials would be visiting their village. They included a panchayat bhavan on their written list of development demands, which they submitted to the chief development officer during this visit (see chapter 4). As of December 2004, however, Nimani's Dalit hamlet did not have a council house.

Fragile Formations

Some women in Nimani took an empowering decision to build a women's center in their village so as to gain visibility for their activities and the program. But their decision was not endorsed by the village chief, who recommended a council house instead, a structure which he had the authority to sanction and resources to construct. He suggested that a council house could be put to a variety of uses, not specific to women or to the MS program; Nimani's MS participants agreed to the change. It is noteworthy that a women's center was passed over for a general use structure, because the former was marked as a women-only space, whereas the latter was viewed as a more inclusive space. This proposal for a supposedly gender-neutral and public council house[9] that would benefit Nimani's Dalit residents as a whole, turned out to be more contentious (and perhaps disempowering) than any of the actors involved had anticipated.

Land emerged as the central focus of dispute, with various families vying for a piece of the village commons on which the council house would have been built. That land was the main point of contention was not surprising, given that it is a critical resource and a symbol of status and power; all influential people in the area, such as upper-caste men, for example, were landowners.

The panchayat bhavan issue caused much argumentation and angst in Nimani and culminated in a fight between some women residents. It is significant that this fight got labeled as a "women's fight" by some residents and by MS representatives, such as Tulsi, and not as a "gendered conflict" overdetermined by class- and kinship-based concerns about private property and the control over resources. Physical altercations among women rarely occurred in the area where I conducted my fieldwork. That this exceptional event took place was a source of anger and regret among Nimani women, and provoked intense reflection on community, kinship, the state, and gender. What does this story about women's struggles for and conflicts over the panchayat bhavan in Nimani tell us about development, empowerment, community, gendered subjects and agency, and collective struggles?

I begin my discussion with the basic premise that identities, communities, and social relationships are not stable grounds on which development programs act; rather, they are formed and informed by development. Identities, quite like communities, are not given, hardened wholes, but fluid and changing ensembles contingently shaped by the intersection of various, sometimes contradictory, relations and discourses of power. Development functions as one among several discourses and axes of identification along which subjectivity and community are articulated; it interweaves with kinship, caste, class, and gender relations to reposition people and remake collectives.

The MS program enters a social field already rife with multiple identifications and affiliations and with development-related symbolism, designations, and fissures. MS is by no means a run-of-the-mill development program. It is guided by a unique philosophy and approach to subaltern women's emancipation, which combines feminist, Freirian, leftist, and even Gandhian elements. Furthermore, in contrast to the neoliberal emphasis on *individual* actualization, self-help, and rights, MS maintains a steadfast commitment to women's *collective* empowerment. And yet, these exceptional qualities of the program do not always translate into smooth functioning on the ground or desired ends. This is a result of some problematic assumptions that underlie MS, of the antagonistic meanings and dynamics of empowerment, and of the wider social and political context in which MS works. The panchayat bhavan conflict in Nimani starkly illustrates the dangers that the MS program faces and unleashes as it attempts to engender empowerment. I now examine the implicit ideas about women's subjectivity and agency upon which MS rests, and show how the program reconfigures identities and social relationships by introducing new modes of identification, and how it exacerbates some hierarchies in the act of challenging them.

MS builds upon the GAD feminist framework, which, as I outlined in chapter 1, called for grassroots empowerment and gender equality as key goals of a newly redefined development. The GAD approach was different from the WID approach in that it disaggregated the singular category of "women," recognized their multiple identities and the uneven impact of development on different women, and shifted the focus away from "women" to "gender." Whereas these theoretical interventions were critical, they might have not gone far enough in challenging the universalisms of WID. For instance, the work of Gita Sen and Caren Grown, which is regarded as having initiated GAD thinking, arguably retains a focus on women (not gender), assumes a binary gender framework (i.e., women versus men), and privileges a commonality of oppression among women, despite foregrounding their multiple identities and particular circumstances (see Hirshman 1995). Furthermore, *recognizing* the complexities of gender identities and *institutionalizing* them into development and political projects are distinct matters. The perils of misrecognition, mistranslation, and false universalisms are ever present, making the practice of gender and collective empowerment a risky endeavor.

The MS program is not always able to avoid these pitfalls. First, MS promotes gender equality but focuses on women's empowerment to achieve this goal. When pitching the program to villagers, MS functionaries often described the program as benefiting families and communities as a whole, not just women; however, men were excluded from village-level MS collectives. The idea, albeit keenly debated within MS, was to empower women first and then encourage cross-gender mobilization around social justice.[10] Although this strategy did not necessarily rest on a naturalized "women versus men" distinction or assume an essentialized antagonism between the interests of these two groups, it did heighten tensions across genders. MS participants in Seelampur block often described men's objections to the program. When MS first began, most men in the area regarded it suspiciously as yet another sterilization program for women (who had previously experienced both forced and "incentive-based" sterilizations). Some raised objections to its "women's empowerment" goal, whereas others considered MS activities a waste of women's time, which could be better spent in agricultural and household tasks. Although many men later changed their opinions and either supported or ignored the program, others continued to criticize it. In Nimani, for example, I noticed that men generally avoided MS meetings; a few occasionally listened to women's discussions or chastised them for lingering and whiling away time on useless gossip. Then there were others, like Bhagwan Das's father, who were hostile toward MS women and challenged their ability to succeed in their development efforts. Even though the program did not take a women-versus-men zero-sum approach to empowerment, where one group gained at the expense of the other, its sole focus on women seemed to amplify antagonisms between genders in certain instances.

Second, the MS program universalizes the identities and oppressions of the marginalized women it names as its clients. It targets poor, landless Dalit women (who are, by definition, passive and disempowered) on the belief that subjects possessing these fixed identities already exist out there. However, as mentioned previously, development programs do not simply target individuals and groups but also produce them (see also Mohanty 1991). The MS program too has this generative effect and constitutes "poor Dalit women" as an essentialized category of development and political subjects. It is taken for granted that members belonging to this category share stable and homogenous gender, class, and caste identities and, as such, will cohere around homologous interests. The MS program both assumes a natural affinity of interests among similarly identified groups of women and wants to forge a spirit of collectivism among them; that is, it hopes to turn a "community in itself" into "a community for itself." The Nimani conflict, however, renders problematic any belief in the commonality of identities and interests among members of "naturalized" and "organic" groups. It depicts how the MS program introduces new status distinctions and reconstitutes power equations *between* women—that is, between MS workers and clients, between MS and non-MS village women, and among program participants. I discuss each in turn, highlighting the fraught intersections of class, kinship, gender, and program participation.

I have previously described in chapters 4 and 5 the ways in which the development industry both presumes and creates problematic distinctions between those who "do" development and those who need and receive it. Siya and Tulsi's attempts to resolve the panchayat bhavan dispute demonstrated how authority and hierarchical relationships are established between MS personnel and clients. These functionaries deployed disciplinary means and exerted command over Nimani women. They recognized the importance of material resources for MS women—the Rs 200 monthly grant that the MS collective received from the government—and repeatedly threatened the women with halting funds if they continued to fight. That Siya and Tulsi succeeded in enforcing temporary compliance through such means contests the idea, described to me by some MS representatives, that subaltern women are inherently "altruistic"—that is, they participate in MS regardless of the fact that the program does not distribute tangible goods (see chapter 2). The government grant, despite its miniscule amount, was clearly significant for MS women. By using disciplinary strategies, Siya and Tulsi also reinforced the impression that program representatives were superior to their clients. Although belonging to higher caste and class backgrounds and having more education than their clients, Siya and Tulsi's relative dominance had much to do with their position as development and empowerment facilitators (thus, by definition, developed and empowered). Their designation as development workers and the associated economic and social status gave them the power to regulate subaltern women's behavior. Nevertheless some MS participants talked back to the authority of MS fieldworkers: Heeravati criticized their ability to punish, and Gulabi challenged their authority by claiming that all women were equal and that their opinions mattered equally.

The confrontation in Nimani also illustrated how the program gives rise to differences and tensions between MS and non-MS women. Piyari and Nirmala (the perpetrators), unlike Meera and Phoola (the victims), did not participate in MS. They had allegedly gone after meetingwaalis, because they had been forcibly kept out of the MS collective.[11] Piyari told me later, in private, that MS women did not do much, other than gossip, and that they were selfish. The only reason they had formed a group was the small amount of money they received from the government every month. In reality, this grant was meant for the development of the entire village; yet nonparticipating women widely believed that MS clients considered that money to be their own and did not want to share it with others. Although the Nimani MS collective had congealed well before the monthly grant started, Piyari's perception that women made a group only for securing the grant and for selfish interests was understandable. MS participants had, after all, equated the initiation of their collective with the peer-group lending and savings activity when I first met them.[12] They also thought of the MS small grant as their personal fund and used it to make loans only to members, leading to the impression that MS did not benefit the village as a whole. Furthermore, some non-MS women believed that class status determined MS membership. Those who were poor, and thus considered as incapable of saving money or paying back loans, were left out of the MS group.

MS clients, on the other hand, claimed that they had invited all female residents of the village to attend meetings and participate in the collective when the program began, but some women chose not to join because they either had no time or did not see any tangible advantage in associating with MS. Once the savings and loan component of the program began, however, a few nonparticipants desired to come on board. At this point, however, MS participants decided against letting them join. They in turn accused nonmembers of wanting to participate in MS for self-interested monetary reasons alone.

MS program dynamics thus fostered novel hierarchies between Nimani's female residents. Participating in MS had a certain status associated with it. Clients interacted with MS staff members and other important outsiders. They attended regular block-level meetings and training programs. Meanwhile nonparticipants did not necessarily have access to the symbolic and material capital associated with being the beneficiary of a development program.

The program also reconstituted familial and class differences *among* MS participants, even as it attempted to bring these women together. For example, Chameli and Beena, who were both MS participants and also sisters-in-law, did not get along with each other because of Chameli's paid job as an MS teacher. Beena confided in me that the entire burden of household work for their extended family had fallen on her shoulders because Chameli was busy with MS work and neglected her share of the household chores. After several confrontations between the two women, the elders in the family decided to break up the extended household into nuclear units with separate kitchens, so each woman would be responsible for her own share of cooking and would take turns feeding the parents-in-law. However, their mother-in-law, Sunehri, complained that now she was taking care of Chameli's household because Chameli had an outside job. MS had altered the dynamics between the women in this family; however, it was not readily apparent to me if these changed familial equations had challenged the existing gendered division of labor. Kinship also caused disagreements between MS women when the projects taken up by the collective were seen to go against the interests of members' families, as the Nimani dispute vividly revealed.

The other main source of antagonism in intra-MS collective dynamics was class. For instance, in Nimani, where the sakhi model was followed, MS created distinctions between those women designated as sakhis, or leaders, and other MS members.[13] Sakhis were chosen for their leadership qualities; trained to organize women in their villages; given information on pertinent issues, such as health, village councils, environment, violence, police procedures and laws, and development programs (which they were expected to share with other women in their villages); and paid Rs 200 per month for their program-related work.[14] The sakhi position was linked with prestige, money, and upward class mobility, rendering it a sore point among MS women. Sakhis in Nimani and elsewhere complained that other program participants did not play active roles and relied on them to raise and resolve all local issues. Non-sakhis, however, argued that because sakhis received special training, information, and money, it was indeed their primary responsibility to do MS work. It was not unusual to hear snide remarks about sakhis' "paid jobs" and lack of enthusiasm.[15]

Class figured as a point of contention among MS participants in another way as well. Heeravati, one of the alleged inciters of the Nimani quarrel, claimed to be the poorest member of the MS collective. She told me that she had been denied loans from the MS collective fund because of class-based discrimination and nepotism: she was poor and did not have any other female relatives in the MS collective. She claimed that MS members looked out for their kin's interests and consistently turned down her loan requests.[16]

Heeravati's allegations of discrimination within the MS collective spoke about the more widespread feeling of class inequality and divisiveness among Nimani's inhabitants, which the residents associated with development programs and which, they claimed, were further reflected in MS collective dynamics. Bhagwan Das raised this issue when criticizing the development-related polarizations in his village. He cited the only government-provided hand-operated water pump in the hamlet as an example, pointing out that it was bored in front of the houses of two village council members because they had money and clout. "[The pump] was not located near the homes of the *asahaya* [helpless] and poor families. . . . All decisions here are based on *pakshpaat* [favoritism]. . . . The residents belong to different economic classes [*aarthik shreni*]—some people earn in the thousands every month and others make Rs 200 or less. . . . People with money have gotten things done for themselves. The government works only for those people who have money." The relatively well-off men in the village, he added, had managed to get government jobs, whereas he, with a college degree but no money, remained unemployed.

The material and symbolic differences between Nimani's Dalit families, along with conflicts over land and other development resources, translated into fractures among MS collective participants. Bhagwan observed, "There is too much jealousy in this hamlet—nobody talks about the common good, anymore. Women also participate in this factionalism and take sides [*party-baazi kartee hain*]. Some MS members' houses are on common land—Kevla's and Chinta's houses, for example. They constructed these houses illegally. [My family] fought a case against them but lost." I commented that because both Kevla and Chinta were MS participants, the MS collective seemed to be the right forum in which to settle this dispute. "That will cause a *yudh* [war]!" Bhagwan exclaimed. "Are you implying that relations among MS participants are not good?" I queried. "No, they are not good," Bhagwan replied emphatically. "These women are together only because of the monthly small grant—because they can only receive that money as a collective. But MS participants are not able to make proper use of the Rs 200 they get from the government precisely because of internal jealousies. . . . They keep blaming one another or gossiping about other women. Women themselves are not concerned about women's development issues [*auratein hi auraton ke vikas ke baare mein nahin sochteen*]!"

Bhagwan conjectured that the disunity within the local MS collective mirrored the interfamily factionalism in his hamlet, which, in turn, was determined by class; he thus directly linked class, kinship, and MS program dynamics and used this to explain why MS women could not derive adequate common good from the program. He also alluded that there was no congruence among MS women, simply because they were women, and held them responsible for furthering gender-based discrimination against women. This was clearly a problematic and non-self-reflexive claim that did not consider how the varied social relations that position women as subordinate inform people's perceptions and practices. Bhagwan's allegations typified men's understanding and critique of women's roles in furthering gender inequality.

Such comments rendered invisible men's participation in entrenching and maintaining patriarchal relations; these discourses about gender served not only to explain but also to construct gender inequality.

Bhagwan's observations, however, do raise important questions about gender and women's subjectivity and agency, shedding further light on the Nimani altercation. Women's gendered subjectivities are not simply derived from their sex/gender positioning but are a complex, contextual, and changing amalgam of the various social relations in which they are placed and in which they move. Indeed, gender, kinship, class, and caste, as vectors of identity and power, attriculate and interpenetrate, and overdetermine subjectivities and communities;[17] this is something that the MS program both partially neglects and cannot control. MS focuses on poor low-caste women. Its strategy rests on the belief that these women will come together in collectives qua "women" and will cohere in strong, lasting groups. It singles out the female identities of women belonging to the same caste, and ostensibly class, and assumes an equivalence of interests among these women. In so doing, however, the program seems to neglect two key aspects of identity formation and mobilization. First, women's gendered identities are contingently fashioned in and through their social positionings as mothers, wives, landless laborers, and development subjects, for example. Women, as material beings, do not simply exist, but are made and remade. Their subjectivities are ever-shifting and processual effects of multiple intersections and layerings that take place in particular contexts (Crenshaw 1991; Hall 1989; Mouffe 1992), which can exert antagonistic pressures and lead to competing claims. Second, the sameness of identities is a shaky ground for political mobilization because (a) identities are not stable, but open-ended and fragmented; (b) the identity categories used for mobilization are products of fraught governmental practices, such as development and the census (Appadurai 1993; Chatterjee 2004; Cohn 1987),[18] and what seem like incontrovertible "facts" about hardened and homogenous filiative and affiliative group identities (e.g., caste and gender) are, in fact, quite fuzzy on the ground; and (c) differences play a critical role in shaping individual and group identities, which means that collectivities cannot but be tenuous and a commonality of interests cannot be presumed but must be discovered (hooks 1984; Mohanty 2002). These realities make the collectivization of women, as "women," a fraught process, as was revealed in Nimani.

Nimani's MS clients' subjectivities as "women" and as "participants" in an empowerment program were overdetermined by their class and kinship identities. These patriarchal relations of power defined gender identities, configured relationships among women, and affected the congruence or divergence in women's interests qua women. Their caste identity, for instance, was shot through with class position and led to charges of discrimination by those who defined themselves as poor against those who were better off. The MS program's naming of certain women as "paid leaders" and the higher class status this symbolized created further tensions. Meanwhile women's class and gender positionings were also shaped by kinship relations. Women's support, or lack thereof, for the council house proposal was defined by their respective families' stance on the issue and desire for private ownership of land.

The panchayat bhavan issue thus illustrated how class-, kinship-, and program-related "gender" (women's?) claims competed with each other and how "common" good clashed with "private," familial interest. MS collective members' identities as women undergoing empowerment *and* united in their fight for gender equality came into conflict with their identities as members of resourceful or resourceless families. These tensions could have been productively explored by Tulsi and Sita, the two local program functionaries. In fact, they rightly named the panchayat bhavan squabble as a family issue; curiously, however, they chose not to further examine the gendered structures of kinship. Perhaps their avoidance of "the family" reflected the challenges that this institution has always posed for feminists. The family, as Sunder Rajan (2003, 99–100) argues, has been one of the most vexed arenas for feminist activism. Even though feminists have powerfully criticized the purportedly natural, nonpolitical, and private nature of the family, in practice, the family ideology has been among the hardest to subvert given its multiple sources of support and power (such as, religion, the law, and capitalism). MS functionaries regularly confront these complications. Familial issues are a key part of their empowerment work. They are, however, forced to tread the family ground with care, given the widespread perception that women's empowerment is an antifamily strategy. Program representatives cannot directly indict and alienate "the family" because of its ideological import; they can and do, however, critique the inequalities and hierarchies in particular families and encourage women to tackle these issues without overtly challenging the idea that the family is essentially a caring, supportive, and natural institution.

Tulsi and Siya viewed the Nimani conflict as a long-standing family dispute over land and specifically asserted that the MS program did not want to get involved in it. In so doing they entrenched the privatized nature of family conflicts and also did not engage with the question of land ownership as a critical node around which social, especially gender, hierarchies were arranged. Didn't the fight in Nimani raise important questions about how gender interwove with class hierarchies, property ownership, the family ideology, and violence, which are central to the program's concern for gender equality and justice, but which Tulsi and Sita neglected to take up? And wasn't MS already implicated in this conflict? I had observed these two program representatives raise family issues (such as the treatment of widows and household violence against women) on other occasions and use them to discuss how familial ties place women in subordinate positions and how state institutions support these hierarchies. In the Nimani case, however, they did not provide a space for reflecting on the links between unequal familial relations, gendered forms of violence, male ownership of land, and state agencies.

Bhagwan Das's comment that women themselves reinscribe prevailing gender norms and hierarchies also raises the related issue of feminist consciousness and women's agency. At first glance, the women in Nimani seemed to subscribe to the dominant ideology that positioned men as "protectors" and women as "weak." They suggested, for instance, that Meera was beaten because she had no male guardian at home and was vulnerable. Moreover, Meera decided not to bring up the dispute with the village council until her husband returned. Such examples could be read as entrenching patriarchal ideas about women's public expressiveness and dependence. I would, however, contend that women's perceptions and decisions were guided by experiential consciousness and pragmatic concerns. Women in Nimani were aware that council members and police functionaries did not pay much attention to women's concerns; hence, they felt that their issues would be awarded more legitimacy if men made the case on their behalf. However, there was little discussion about how this pragmatic strategy might reinforce gender subordination and norms.

Perhaps the most obvious example of women's participation in reinscribing gender subordination and of the complexities of feminist consciousness and agency was their complicity in violence against women. One could contend, for example, that it is not in women's strategic gendered interest (Molyneux 1985) to physically assault other women and that all women should be aligned against such violence. Nimani women, however, were not just instruments of but also active participants in gendered and class violence. Nirmala and Piyari threw stones at Meera and Phoola and, along with Heeravati, urged the men in their families to physically harm Meera. Meera and Phoola got their retribution when a policeman beat up Nirmala, Piyari, and Heeravati; "justice" had apparently been served by this official act. Meanwhile the men who had actually beaten Meera escaped punishment and were nowhere to be found.

Violence against women has been a key issue for feminist movements around the globe; it is considered a common ground that has united southern and northern groups under the "women's rights are human rights" banner (Bunch 1990; Keck and Sikkink 1998). Mobilizing against gendered violence is also considered an important marker of feminist consciousness. How then does one view the Nimani incident, where women participated in violence against other women, through a feminist framing? I argue that this dispute complicates straightforward notions of "proper" women's consciousness as essentially nonviolent and egalitarian. It forces us to reexamine truisms about feminist agency and to analyze the sometimes paradoxical effects of women's struggles. What implicit definition of feminism does one deploy when dismissing some women's acts as antiwomen or even antifeminist? How does one approach the thorny issue of women's apparent complicity in violence, not only critically examining its retrogressive effects vis-à-vis gendered equality but also paying attention to how this complicity might be the ambiguous result of the complex and open-ended articulation of the multiple aspects of women's positionalities? How do patriarchal social relations and class inequalities in which women are situated and become subjects influence their actions and feminist consciousness?

Take Bhagwan's allegations against women, for example. Although he highlighted women's role in furthering gender inequality, he did not bring up the roles that men and gender and kinship relations play in reinforcing patriarchy; some women in Nimani, however, did. Phoola held men responsible for what became labeled as women's fights and accused them of using women as fronts in land feuds. Kevla and Gulabi agreed with Phoola's observation, even though they also reasoned that Meera was assaulted because she had no male guardian to protect her. Whereas they subscribed to patriarchal discourses that position men as powerful and women as subordinate, they also understood how women unwittingly become involved in fights that are essentially between men over resources. MS participants complained that ever since the program began in the village, their men took less and less responsibility for community problems and development issues. "Men think that we have become [strong] like lions [because of MS] and we will be able to do anything," remarked a frustrated Gulabi. But when women's empowerment-based MS activities were inconvenient or raised uncomfortable questions about who controlled what resources, as occurred in the Nimani conflict, some men, like Bhagwan Das's father, slandered women and challenged their abilities to do anything beneficial for the village.

Even though they conveniently used women's empowerment to justify stepping back from communal roles when needed, men did not necessarily allow this empowerment to encroach upon their dominance in household decision making. Gulabi told me that her daughter-in-law wanted to attend college; although she supported her daughter-in-law's desire, she was unable to counter the objections of her son. He had failed to graduate from high school and did not want his wife to be more educated than him. "Can't you talk to him?" I asked Gulabi. "I can, but I am afraid," replied Gulabi, "I have no say at home." Even though Gulabi took a leadership role in MS activities and was a designated sakhi, she was not able to influence decision making at home. This example once again demonstrates the particular dilemmas that the family, as a site for the reproduction of inequalities, presents for feminist empowerment work (as I mentioned earlier). It also shows that empowerment in one context does not easily translate into another—that a change in women's self-image and public image through consciousness-raising activities may not influence their power and status across various social contexts. MS women often spoke about gender equality and yet were not always able to implement these ideas in their own households.

Nimani's MS participants also understood that violence against women was a complicated matter in which state institutions and class and caste inequalities were implicated. For example, they criticized the police for not taking women's issues seriously. They also spoke about how their class and caste location impinged upon their public presence and mobility. As landless Dalit women they could not afford the luxury of staying at home because their very survival depended on working on farms owned by upper-caste men. However, their mobility and access to public places, such as the Farmers' Assistance Center, were restricted by prevalent gender norms and threats of male violence. They used me as a point of comparison, explaining why they would never enjoy the kind of mobility I had, given my visibly embodied caste and class identity. "Men will probably not trouble you much if you walk down the road here," Phoola pointed out matter-of-factly. "They would not mistreat an upper-caste woman." Certain women's bodies, in other words, were accessible to certain men only, and this was determined along class and caste lines. Landless Dalit women were the most vulnerable to violence by men from varied class and caste backgrounds because of these women's multiply marginal social location.

Nimani women clearly understood that caste-and class-shaped gendered violence and implicated men and state officials in configuring relations among women. Despite this knowledge, however, they sometimes seemingly colluded in furthering violence against women and thereby participated in reinforcing social hierarchies. Rather than characterizing their actions and consciousnesses as necessarily antiwomen or as "nascently" feminist, I want to reconsider what counts as women's agency and feminist consciousness.

Agency, I argue, must be examined in the specific contexts in which women are positioned as gendered beings and in which they act—contexts that are overdetermined by a host of discourses and relations of power. Women's social agency, Chantal Mouffe writes, needs to be seen as the "articulation of an ensemble of subject positions, corresponding to the multiplicity of social relations" in which women are situated (1992, 376). Women are constructed as subjects through varied and often competing discourses that are in "contingent and precarious forms of articulation" (Mouffe 1992, 376). These contradictory subject positionings translate into ambiguous actions on the part of women in different situations—actions that sometimes deepen gender inequalities even as women attempt to comprehend and contest these hierarchies. The panchayat bhavan struggle and the accompanying conflict in Nimani generated critical reflection among MS participants on gender relations within the community that positioned women as pawns in men's relations with other men and turned women against each other. This issue also resulted in highlighting gender-based discrimination by state agents, including policemen and local functionaries such as the land records officer and the block secretary. However, the extent to which this conflict enabled women to openly challenge the various institutional mechanisms and social relations that defined them as subordinate beings and to directly engage their own implicatedness in gendered violence and inequalities, remained less clear.

Final Thoughts

In this chapter I described the struggles and confrontations that took place in the Dalit hamlet of Nimani over the building of a village council house, or panchayat bhavan. The process for building this bhavan was initiated by some MS participants but opposed by other participants and nonparticipants. My purpose was to analyze the knotty and mutually constitutive relationship between subjectivity, community, and development and thus to inquire into the strategy of feminist collectivization, a hallmark of the MS program's approach.

The "community," in both pro- and antidevelopment scholarship, is seen as a romanticized and unified whole and as a critical actor that either services development or confronts it. The mainstream development literature on social capital views social networks among people and communities as the perfect antidote to poverty; the practitioners of this ideology focus on identifying already existing networks and communities, building their survival capacities, and using them as vehicles for development. Meanwhile, the critical development literature celebrates marginal, autonomous communities as utopian places where alternatives to development are imagined and lived. Although these two standpoints differ in how they view communities—either as non-political, civil-society networks that facilitate development or as deeply political actors struggling against development and surviving despite it—they also share the basic premise that communities precede development and that they are essentially homogenous actors, united in their goals and interests. These assumptions also find their way into the work of some GAD feminists, which positions women as a given development group. This is a community made up of individuals possessing a similar gender identity and sharing the universal, strategic goal of gender equality and justice.

These various perspectives on community not only privilege similarity over difference, where communal identities are concerned, but also overlook how development configures contentious communities. Groups that critically engage with and/or demand development are not natural, autonomous, and homogenous entities that confront development; they are themselves forged by modern governmental regimes. Development, in fact, operates as a staging ground upon which solidified administrative definitions of *enumerated* communities, often premised on so-called natural filiation (such as caste, kinship, and religion), tangle with the more slippery, fluid, and fuzzy material and ideological workings of communal membership (Chatterjee 1993, 223; Chatterjee 2004).

Furthermore, defining communities as preexisting and internally coherent groups of identical actors glosses over the hierarchies and fissures that exist within them. How are the margins within these collectives drawn and redrawn? How is membership delimited and what conflicts of interests emerge between differently positioned members? Where does individual interest clash with the "greater common (or communal) good" and how are these defined anyway? Indeed, to what extent can "the community" ideal be relied upon for democratic, egalitarian, and representative political action, as is so often assumed? These are the thorny questions that face many grass-roots and feminist struggles today and they reinvoke longstanding debates about identities and collective activism.

My ethnography of the makeup of Nimani's Dalit hamlet reveals the sedimented and ever-changing hierarchies of gender, class, and kinship that structure this caste-segregated residential community; these hierarchies are also reflected in the composition and dynamics of the local MS collective. My work also demonstrates the ways in which development works into and reconfigures identifications and affiliations. This is a process simmering with tension and leads to perilous and unpredictable, not predetermined, outcomes. Although the women's center/council house project in Nimani failed to materialize, it resulted in bringing to the fore the complexities of subject and community formation and agency.

Women's gendered identities, as I illustrated earlier, are a contradictory amalgam of different social relations, such as caste, class, and kinship; these relations are not compartmentalized wholes but shaped in conjunction with each other. Women's subjectivities are contingent upon the specific ways in which these power relations articulate in particular contexts; these subjectivities not fixed but open-ended. Because women's actions are performative (Butler 1999) and do not stem from fully formed, centered, and stable "cores," their consequences are anything but given and sometimes paradoxical. The conflict in Nimani troubles simplistic understandings about women's unequivocally "positive" gender agency, in the sense that they will always and only look after their common interests as women and militate against gender subordination. Women do not necessarily agree upon common interests, thus privileging their gender identities over other affiliation; they are also not *essentially* nonviolent. Women's acts can occasionally further patriarchal ideologies and practices.[19]

And yet, as I argued, women's agency needs to be examined in the context of their ambiguous subject positionings by various discourses of power. As Urvashi Butalia contends, "our understanding of agency . . . needs to take into account notions of the moral order which is sought to be preserved when women act, as well as the mediation of the family, community, class and religion" (Butalia 1993, WS-24); state agencies and governmental practices, I would add, are also key mediating factors. Thus women's shifting positionings in different institutional and discursive settings and the competing claims these generate are at stake when considering the question of women's agency.

The Nimani dispute, as I have shown, problematizes the notion of an essentialized and unified community of women. The MS program, however, both assumes and attempts to create precisely such a homogenized and organic community among Dalit women. MS desires to empower these women through collectivizing them but risks ignoring their already fragmented and changing identities and interests. The program's strategy of collective mobilization assumes that women will come together as individuals, realize the social nature of their oppression through consciousness-raising activities, and then take collective action against gender oppression.

Feminist and other tactics of collectivism, as Wendy Brown (1995, 194) writes, are based on a "conviction about the inevitably radicalizing effects of collectivizing subjects previously isolated and dispersed in their oppression." She further suggests that "[t]his conviction . . . presumes a transcendental subject, a subject who simply *moves* from isolated to collectivized conditions, as opposed to a subject who is *produced* or engendered by these respective conditions" (194). This is a trap that MS is not always able to avoid. The program sometimes ignores how different collective identifications are already implicated in women's individual identities when they join MS or how affiliation with MS rearticulates existing identities, while instituting new ones. The Nimani case illustrates that participation in MS, and in other development programs, transforms class, kinship, and gender relations, reconfigures status equations, and alters relations between women; not all these shifts necessarily challenge social inequalities and gender subordination, which is the purpose behind the MS program's empowerment vision.

The Nimani case reveals the difficulties of collectivization. Programs that seek to instate group-based processes or mobilize specific communities of people presume the existence of transcendental individuals who have a set of "natural" identities and are able to easily prioritize certain identities or allegiances over others; this, however, is not tenable in practice. In the case of MS sanghas, I have suggested that women's varying positionings shape how they come together in the context of the MS program and which issues they take up as a collective. This results in a messy and contradictory process of collective conscientization on the ground. It tells us that the dynamic of group empowerment and mobilization in MS specifically, and other forms of feminist politics, cannot but be a fraught processes, and collectivities cannot but be fragile and transient. The ephemerality of subjectivity is reflected in the ephemerality of collectivities. This is what MS staff members face and attempt to negotiate as they seek to engender and support women's activism that has emancipatory, justice- and equality-based goals.

That the MS program's project of collectivization is sometimes frustrated in practice should not be seen as evidence of either the program's failure or as an indictment against collective conscientization per se. Rather, I believe that the program's unequivocal support of collective mobilization in our era of high individualism is absolutely crucial and potentially subversive of dominant ideas. The broader context in which MS works is traversed by statist and media discourses that venerate individual entrepreneurialism and rights, self-interest, and personal uplift. The self that such hegemonic neoliberal discourses and practices target and seek to improve is an autonomous individual, and not a collectively inscribed and embedded "social" subject. And here is a program, MS, which recognizes social subjectivity and the power of collectivism and stands against neoliberal individualism; however, it is unable to cordon off these hegemonic discourses. The terrain upon which MS operates (and also constitutes) is full of contradictions. The program, for instance, has to contend with the juridical apparatus of the state on the one hand, which primarily confers rights on individuals, and with group mobilizations, on the other, which open up new possibilities for conceptualizing collective rights that the state may not recognize or guarantee. Whether and how these contradictions can be reconciled in practice is tricky. However, I see MS's commitment to the strategy of collective consciousness raising and promotion of collective rights, given the context in which it works, as an important challenge to the unmitigated neoliberal support for individual entrepreneurial advancement.

While my analysis of subjectivity, agency, community, and collectivization is grounded in the specific workings of the MS program, my conclusions also have broader implications for feminist projects and struggles. Recognizing the shifting, contradictory, ensemble-like, and non-essentialist nature of women's subjectivities and complicating the idea of a community does not foreclose the possibility of emancipatory political action undertaken collectively by women (hooks 1984; Mouffe 1992). What it does foreclose is the option of assuming, *a priori*, that women's identities are identical and given, that their interests are shared, that they will easily band together in unified collectivities, or that their collective actions will have anticipated results. It also troubles any singular and hegemonic definitions of the ideal feminist subject and project. If various institutions, practices, and discourses participate in constructing gendered subjects and women's subordination in different ways, then feminist struggles have to be differentiated and fought on multiple fronts, as "wars of position" (Gramsci 1971; Hall 1997) even though they can be tentatively linked under the banner of gender egalitarianism and social justice. Such feminist projects can only be based in precarious commonalities and solidarities forged in and through political struggle, and in unities that are constructed, not presumed (hooks 1984; Mouffe 1992; Mohanty 2002). It means that collective feminist politics must be a politics of ephemerality, where solidarity functions as a vanishing and reappearing horizon but which, nonetheless, remains a vital mobilizing factor and vision that indeed makes political struggle possible.

Conclusion

Terra Incognita, or a Politics without Guarantees

Even as I write this conclusion, much is happening in the field of popular politics in India. 2007 and 2008 have witnessed tense protests and often bloody confrontations between government representatives, the police, corporate agents, and marginalized actors over the juggernaut of state-abetted, procapitalist neoliberal development. In the eastern Indian state of West Bengal, for example, government acquisition of agricultural land for industrial development has caused much angst and struggle. Land that comes under "Special Economic Zones" is being taken away from agriculturalists and awarded to industry on highly lucrative terms for the latter. Farmers and peasants who depend on this land for their livelihood are facing serious issues of compensation, resettlement, and survival. Meanwhile, in Maharashtra and Andhra Pradesh, in western and southern India respectively, farmer suicides continue unabatedly. The victims are peasants who can no longer depend on traditional crops for their livelihood, who have switched to cash crops but cannot afford the recurrent costs of seeds, pesticides, and irrigation, or who are faced with crop failure. Crushed under the weight of mounting debt attributable to inimical agricultural developments, theirs is a deadly form of protest. Finally, Bihar, Jharkhand, and Madhya Pradesh, in eastern and central India, recently saw demonstrations by street hawkers and small vegetable vendors against corporate giants such as Reliance Industries, which are opening large fresh-food chain stores all over India and are threatening the livelihoods of the former. These battles yet again upend conventional understandings of supposedly antagonistic ideological perspectives as left parties, such as the Communist Party of India (Marxist), a leading member of the ruling Left Front government in West Bengal, take on the mantle of proindustrial capitalist development with a zeal heretofore unseen, whereas a Hindu right-wing party, the Shiv Sena, sides with farmers in Maharashtra against forcible land acquisition by the government on behalf of corporations. Regardless of what motivates such moves—opportunism or political expediency or something else—what such muddiness and ideological incongruities make clear is that development remains a crucial rallying point for politics and struggles in India.

Development, as I argued in this book, is neither an obsolete nor simply a regulative discourse, but a fertile, contentious, and unpredictable site on which both conforming and unruly subjects, communities, and struggles take form. Although the actors so shaped may not be antidevelopment per se, many do challenge hegemonic technocratic and economistic definitions of the term by inserting critical questions about justice, redistribution, equality, and ethics. The modern regime of development is thus an important stage on which a remoralized politics of citizenship is enacted and where rights and entitlements are negotiated.

The protests I just mentioned and the everyday resistances I recounted throughout this book constitute the struggles of marginalized subjects in India—landless Dalit women, farmers, peasants, and informal sector workers—against being made invisible by the forces of neoliberal globalization and over the meaning of just and equitable development. These actors constitute India's large and vibrant political society, which Partha Chatterjee (2004, 74) describes as a "site of negotiation and contestation opened up by the activities of governmental agencies aimed at population groups." Political society politics, he argues, is generated by the very same technologies of governmentality that attempt to depoliticize and discipline populations in the name of administration and efficiency.

This book has grown out of Chatterjee's ideas about popular politics and its connectedness with governmental regimes, and has engaged similar concerns. I presented a slice of state- and development-driven politics in India and narrated stories about what takes place when marginalized women's empowerment is mobilized as a governance mechanism by the state in partnership with women's groups and NGOs. Unlike much scholarly and even journalistic writings about subaltern subjects and popular politics in contemporary India, my book focused specifically on women as central actors on the political society stage. In so doing, I heeded the call made by several postcolonial feminists, especially Chandra Mohanty, to think critically and carefully about the relationship between subaltern women's oppression and agency, and to link the micropolitics of their everyday lives and struggles with broader translocal political-economic processes.

I refrained from calling subaltern women's activism a "politics of the governed," and this marks a point of distinction between Chatterjee's work and mine. In using the phrase, "the politics of the governed," Chatterjee (2004) distinguishes between those who govern and those who are governed and examines the survival and justice-oriented battles that the latter engage in. My work, by contrast, shows that an absolute binary between these two sets of actors is not tenable in practice. Indeed, the logic and dynamics of neoliberal governmentality rest on the impossibility of such a clear divide. Neoliberalism, like any hegemonic cultural project, works by annexing social subjects of all kinds—individuals, groups, NGOs—to the endeavor of rule, which entails inculcating habits of self-governance; such entities, although less advantaged than the state and subordinated to it, are critical nodes in the network of neoliberal governance. I would, therefore, venture to call subaltern women's activism a "politics engendered by governance."

In this book I revealed the on-the-ground messiness of who constitutes the government or mai-baap or sarkar and who does not, of what the state is and what it is not, through ethnographic vignettes culled from the MS program. The shifting, discursive, and public cultural nature of state and government boundaries, which we tend to take as given and solid, was vividly illustrated to me on the silver screen in India.

Cut to December 2004, New Delhi: Just about everyone I meet and who knows that I belong to that rather innocuously named but increasingly sought-after category of individuals, "Non-Resident Indians (NRIs)," advises me to watch the recently released Hindi movie, "Swades: We, the People".[1] *I am intrigued by the title. Swades translates as homeland. The word also has historical connotations of anticolonial resistance, of Gandhi's rejection of manufactured imports and promotion of swadeshi, or home-made products, and finally of his call for self-rule and freedom. It remains a politically loaded term in reglobalized, postliberal India and is often deployed by groups struggling against transnational corporations and capitalist globalization. The subtitle, We, the People, is equally interesting. It is the phrase with which the* "Preamble" *to the Indian constitution begins and obviously brings to mind democracy. If the title and subtitle of the film are not provocative enough, I am told that I must see this movie because of how it represents and recuperates the diaspora (upper caste, educated, technologically savvy and male) and ties it to the project of national development. I need no further convincing. I drag my mother to one of the plush multiplexes, which dot the landscape of redeveloping Delhi, to watch this film. . . .*

Swades tells the story of how a north Indian village, Charanpur, fractured by caste divisions, is unified and developed through the interventions of an NRI male, Mohan, who returns to India from the United States in search of his childhood caretaker, Kaveri Amma. He is guilty of having abandoned her and wants to bring her back with him to the United States. He is, additionally, nostalgic about "homecoming." He finds Kaveri Amma in Charanpur, where he also finds and falls in love with Geeta, the young woman with whom Kaveri Amma lives. Geeta is an idealist who is doing her part to help develop the nation; she is city-raised and educated but chooses to live and teach in Charanpur village. Mohan, partly inspired by Geeta, instructs the residents of Charanpur to overcome their caste rivalries and to take charge of their own development.

Electricity symbolizes development in this film and Charanpur lacks reliable power. The residents have learned to deal with frequent power outages and are also taking steps to address the situation. They question the local BDO during one panchayat, or village council, meeting about what steps his office is taking to alleviate their power-related problems. The BDO tells them that an administrative report has been prepared and that work will be done in due time. The predictability of this "classic" bureaucratic response made me smile. One panchayat member responds that indeed something must be done soon or they will have to take up the issue with higher-ups. But Mohan, the protagonist, who is attending the first panchayat meeting of his life, is dissatisfied with this exchange and two scenes later takes up the matter with Geeta.

Set up as a debate between Mohan and Geeta over development, this scene unfolds in Kaveri Amma's kitchen. Kaveri Amma serves lunch to Geeta and Mohan and listens in on their heated discussion on "values and traditions" [sanskaar aur parampara]: are they good for the nation or impediments in the path of national development? Mohan believes that values and traditions "have shackled the nation and are preventing it from moving forward" [desh ko jakde hue hain; aage nahin badne de rahe hain]. Geeta takes the opposing stance, arguing that without traditions and values, the nation would be "like a body without its soul" [jaise aatma bina shareer]. Mohan reminds her that "We are plagued with problems," such as caste discrimination, illiterarcy, overpopulation, unemployment, and corruption, and concludes that "we are yet underdeveloped. . . . It is pathetic!" Geeta responds, "The sarkar [government or state] is trying to find solutions to these problems." But Mohan cuts her off: "Yeah, yeah, we'll see what solutions the sarkar finds." He rants about the woefully lacking infrastructure that can barely cope with one-fourth of the country's population. Geeta reiterates: "The government is trying; it is designing [development] schemes [yojnayen]." Mohan continues, "Like hell it is trying [kya khaak koshish kar rahi hai]! Schemes! Does the government's sole responsibility lie in designing schemes and collecting funds for them? Are *these schemes getting implemented at the 'grassroot' level, are they reaching the common man* [aam aadmi]*—isn't it the state's duty to ensure these things?" "Yes it is," responds Geeta and then retorts, "But what do you think the sarkar is* [sarkar ko tum samajhte kya ho]*? The sarkar is a 'system' of which the public* [janta] *is a part. I, you, this village, everyone who lives here, are a part of this system. If there is something lacking in this system* [koi kami ho], *then it is as much our esponsibility to set it right as that of the sarkar's." Kaveri Amma nods in agreement: "Even God can't help those who do not know how to help themselves."*

Mohan takes this lesson in participatory governance and self-help forward. He works to end caste factionalism in Charanpur and urges the residents to work collectively to electrify the village. He conveys his message through a song, using the metaphor of stars: each star in the sky looks beautiful on its own, the song goes, but acting together stars light up the entire night sky. After some persuasion the residents of the village follow his advice. Instead of depending on the sarkar for electricity, they band together in groups based on traditional caste professions and build a small-scale hydroelectric power-generation unit. In the end the village gets electrified (em-powered? enlightened?) through the collective efforts of its residents, acting under the tutelage of the technologically trained, "nativized" son who subsequently quits his National Aeronautics and Space Administration (NASA) job and returns to India permanently.

The movie conveyed important lessons on collectivism and of a specific kind of empowerment. Its assertion that reliance on the government for development was not good, its emphasis on a caste-based division of labor, and its construction of self-help under the sign of "tradition" mapped onto the body of the (rural-oriented) female protagonist were among the issues that made me uncomfortable. What struck me, however, was the movie's take on what constitutes the sarkar. It clearly implicated social collectivities (villages) and individuals as participants in the broader "system" of government and governance, who had to assume the collective responsibility of developing the nation. What part of this message reflected a present-day reworking of Gandhi's ideas, I wondered, and what part took from other ideologies, like neoliberalism? What complex articulations were instantiated in this popular cultural text?

Neoliberalism, as I have argued in this book, does not look the same or work in an identical manner everywhere but layers into other histories, cultural grids, and political projects and to surprising effect. The Indian case, for instance, complicates the supposedly universal consequence of neoliberalism on state privatization and dewelfarization. Although the Indian state has indeed devolved some welfare functions upon NGOs and GONGOs and is promoting new kinds of development programs that focus on empowerment and self-help rather than giving "handouts," it can hardly be called a state rid of welfare. Not only do welfarist assumptions underwrite the governmental logic of empowerment in India, as I illustrated, the state is also extending redistributive programs because a long history of popular politics and populist election rhetoric in postcolonial India demands it.

In 2005, for example, the government passed the National Rural Employment Guarantee Act, which ensures a minimum of one hundred days of unskilled, manual wage work (at the stipulated minimum wage) annually to at least one adult member of every rural household.[2] More recently, India's prime minister, Dr. Manmohan Singh, announced new antipoverty programs during his speech on the occasion of India's sixtieth Independence Day celebrations (August 15, 2007). Iterating that "Gandhiji's dream of a free India would only be fully realized when we banish poverty from our midst," Dr. Singh shared his vision of a new "caring India," which is

> not divided by caste, creed or gender. An India in which the creativity and enterprise of every citizen can find its full and free expression. An India in which the weak and downtrodden are empowered, the disabled find support, the destitute find succour and every individual is touched by the hand of progress and development. An India in which no person or region is left out of the journey of development and progress. (Singh 2007)

Noting that over the last three years his government had "significantly increased public expenditure in the social sectors [which] . . . is in line with our commitment to the welfare of the *aam aadmi* [common man]" (Singh 2007), he promised pension plans, programs in health care and education, and rehabilitation packages aimed at the poor. That the prime minister used the symbol of "the common man" and invoked the empowerment of "the weak and downtrodden" to argue for a more inclusive development paradigm in a new "caring" India is unsurprising. It would be hard to fathom an Independence Day speech delivered from the Red Fort in Delhi that did not mention the misery of the aam aadmi and his [*sic*] need for development. But what is equally important is that political society protests *compel* state representatives to renew their commitment to equitable national development; they force the government to reaffirm the (largely rhetorical) promises it makes about a progress that benefits all and not just a few. Indeed, the prime minister's speech not only reiterated the postcolonial Indian state's welfare responsibilities toward disadvantaged groups, but also indicated an expansion of its redistributive role in the years to come.

The generic descriptions of neoliberalism as "dewalfarization" or "roll back," then, do not adequately capture the complexity of state transformation that is underway. The Indian case points to the troubled travels and contradictory effects of neoliberal ideologies and underscores the ongoing need to examine (1) which sets of neoliberal ideas circulate easily and which do not, (2) how they confront other political rationalities and histories in different places, recuperating them or sitting uncomfortably with them or not fitting at all, and (3) what specific results ensue from these easy and not-so-easy conjunctures. The articulated nature of neoliberalism and its ambiguous, uneven effects are precisely what I have highlighted in this book, using examples drawn from the MS program.

MS, as I stated at the very beginning, cannot be viewed as a typical neoliberal program; rather it is an overdetermined product of multiple forces and ideologies not limited to neoliberalism. As an initiative that focuses on collective empowerment, it borrows from diverse frameworks, including feminist consciousness raising, Freirian pedagogy, leftist grassroots mobilization, and even Gandhian self-making and liberation based on local socio-moral worlds. Yet MS also operates in a context where the empowerment of individuals and communities is widely promoted as a mainstream technology of neoliberal development and governance. This program thus packs contingent and curious ideological confluences, appropriations, and disarticulations, which upset any preconceived notions about what empowerment may mean or what its outcomes may be.

Cut to December 2004, Begumpur, U.P.: I arrived in Begumpur with the intention of meeting with friends and acquaintances: MS staff members, the residents of Nimani village, and others whom I had gotten to know during my prior fieldwork. As I stood at the reception desk of my motel, completing the check-in formalities, I heard a familiar voice. I turned around to find Mallika Mehta, a long-term MS functionary, conversing with a group of people whom I did not recognize. I signaled to Mallika with a wave and she beckoned me over to where she stood. We hugged each other warmly and she introduced me to her colleagues, explaining that they were part of a team conducting an evaluation of the program in Seelampur block. With a promise to catch up with me later, she and the others departed for a meeting. One of the MS drivers, Raja, who knew me well, stayed back in the lobby. He updated me on some of the recent goings-on in MS over a cup of tea. Raja told me that most of the district-level staff had changed. Some field-level sahyoginis were still with the program, but others had joined the Total Literacy Campaign. MS had been phased out of Seelampur block, but block-level meetings with former program participants still took place on a monthly basis. He also mentioned that MS salaries had been doubled across the board. He was currently drawing a monthly salary of Rs 4,800 as opposed to his earlier salary of Rs 2,000. Sahyoginis, resource persons, district program coordinators and others had received similar raises. Raja felt, however, that the program was not operating as smoothly as it had in the past and complained that some of the district-level employees had slacked off. Our conversation ended abruptly as Raja was sent on an errand.

Mallika met me in my room later that evening and we spoke about what was going on in our lives and in MS. She told me that the program had undergone many changes, some good and others not so good. The U.P. program had expanded and was working in some new districts. Mallika lamented that "the kind of solidarity and cohesiveness that had existed in the program earlier was now lacking [pehle jaisa judaav nahin hai]." *But, she opined, that was bound to happen given that the people associated with the program had changed and the context was different. She was taking the transformation in stride. The one thing about MS, however, which she continued to appreciate, was the space it allowed for creativity to flourish: "the program lets people try out different things, even if they ultimately fail." Mallika used an example from her own life to illustrate the importance of creative, novel ideas for personal growth and social change.*

The new, exciting development in her life was her participation in the American pyramid-structured business scheme, Amway. Mallika readily admitted that potential monetary gain contributed to her excitement. But what she emphasized was the manner in which Amway had "converted" her attitude and thinking. She told me that participating in Amway had given her the confidence to talk to anyone and to not take "no" for an answer. Moreover, she admired how Amway had brought out women, especially housewives: it had given them the opportunity to do something outside of their daily household routines. The most important and admirable aspect of Amway, however, was the discipline it taught. Mallika explained that Amway distributed books, which participants were supposed to read everyday, and tapes, which they were expected to listen to (without rewinding, she stressed). She followed this regimen to a "T." Self-discipline was reflected at Amway's national meetings as well. Mallika informed me that these meetings were attended by thousands of members but were so well organized and disciplined that police forces were not needed to watch over them. Nobody touched, fondled, shoved, or harassed women, Mallika stated, with a note of incredulity in her voice. She recounted many Amway success stories of people going on cruises, being showered with flowers, quitting jobs at Oracle in America, returning from Australia to India and making Rs 300,000 a month as Amway entrepreneurs. "I hadn't even dreamt about this!" Mallika exclaimed. What came next caught me unawares.

Mallika told me that Amway appealed to her because it was just like the MS program. To allow women to emerge out of their shells, to generate a collective spirit among them, to develop new skills and creativity, to speak boldly in public, to change one's own self-image and life and that of others, and to organize: these were, after all, the things that MS aspired for and taught. For her Amway represented an expansion of her horizons and a disciplined means for personal betterment, awareness raising, and collective regeneration. In this respect, she opined, Amway was just like Mahila Samakhya. In fact, she was able to not only orient herself better to Amway because of her previous experiences with self- and social empowerment in MS, but also to implement insights from Amway into her MS work.

After Mallika departed, I recalled a personal run-in I had with an Amway representative in New York City in 1993. Even though I did not sign on to the Amway "way," I remembered the near evangelist zeal with which this individual conveyed to me the principles of self-advancement through business and group support that his organization stood for. But I had never imagined that Amway, an American pyramid-structured business scheme based on self-actualization through entrepreneurial means and attitudes, could be likened to MS, an innovative, feminist, collective, grassroots empowerment initiative for rural women in India. To my mind they could not be more different. And yet here I was, faced with the unlikeliest of comparisons between the empowering efforts and outcomes of both Amway and MS. Mallika's musings forced me to confront the surprising conjunctures of apparently incompatible initiatives and ideologies under neoliberalism. Our conversation vividly revealed how counterhegemonic and hegemonic ideas about personal and social betterment and about development through market-based action, discipline, and collectivism could be condensed and rearticulated into a translocal ensemble called empowerment. Along with the oppositional connotations of the term came a whole set of other signifieds that made empowerment a less obviously "alternative" strategy. Furthermore, these peculiar confluences and layerings, which overdetermined and destabilized the very meaning of empowerment, translated into unexpected effects.

The consequences of using empowerment as a governmental tool are paradoxical, as I have argued and elaborated in this book. Mallika Mehta's comments reiterated for me, once more, how MS becomes implicated in broader neoliberal processes, despite its creative approach to empowerment and its feminist goals of gender equality and just social transformation.

The contradictory and uneven results of state-partnered women's empowerment raise the vexing issue of how to think about feminist collaborations with state bodies in alternative projects for social change; I turn my attention to this question in concluding this book. The state, as Mary John (1999, 108) points out, has been the "most constitutive site of contestation" for Indian feminists. How, then, does one make sense of feminist-state alliance, in the shape of a GONGO, on the governmental project of women's empowerment? What are the dangerous and transformative possibilities unleashed by this form of state-directed feminist political activism at this particular moment?

My point in raising this important issue is not to dismiss Indian feminists' partnering with the state as "bad." Such an unreflexive, evaluative stand, as I stated at the beginning of this book, is both analytically and politically unhelpful, and is one that I, as a feminist, am unwilling to take. Indeed, advocating feminist disengagement from state institutions during the neoliberal era, as many Indian women's movement activists and scholars have argued, is troublesome and ill-advised (Agnihotri and Mazumdar 1995; Menon-Sen 2001; Nagar and Raju 2003; Sunder Rajan 2003). In India, as elsewhere, the forces of economic liberalization are increasing poverty and inequalities, and making the survival of marginalized women tenuous. The abject life conditions of disenfranchised women and their continued demands for state-assistance and entitlements force us to contend seriously with state-centered feminist politics. Subaltern women, "caught in the travails of a rapidly changing society," as Sunder Rajan (2003, 91) suggests, "are desperately *in need of* the services . . . that only the state can provide in the [quantity] and at the cost that can answer to such a massive (and as yet unrecognized and unmet) demand."

To my mind the important concern in the context of neoliberal globalization is not *whether* feminists should engage the state, but *how*. In other words, how do Indian feminists sustain their critical and wary relationship to the postcolonial state, honed over many years of activist work, "without . . . relinquishing that relation" (Sunder Rajan 2003, 215)? It is precisely in this spirit of critical self-reflexivity that some women's movement activists participate in the MS program, as I detailed in this book. Although these women remain deeply skeptical of masculinist state agencies and policies and aware of their own complicated locations as GONGO representatives, they view their involvement in MS as an innovative feminist experiment with state structures. The crucial question that drives their work, as Meera Srinivasan, a New Delhi–based woman associated with MS, put it, is: "Can a [women's empowerment] program sponsored by the state sow the seeds of some change? Is that possible?" I now take my cue from Srinivasan and inquire into the actual and potential effects, the risks as well as the opportunities, of involving state institutions in feminist projects for radical social change in the broader context of neoliberal governmentality.

I begin with the risks. MS faces the danger of a bureaucratization of empowerment. Carrying out empowerment as a professionalized, governmental intervention means instituting hierarchical structures and using statist proceduralism. These structures and practices, however, are enmeshed within the inequality-producing logic of bureaucratic state power (Brown 1995). Their proliferation through the program creates hierarchies among MS staff members and between them and their clients, which run counter to the program's egalitarian, equality-oriented outlook and goals. These hierarchies and tensions challenge program representatives to contend with an expansive framework of feminist solidarity and equality that is "attentive to power differences within and among the various communities of women" (Mohanty 2002, 502).

MS also encounters the ever-present danger of a bureaucratic takeover of the program. My informants complained about increased state intervention into the program. Unsympathetic government officials subvert the program's flexible, open-ended, and radical strategy of empowerment, turning it into a target-driven approach. For instance, the government desires hard evidence for the success of empowerment, which means that the program's broad focus on empowering conscientization and "education" is often reduced to literacy, because literacy is a tangible, measurable variable. Another opportunity for subversion arises when officials use MS collectives as ready-made vehicles to implement other government programs, such as those focusing on peer-lending and microenterprise, or to demonstrate their commitment to grassroots or civil society participation. Seema Gupta of MS underscored this when she pointed out that "[Government officials see MS] as a sort of implementing agency. [They have] various other schemes. Their only worry [is] that 'we have money but we don't have a network.' And now they have a network of all these women's collectives in place." Prabha Kishore also criticized the usage of MS by state representatives: "I feel that the whole purpose behind the government running these programs is that it can create a pool of sensible women voters. . . . They need women who can vote sensibly and who can talk—so that the government can say to the world, 'See, our women are so empowered.'" The danger is that state agents treat MS in an instrumentalist and tokenizing manner and appropriate the program, as needed, to project a gender-sensitive, feminist, and participatory face. However, as Seema Gupta alleged, "[Government officials] are not giving importance to the innovativeness of MS; they are not giving importance to women's intelligence and strength or to their ways of doing things. They are simply making use of those things so that they can claim that they have made all these innovations."

Besides the hurdles posed by government functionaries, who monopolize program resources but view women largely as symbols and tools and do not support their empowerment, the usage of empowerment as a governance method by the state also imposes limits on its definition and deployment as an activist tactic against oppression. For instance, Anil Bordia, suggested that

> By and large it will be true to say that empowered women would almost always take up causes which are humane, which are in conformity with law, and which are forward looking. I would not say the same for all sections of society because the CPI–ML people and the People's War Group [radical leftist organizations] are also empowered in a sense, but they do not always take a stand which is within the framework of law. But in the case of women, I . . . know of no case where empowered women have . . . taken the law in their own hands or have acted contrary to . . . government policy; in fact, that is a good test of what policy should be.

Bordia's distinction between the implicitly illegitimate empowerment struggles undertaken by radical groups and the desirable empowerment mobilizations of subaltern women reveals how state-initiated programs can potentially serve as vehicles for turning women into law-abiding, disciplined, and responsibilized citizen-subjects (Cruikshank 1999), who use legitimate civil society mechanisms to fight for their rights. These women are denizens of political society in India, which is a relatively unregulated, negotiational domain of politics and is not governed by the norms of elite civil society (Chatterjee 2004). Their tutelage under empowerment programs can be seen, perhaps cynically, as yet another aspect of the modernizing, pedagogic project of the state that aims to equip subaltern women to function as good members of civil society and to deal with formal political institutions as proper citizens. MS, in fact, trains its clients to participate in local legislative bodies. Might this signal a *formalization* of political society mobilizations, which seeks to deradicalize them and bring them in line with normative civil society?

These potentially disempowering effects of employing empowerment as a category of governance have led some feminists to contend that states should stay out of grassroots empowerment (Moser 1993) and others to argue for feminist distancing from state programs (Brown 1995).[3] Do these assertions, however, assume that states are bad and obviously disempowering agencies and, as binary logic dictates, nonstate bodies are good and empowering? My work shows that the neoliberal blurring of the boundary between state and nonstate spheres makes it difficult to make simplistic judgments about these entities or to determine in an absolute fashion whether states should participate in women's empowerment and whether feminists should get involved with state institutions. The governmentalization of empowerment is not simply a reflection of direct state involvement but also an instance of the neoliberal practices of governance that suffuse society at large. If we are to rethink the state conceptually in order to see that state and nonstate entities are part of the same apparatus of government, then we need to examine the politics and paradoxes of empowerment programs undertaken by all kinds of institutions, including NGOs. NGO-initiated programs, after all, do not operate in a hermetically sealed context unaffected by state representatives and practices or by international funding-agency agendas; neither are they, by definition, necessarily more participatory or accountable. Prabha Kishore, in fact, challenged the problematic "bad state/good NGOs" dualism when she suggested that NGOs were only concerned about money and not meaningful development, and that they, just like the state, tokenized women.

> First the government used [women] for votes [as vote banks], and then it used us for sloganeering. Then NGOs used us for protests against alcohol, in the Sarvodaya movement, in forest protection movements, and in other kinds of movements. Once they have used us, they tell us to back off and go back [to our usual existence]. This has always happened. When they needed *shakti* [female power], the

> Gods created Kali [the Hindu goddess who personifies shakti]. And when she did what she was supposed to do, she was told to go and sit in a temple. "Now you are not needed; now people will worship you and you can be happy." And she was locked up in a temple.

Using the theoretical lens of governmentality complicates the feminist debate on disengagement from state structures in another way as well. What does it mean, for example, to be co-opted by an entity that cannot be clearly demarcated or to seal oneself off from governmental processes that permeate the entire social formation? Indeed, the latter may not be an option; rather it may be more useful for activists to assume tactical positions within regimes of governance.

One productive way to approach these knotty issues is to ask what kinds of subjects are being produced by the governmentalization of empowerment and the resulting increase in interfaces between subaltern women and state agencies. Do women's "expanding relationships [to state institutions and processes] produce only active *political* subjects, or do they also produce regulated, subordinated, and disciplined *state* subjects?" (Brown 1995, 173). My analysis of the MS program substantiates Partha Chatterjee's claim that governmental programs do not simply fashion bureaucratized and passive state subjects. In postcolonial contexts these programs are generative in that they produce active, sometimes dissident, political actors and provide the ground for political society mobilizations in which marginalized subjects make claims on the state, negotiate over entitlements, and contest social hierarchies. Governmentalization does not depoliticize so much as it spawns openings for a subaltern politics of citizenship that may take new, unexpected forms.

This book has elucidated the kinds of politicization and empowerment that occur "behind the backs of or against the wills of even the most powerful actors" (Ferguson 1994, 18). MS women come to understand and challenge state-supported structural inequalities; they actively engage local mafias (which exceed the conventional confines of the state but involve particular bureaucrats) and connect them with gender and other forms of hierarchies; and finally, they learn statist languages and practices and use them as potentially subversive tools for demanding accountability. These processes, albeit complicated, can be empowering in that they help women formulate tactics for contesting locally entrenched power equations. These tactics allow women to negotiate a broader, if contingent, notion of empowerment that is not exclusively about changing women's individual or collective gendered situations but about understanding and confronting the overlapping structural inequalities (of class, caste, and gender, for example), which shape individual and collective realities and within which state officials are mired. Empowerment is about taking up fights for issues that extend well beyond the scope of "women's rights" defined narrowly, insofar as these are centered on mechanical ideas of gender equality. Although certain officials and local elites may not endorse this kind of women's empowerment or take it seriously, such processes, once initiated, may not be easily reined in. Shakti once released, to extend Prabha Kishore's analogy, cannot be locked in a temple after she has served her intended purpose.

Empowerment takes on a life of its own; it erupts, interrupts, and exceeds neoliberal, regulative logics. Women undergoing collective empowering processes act in ways that may refuse to adhere to any preconceived dominant script and may, thus, confound expectations. To quote Prabha again, "Our work is to motivate women. . . . If they are motivated in the 'wrong' way, it is not our fault—[that] is what we tell the government [when questioned]!" Empowerment, thus, is an "excess," a moving target whose meaning is continually redefined through subaltern women's struggles. It has an ambiguous and open-ended quality that manifests in multiple and conflicted ways in women's lives. The governmentalization of empowerment, therefore, may not just mean a potential formalization of subaltern political society; it might also open the door for a substantive *democratization* of elite civil society and state institutions. These bodies have generally looked down upon political society—because it does not conform to the formal, hegemonic norms of political participation and is not disciplined—and have largely kept it at bay except during election time. But the political society activism that I have elaborated on in this book challenges such an instrumentalist admission and criticizes the normal business of government-at-a-distance (Rose 1996). Subaltern mobilizations, in fact, enable a populist "demotic" politics (Clarke 2007, 13)—which speaks the language of the aam aadmi or the common person—to leach into the elite, formal realm of nominal "democratic" politics and to force a convergence.[4] Indeed, popular struggles compel democracy to function and look like it is really meant to: not an exclusive and regulated domain of polite conversation indulged in by privileged members of society but an unruly political theater and "an absolutely, bloody-unending row" (Hall 1997, 65).

When poor rural Dalit women struggle against violence or against upper-caste control over land or when they insist on obtaining development entitlements, they try to make state agencies and representative political institutions do what they are supposed to do—that is, guarantee their constitutional rights and survival. They protest oppression and invisibilization, and demand recognition as legitimate citizens. Furthermore, their political practices articulate a vision of an ideal citizen that cannot be contained within the liberal and neoliberal logics of citizenship. Disenfranchised subjects, as I have shown, refuse to inhabit a legal identity that is abstract (decontextualized), generically equal, and self-interestedly entrepreneurial. Rather, by basing their rights claims in their unequal and different status and by using moral notions of personhood, community, and solidarity to appeal to the powerful, subaltern actors fill the legal container of citizenship with locally meaningful, ethical content.[5] This remoralized politics of citizenship also conjures an ethical state. By critiquing the state "as is" (i.e., administered by people who have power and abuse it to maintain their economic, social, and political dominance) and by consistently referencing the (promised, but largely failed) welfare state that "never was," the subaltern actors I described in this book discursively materialize the state as it "ought to be." This ethical state "must be reflected not only in the original mandates of a constitution but in a government's repeated and alert responsiveness to the varied needs of different but equal people according to a calculus that transcends cost benefit, a (self-) control that checks the abuse of power, and an impersonality that yet accepts responsibility greater than that of any guardian" (Sunder Rajan 2003, 112). As Anil Bordia rightly signaled, the issues that marginalized women take up in their fights for rights and survival and how they implicate state officials in these issues could indeed serve as critical markers for how official policies and practices, state and civil society institutions, and citizenship must be transformed if the goal of social emancipation and the promises of substantive, not nominal, democracy and equal rights are to be realized. The alternative envisionings of governance, development, personhood, belonging, and a just society put forth by subaltern women's politics and protests are, perhaps, unintentional and empowering fallouts of governmental programs.

If the story I told in the book did not sound like a "simple story with a happy ending", it is because "no story about political society [and governmental technologies] ever is" (Chatterjee 2004, 67). Empowerment as a quasi–state-implemented governmental strategy is a double-edged sword that is both promising and precarious. Feminist collaborations with state institutions on women's empowerment are opening critical vistas for challenge and change. However, the dangers involved in these projects mean that one cannot be overly celebratory or sanguine about their liberatory potential: they provoke a politics that does not come with any guarantees. My analysis of the MS program, as an example of the articulation of different political projects and actors around the theme of empowerment in liberalizing India, suggests that there is indeed no "system of safeguards that offer us a zone of comfort when we engage in political action" (Dean 2001, 62). But the murkiness of political praxis today and its known and unknown risks do not imply that such actions are futile and should not be taken. My work illustrates that many MS women, both employees and participants, are keenly aware of some of the dangers their work inheres and attempt to confront and negotiate these counterproductive possibilities and perils on a daily basis.

The world of neoliberal governmentality, in which projects such as MS operate, makes empowerment a risky maneuver to undertake. Empowerment has layered histories and multiple avatars: a leftist strategy for political conscientization and class-based politics, a feminist strategy for awareness raising and gender equality, and now an entrepreneurial strategy for development and self-improvement. Critical analyses of how these contentious meanings overlap and clash in different contexts and what dangers they pose are crucial for activists and scholars alike. The outcomes of these intersections are neither given nor unproblematic, and they point to the need for exerting constant vigilance when engaging in the politics of empowerment, on the ground and in theory.

Notes

Introduction

1. The quotes around the word *empowerment* here denote its open-ended and contested meaning in varied temporal and spatial contexts. Subsequent appearances of this term will not be in quotes although the same considerations apply.

2. Mahila Samakhya translates as "Women Speaking with an Equal Voice." In this book I follow my informants in referring to this program as MS.

3. The Indian government's Ninth Five Year Plan, launched in 1997, formally promoted empowerment as a development strategy.

4. While studies of neoliberal governmentality have largely focused on modern Western democratic states (Dean 2001), there is a growing literature on colonial and postcolonial governmentality. For example, see Chatterjee (2004), Das and Poole (2004), Ferguson (1994), Ferguson and Gupta (2002), Gupta (2001), Hansen and Stepputat (2001), Mitchell (1991, 2002), Ong (2006), Paley (2001), Scott (1999), and Stoler (1995).

5. See Clarke (2007). Mohanty (2002) also underscores the dialectical relationship between the particular and the universal and makes a similar case for paying attention to specific contexts and cases to understand global political-economic processes such as capitalism.

6. Although Chatterjee seems to make a clear distinction between those who govern and those who are governed, in this book I demonstrate that such an absolute binary is untenable under governmental regimes. Governmentality operates through including individuals and other social actors in the project of rule. This broad field of governance renders impossible a strict and a priori divide between the rulers and the ruled; indeed, it then becomes important to analyze where this line gets drawn, how and by whom.

7. Chatterjee defines *political society* as a zone that straddles the boundary between legality and illegality and emphasizes, in particular, the contradictory moves made by those who, on the one hand, clearly break the law (for example, by squatting on land) and, on the other hand, make rights-based claims. Illegality does not make a similar appearance in my work. This book concerns the entitlement and rights-based struggles of those subjects who may not have access to the formal legal system, but who also do not sit on the fence of legality or obviously break laws.

8. Ida Susser, in her study of Norman Street, New York City, conducted well before welfare reform in the United States, argued that the most "striking feature" of the politics of the working poor is "the organization of collective protest to demand essential resources from the state" (1982, 9). My work reveals similar dynamics at work in contemporary India, but also differs in crucial ways. Susser studied working-class welfare recipients in the United States and claimed that their political action was conditioned and "dampened" by dependence on welfare and the fear of losing benefits (1982, 77). I, on the other hand, worked with those who have largely been left out of redistribution programs in India or have never received the promised benefits. The activism of this population is quite different given that they have nothing to lose. Born out of material vulnerability and socioeconomic injustice, they enact a moral politics of rights and citizenship that demands fair access to basic needs.

9. Piven and Cloward (1971) made an analogous argument about the erstwhile U.S. welfare state.

10. For example, see Bourdieu (1999); Cohn (1987); Coronil (1997); Corrigan and Sayer (1985); Das and Poole (2004); Fuller and Benei 2000; Geertz (1980); Hansen and Stepputat (2001); Herzfeld (1992); Joseph and Nugent (1994); Nandy (1992); Navaro-Yashin (2002); Steinmetz (1999a); Stoler 2004; Taussig (1997); and Taylor (1997).

11. Macrological state-centered theories that focus on political parties, bureaucratic organization, and capital cities have, until recently, dominated South Asian scholarship (see Alavi 1972; Bardhan 1984; Brass 1990; Kohli 1990).

12. See Bhattacharjee (1997); Ferguson (1984); Gal and Kligman (2000); Gordon (1990); MacKinnon (1989); Orloff (1999); and Piven (1990) for analyses of different Western state bureaucracies and laws. There exists a rich feminist literature on the gender of the postcolonial Indian state, which complicates both the nature of the state and feminist engagements with state institutions. These analyses approach the state through specific policies, laws, and agencies. For example, on legislation regarding the repatriation of women "abducted" during Partition, see Butalia (1993) and Menon and Bhasin (1993); on forced hysterectomies and prostitution, see Sunder Rajan (2003); on the politics of protection, see Pathak and Sunder Rajan (1992); on female feticide, abortion, and rape laws, see Menon (1996, 2004); on development planning and gender, see Chaudhuri (1996) and John (1996); and on violence in the context of a state-initiated women's empowerment program, see Mathur (1999).

13. See also Crush (1995); Gardner and Lewis (1996); Mitchell (1991); Shrestha (1995); and Sachs (1992).

14. Identity formation, as Stuart Hall (1989 and 1997) suggests, involves an interplay between being positioned and (re)positioning in and through discourse.

15. Hall used this term when talking about identity politics. Identities, he argued, are not essences but unstable positionings in discourse. Therefore, "there is always a politics of position, which has no absolute guarantee in an unproblematic, transcendental 'law of history'" (Hall 1989, 72).

16. In addition to bell hooks (1984), who makes a powerful case for starting from the perspectives of those on the margins of society, Gita Sen and Caren Grown (1987) and Chandra Mohanty (2002) have also made this point.

17. Here, I am guided, in particular, by the works of Butler (1999); Hall (1989 and 1997); Hall and Held (1990); Mohanty (1991 and 2002); and Mouffe (1992). My work is equally influenced by the following scholars, who examine gendered subjectivity in the context of (post)colonial public culture, policy, and the law: Alexander (1991); Butalia (1993); Mani (1989a, 1989b); Mankekar (1993); Menon (2004); Menon and Bhasin (1993); Sarkar (1991, 1995); Sarkar and Butalia (1995); and Sunder Rajan (2003).

18. Program representatives occupy an important place in the development dynamic. They are positioned as intermediaries, who mediate between various (incommensurable?) groups of actors, translate policy agendas on the ground, and mobilize these visions in both expected and subversive ways. My interest in how a concept as abstract as empowerment is discursively defined, implemented as a policy strategy on the ground, and to what effect, necessitated taking a close look at MS functionaries.

19. The Indian bureaucratic setup is divided into hierarchically arranged administrative levels. At the apex of this structure is the national level, below which lies the state level. Each state is divided into several districts and each district is, in turn, composed of many blocks. A block is the lowest administrative subdivision in this hierarchy and consists of roughly a hundred villages. Each village has its own elected *panchayat*, or village council, which takes decisions on locally relevant development and legal issues.

20. I conducted interviews in Hindi, Bhojpuri (a dialect of Hindi spoken in eastern U.P.), and English.

21. Dutch funding for MS lasted through 2007. The Cabinet Committee on Economic Affairs of the Indian government recently announced the continuation and future expansion of the program as part of its eleventh Five Year Plan (2007–2012). The program costs, totaling Rs 210 crores, will now be shared by the Department for International Development (DFID) of the UK and the Government of India (http://www.igovernment.in/site/rs-210-cr-for-%E2%80%98mahila-samakhya%E2%80%99-plan/; accessed on May 10, 2008).

22. Unlike WDP, which is a state government program, MS is an Indian government program.

23. In U.P., MS operated in ten districts in 1998–1999. Funding for these districts was provided by the Dutch government and the World Bank (through its support of the Indian government's Education for All program). MS now operates in fewer districts because a new state, Uttaranchal, was carved out of U.P. and some of the older program districts fall under the jurisdiction of the new state.

24. *Dalit*, which literally translates as broken or crushed, is a commonly used term referring to the oppressed or downtrodden people at the bottom of the Hindu caste hierarchy. Until the rise of a self-conscious Dalit movement a few decades ago, this

group was variously identified: *outcastes* (which is a mistaken term because, although not belonging to the four main Hindu caste divisions [*varnas*], Dalits are very much a part of the caste system); *untouchables* (because they largely engaged in occupations deemed "polluting," such as leatherwork and scavenging); *Harijan* (children of God, a term coined by Gandhi); and *Scheduled Castes*, a term invented by the British colonial state in 1935 and commonly used in postcolonial government documents. In contrast to the above labels, *Dalit* is a political and activist term of resistance, chosen by the people so identified, which aims to mark injustice and struggle and does not have the patronizing connotation that Harijan is seen to carry. According to the 2001 Indian census, the total population of *Scheduled Castes* equaled 166.6 million (http://www.censusindia.gov.in/Census_Data_2001/Census_data_finder/A_Series/SC_ST.htm; accessed on May 10, 2008). Dalits in India today continue to suffer serious violence, social discrimination, economic marginalization, and de facto disenfranchisement (Human Rights Watch 1999), despite Indian constitutional articles that abolish untouchability and protect against discrimination in public places and despite the state's reservation policies that institute quotas for Dalits in educational institutions, political bodies and government jobs. Dr. B. R. Ambedkar, the architect of the Indian constitution, was a venerated Dalit leader. The last two and a half decades have seen the rise of other prominent Dalit political figures in North India, notably the late Kanshi Ram and Mayawati, who are associated with the Bahujan Samaj Party (BSP). Guided by the political philosophy of Ambedkar, the BSP represents the concerns of Dalits. Since its founding in 1984, this party has emerged as a major player in U.P. politics, winning a majority of seats in the state assembly elections in 2007. Mayawati is the current chief minister of U.P., heading a coalition government. See also Mendelsohn and Vicziany 1998.

25. The term sahyogini literally means one who assists or helps.

26. The organizational structure of state-level MS societies mirrors the administrative subdivisions of the government.

27. The district- and state-level program managers are assisted in their work by a team of resource persons, consultants, accountants, drivers, administrative assistants, and messengers.

28. During the initial years of the program some of the state project directors were government bureaucrats.

29. The ex officio members include representatives from the Departments of Education, Women and Child, and Finance, for example.

30. The program in the state of U.P. was initially implemented in three districts through well-known local NGOs. This strategy was later altered by setting up a registered MS society in the state that took over program management from the NGOs.

31. This structure was arrived at partly because of the lessons learned from the WDP in Rajasthan, which suffered from state interference and ultimately co-optation. To prevent a recurrence of this scenario, MS planners decided on a semiautonomous structure for the program.

32. This perception of MS as a non–target-driven project is changing. A number of my informants told me that the program was becoming increasingly target oriented.

33. MS selects program blocks that have a relatively high proportion of low-caste residents and a low representation of NGOs.

34. According to the 1991 census of Seelampur block, 18 percent of the female residents were literate as compared to over half the male residents.

1. Empowerment Assemblages: A Layered Picture of the Term

1. These ideas of assemblage build on the work of Deleuze and Guattari (1987).

2. The Cairo conference dealt with population and reproductive rights and Beijing with gender issues within development.

3. Here the GAD advocates build on Steven Lukes' (1974) discussion of power.

4. Molyneux (1985) challenged a homogenizing and essentialist conception of women's needs, arguing instead for a shift in focus to gendered needs and interests. The latter were related to people's gender positioning within societies and could be either practical or strategic. Women's practical gender needs were related to their immediate living conditions, concerned survival and basic needs issues, and were important to address. But fulfilling these needs did not necessarily challenge accepted definitions of gender roles or establish a more gender equitable society. Strategic gender needs and interests could be identified through critically analyzing particular systems of gender subordination and their intersections with other forms of hierarchies. This analysis would enable struggles that directly contested entrenched gender norms.

5. GAD feminists linked practical and strategic gender needs, arguing that tackling the former could serve as an entry point into addressing the latter (Batliwala 1994; Kabeer 1994).

6. Most MS sahyoginis are selected from the rural areas in which they work; but unlike their clients, many have high school degrees and generally belong to lower-middle-class and lower-/middle-caste families.

7. Some people associated with the MS program had previously participated in Gandhian student and social justice movements, and they brought these experiences to bear upon their work in MS.

8. I do not examine what Gandhi's ideas have historically meant for different groups of people or how these ideas have been translated into practical programs by various Gandhian leaders. These important issues have been addressed by others. For example, see Amin (1984) and Fox (1989).

9. The claim, made by scholars such as Chatterjee (1986a) and Nandy (1983), that Gandhi symbolized a truly indigenous and autonomous form of resistance to modern civilization and articulated a unique vision of a free society has been complicated by others (see Bose 1997; Bose and Jalal 1998). They show, for instance, that Gandhi's idea of the village republic was borrowed from the work of Henry Maine and others.

10. Truth, for Gandhi, was both relative and transcendental: it stemmed from the lived experiences of moral individuals and was also universal; it was experimental, yet unchanging. Truth could not be found in scriptures or in history, and it could not be accessed through science but found in the experiences of morally lived lives (Chatterjee 1986a, 96–97).

11. Gandhi's vision got sidelined by the postcolonial nationalist state that took over the reins of development as its duty. Not only did the state exist to serve development, but indeed development served to legitimize the state (see Bose 1997).

12. Chatterjee (1986a) also contends that whereas Gandhi rejected modern political institutions in *Hind Swaraj*, he later saw some advantages to working inside state institutions. Those on the inside could point to the wrongs of the government and prevent harmful legislation from being enacted (1986a, 114). However, Gandhi continued to emphasize that a true moral leader should work outside of state structures (1986a, 113).

13. Liberal thinkers, such as Mill, also promoted the idea of trusteeship to justify colonial rule, whereby modern, educated trustees could teach and lead unenlightened colonized people (Cowen and Shenton 1995). But Gandhi's notion of trusteeship was quite different from that of liberal thinkers, grounded as it was in local moral worldviews rather than in universalistic enlightenment ideals. Furthermore, Gandhi's satyagrahi leaders were not only supposed to follow the collective will of the people, but also to lead by example and not govern over people.

14. Although Gandhi desisted from claiming that modern education in the sciences, for example, was utterly useless, he argued against making a "fetish" of it (Gandhi 1997, 102).

15. There are interesting convergences between Freire and Gandhi, in the historic role of the oppressed to liberate themselves and others, in getting rid of the fear that grips the oppressed, in viewing struggle as an act of love, and in rejecting possessive individualism and materialism. They both also articulate projects of liberation, which are firmly pedagogic.

16. The establishment of the Inspection Panel in 1993, for example, was part of the World Bank's reinvention, which made it possible for it to position itself as a champion of the environment and of the rights of marginalized groups and as a more accountable institution (Clarke, Fox, and Treakle 2003). The Panel is a unique instrument that allows civil-society organizations and the people affected by Bank-funded projects to challenge the World Bank if they can prove that the projects the institution funds are noncompliant with its own environmental and social policy guidelines.

17. McNamara also briefly promoted the social dimensions of development during the 1970s through such mechanisms as the basic-needs approach (see Finnemore 1997).

18. Gender, as Buvinic, Gwin, and Bates (1996) argue, was more palatable to the male staff at the World Bank because it included men. The quick move from women

to gender at the World Bank and other international institutions was criticized by some feminists, who argued that it allowed these agencies to depoliticize the meaning of gender as a relation of subordination, sidestep a focus on women, and emphasize men's exclusion (Baden and Goetz 1997). This has indeed happened at the World Bank, which has recently called for "menstreaming" development: a purportedly more inclusive approach to development and gender equality that takes into account men's gender issues (World Bank 2006c).

19. It is not insignificant that the World Bank took the concept of "comparative advantage," which offers an economic rationale for the benefits of free trade, and applied it to the field of social empowerment. For a critical discussion of the World Bank's text "Empowerment and Poverty Reduction: A Sourcebook," see Horwitz (2003).

20. Despite its talk about social development, no more than 9 percent of the World Bank's budget in 1999 was devoted to social programming (World Bank 1999).

21. This issue gets to the heart of the conundrum that the MS program poses: it is a *government-sponsored* project for women's emancipation and empowerment (see chapter 3).

22. The narrowing down of the feminist empowerment mandate through institutional priorities is evidenced by the Gender Empowerment Measure (GEM) used by the UN to assess gender equity in various countries (see Bardhan and Klasen 1999). This involves measuring women's representation, relative to men, in national political institutions; in administrative, technical, and managerial positions; and their share of earned income. The extent to which GEM is able to capture the processual nature of empowerment is questionable. Furthermore, GEM uses a universal standard to evaluate a process that is supposed to be contextually specific and self-defined.

23. Even self-defined collective change is complicated in that it assumes a commonality of interests. I argue in chapter 6 that these interests are not transparent and that establishing "common interests" is itself a part of the process of struggles.

2. Engendering Neoliberal Governance: Welfare, Empowerment, and State Formation

1. A block office is the seat of the block-level administration, which comprises of the BDO, a government appointee, and a team of assistants.

2. I have changed the names of all individuals in this book except Anil Bordia, who is a well-known public figure widely associated with WDP, MS, and other innovative development programs. I follow local naming conventions throughout this book, shifting between full names and first and last names of my informants. Some of my informants, depending on their social and geographical location, did not use last names for self-identification. The "Rani" in Meena Rani's name, for example, is not her last name but is considered an extension of her first name that refers to her gender. I use given names for such informants and no last names.

3. The 73rd and 74th constitutional amendments in India reserve 33.3 percent of the seats in local elected bodies for women.

4. DWCRA is one of the largest state-run development programs for poor women. Under it, women are organized into peer groups and are provided skills training, after which they become eligible for peer group loans (through the Integrated Rural Development Program) for starting income-generating work.

5. MS staff members used the Hindi word sashaktikaran and the phrase *mazboot banana* [to make strong or strengthen] interchangeably to describe empowerment.

6. A block chief is the elected head of a block.

7. For analyses of the impact of the Indian political context of the 1970s and 1980s on feminist activism see Agnihotri and Mazumdar (1995); Gandhi and Shah (1992); and Philipose (2001). Agnihotri and Mazumdar (1995) argue that the contemporary Indian women's movement has been influenced by (1) the crisis of the state brought on by the Emergency, (2) the rise in the late-1970s of civil rights movements across the country, (3) a significant increase in women's organizations in the 1980s and the resultant inclusion of women's issues in the official agenda, (4) the rise in fundamentalist movements that deploy essentialist notions of tradition, culture, and gender, and (5) the deepening crisis of the state and society during the 1990s due to the global spread of free-market capitalism and liberalization policies.

8. Some of my informants reported that district- and block-level MS offices have indeed enjoyed relative autonomy from the New Delhi–based Government of India in their everyday work; however, local-level government officials have intervened in the day-to-day administration of the program.

9. In discussing the pros and cons of state and nonstate bodies, my interlocutors invoked smaller NGOs and women's organizations. NGOs, however, come in all shapes and sizes. Large transnational NGOs, for instance, operate virtually as state bureaucracies and can challenge the authority and sovereign control of states.

10. What I offer here is not a definitive statement on the gendering of state and nonstate institutions, but an interpretative analysis. Instantiations of gender categories and categorizations are fluid in practice and thus hard to pin down or demonstrate. One has to rely on analogical evidence and structural correspondence. This is where scholarship, public discourses, and ethnographic observations about states, NGOs, and gender come in handy, and I rely on these to postulate the complicated and indeed emergent gendering of the state and NGOs under neoliberalism.

11. Fisher (1997) reviews these commonplace assumptions in the literature on NGOs, critically analyzing both mainstream depictions of NGOs as depoliticized social actors who can solve all development problems and laudatory representations that position NGOs as alternative, radical, antidevelopment agencies.

12. The discourse on protection is a crucial part of the postcolonial Indian state's patriarchal self-representation. For example, see Pathak and Sunder Rajan 1992; Menon and Bhasin 1993; and Sunder Rajan 2003.

13. The ambiguous gendering of state and nonstate arenas under neoliberalism, might also hint at the complex reworking of dominant gender norms of masculinity and femininity in the current moment.

14. It is difficult to provide an accurate count of Indian NGOs or their growth over time because not all of them are formally registered. Furthermore, to have a nonprofit status, an Indian organization can be registered under any one of five acts: the Societies Registration Act of 1860, the Indian Trusts Act of 1882, the Cooperatives Societies Act of 1904, the Trade Union Act of 1926, and the Companies Act of 1956 (Sen 1993).

15. Clearly, southern state actors are not simply victims of externally imposed SAPs. Governing elites in India, for example, have embraced these reforms and have benefited from them. Yet their enthusiasm has to be seen within the context of the enormous clout that institutions such as the IMF and the World Bank carry and their ability to pressure southern states into adopting their expert recommendations.

16. The Foreign Contributions Regulation Act of 1976, for instance, requires NGOs receiving foreign funds to register with the government and accept state monitoring (Sen 1993).

17. A number of my informants believed that the government began paying more attention to women's issues once Rajiv Gandhi came to power. For many, Gandhi and his team of technocrats represented the promise of a "modern" India. They initiated the process of economic liberalization and also pushed for the application of modern technologies, such as computers, in national development. It is, therefore, important to look at how the political ideologies of the party in power reconfigure the ideas and practices of development and empowerment.

18. Within WCD, as one bureaucrat noted, the women's bureau has less clout than the children's bureau, which is responsible for administering the ICDS program. ICDS is one of the largest programs focusing on preschoolchildren and maternal health issues in India. It views children as a national asset, and considers an investment in their human capital development as crucial for the nation's future (see Gupta 2001). Women, as mothers, are important only as secondary players in the development of children.

19. ICDS runs *anganwaadis*, or preschools for children, where they receive food, among other things. It also monitors and provides for the health needs of the children and their mothers.

20. My point is that elected and appointed officials at the block and district levels, given their locations and entrenched interests, can subvert the policies designed by New Delhi-based bureaucrats; such dissension between different levels of the state illustrate its nonunified nature.

21. When I told local MS staffers about this conversation, they were furious. They informed me that they had attempted to meet the BDO many times and sent him invitations for MS events, but he had ignored them.

22. This instance also illustrates the complex and contextual nature of empowerment. Just because a woman is powerful in one situation does not imply that she will be able to act in an empowered manner in another context with different people, power dynamics, and needs.

3. Empowering Moves: Paradoxes, Subversions, Dangers

1. See Ferguson (1994) on how development operates as an antipolitics machine that takes the highly political question of powerlessness out of poverty, thus turning it into a matter of neutral expert intervention and management.

2. After a year of employment with the program, staff members became eligible for a matching savings program, the "Provident Fund," from the government.

3. In 1998 the minimum wage for skilled work was Rs 54 per day. Assuming a 25-day work month, this translated into a monthly earning of Rs 1,350. MS sahyoginis earned Rs 1,500 per month for working longer hours. In addition to their honoraria, they received a travel allowance of Rs 300 per month.

4. The official's remarks are significant because most of the employees at the lower end of the organizational hierarchy come from rural, lower-class, and sometimes lower-caste backgrounds; this official seemed to be mapping educational levels and skills onto caste and class positions.

5. A similar unionization-related incident happened in the context of the empowerment-oriented, state-initiated WDP. At a unionization meeting of WDP's women "volunteers" in 1992, state authorities confronted the women and, under the threat of program closure, forced the meeting attendees to submit written promises that they would not unionize (Sathin Union Representative 1994). But when these scare tactics failed to stem the unionization tide in a particular program district, government officials sent letters to the husbands of women volunteers. The officials effectively ordered the men to prevent their wives from unionizing and threatened that the government would not be held responsible for what might happen to the women (WDP Fact Finding Team 1992).

6. Program functionaries at all levels regularly compiled reports about their interventions, which sought to capture, both qualitatively and quantitatively, the results of their empowerment strategies. Whereas they saw the qualitative dimension of these efforts as the most important method of ensuring critical program feedback and recording change, they also complained that externally imposed targets were subverting the radical goals of the program.

7. In chapter 5 I analyze subaltern narratives about the failure of development and their demands for it.

8. See Gupta and Sharma (2006) for a detailed analysis of this partially "failed" census encounter.

9. Memories of the Emergency period and the forced sterilizations that ensued were alive in social milieus in which MS operated. In fact, many MS fieldworkers told me that when they first arrived in some villages to introduce themselves and the program, they were questioned by Dalit residents about whether they had come to sterilize women. A fieldworker mentioned that in one village all female residents hid in their homes. After much coaxing these women emerged from their houses and told the MS representative that they had hidden because they feared getting pressured into sterilization. Their previous encounters with development functionaries who promised them "incentives" in exchange for sterilization indelibly shaped their imaginations of the state and of development and colored their interactions with MS personnel.

10. Government-issued liquor licenses constitute a women's issue because there is a correlation between the sale of alcohol, women's workloads, and violence against women. In the last decade women have led and participated in several antialcohol movements across India (e.g., in the southern state of Andhra Pradesh). This issue has become significant enough to force some regional political parties to include antialcohol stances as part of their official agendas to garner the support of women voters.

11. For a discussion of the Bhanwari rape case, see Kanchan Mathur (1999).

12. See also Ida Susser (1982), who argued in her study of Norman Street in New York City that the politics of the poor concerns learning how to deal with the government.

4. Staging Development: A Drama in North India

1. India is the World Bank's largest single borrower with a cumulative loan portfolio of over US$60 billion (World Bank 2005).

2. I broadly group feminist and queer theorists' ideas about the performativity of gendered identities with postcolonial studies scholars' analyses of colonial mimicry and modernity under the "performativity" studies label because of how these scholars deploy poststructuralist ideas about difference, reality effects, and the unstable relationship between signifiers and signifieds.

3. I had spent eight months conducting in-depth research in Nimani when the World Bank visit took place.

4. For example, see Cooper and Packard 1997; Ebron 2002; Grillo and Stirrat 1997; Moore 1999; Sivaramakrishnan and Agrawal 2003; and Walley 2004.

5. Ebron (2002), Elyachar (2005), Sivaramakrishnan and Agrawal (2003), and Walley (2003) are exceptions. Other anthropologists have examined development events as secular rituals that help stage authority and shape political ideologies (Moore 1977) and particular visions of nationhood (Tennekoon 1988), but they do not analyze the performativity of development per se.

6. Butler (1999) builds on the work of Austin (1962), Victor Turner, and practice theorists such as Bourdieu (1977). Her idea of performativity has had a major impact

on recent feminist and anthropological studies of sex/gender systems and performance (see Morris 1995).

7. In marking a distinction between studies of performance and performativity, I do not wish to deny their conjunctures (see Morris 1995). The notion of performativity is presaged in some accounts of performance. Although Goffman (1973, 252–253) sometimes assumes a core human self that lies behind the performed and socialized self, he also posits that the self is a "performed character" and a "dramatic effect." Similarly Geertz (1973, 451) contends that "art forms generate and regenerate the very subjectivity they pretend only to display."

8. Avant-garde performances are an exception, because they blur the distinctions between onstage shows and external realities (see Beeman 1993).

9. The lens of performativity has been used in a similar way by scholars who study the workings of capitalism (Gibson-Graham 1996) and markets (Callon 1998; Miller 2002), for example.

10. I describe the reasons for these tensions in chapter 6.

11. *Avaas* refers to subsidized housing constructed for people living under the poverty line who qualify for a government-sponsored housing project, the Indira Avaas Yojana.

12. Stacy Pigg (1997) provides a provocative example of development's modular thinking. She shows how planners construct the generic category traditional birth attendant (TBA), assume that TBAs exist in every "traditional" society, and use this category to design programs in Nepal.

13. One way these hierarchies were elaborated was through aesthetic markers, showing that development is as much an aesthetic project as a politico-technical program for social change (Ebron 2002; Scott 1998). The actors' appearance, mannerisms, and speech style communicated relative scales of modernity. Take the women's clothing, for example. MS fieldworkers were attired in polyester saris commonly worn by women in the area, including their clients. However, these staffers draped their saris in an urban and modern way to mark their less "common" and more developed status relative to their rural clients. MS managers and female government administrators wore relatively expensive saris, also draped in a modern style, which conveyed their higher standing vis-à-vis other women.

14. Despite its current agenda of decentralized, participatory development and privileging of civil-society groups, the World Bank tends to work primarily with state actors (Fox and Brown 1998).

15. Elsewhere I discuss how the empowerment approach fits within the neoliberal framework promoted by international development institutions such as the World Bank and how this is reshaping the state and governance (Sharma 2006).

16. The appropriation of feminist and leftist languages and methodologies of empowerment by powerful institutions has also meant an increasing mainstreaming, bureaucratization, and professionalization of these strategies, as Seema Singh, an MS functionary, clearly expressed (see also Alvarez 1998; Nagar and Raju 2003).

17. Program monitoring also acknowledges the threat of subversion that plagues development. Why else would program functionaries and clients need to be constantly surveilled?

18. These questions have been central to anthropological methodologies since the discipline's turns towards self-reflexivity (see Gupta and Ferguson 1997), but are not always reflected in development practices.

19. I did not have access to the World Bank's report on this visit to the MS program. Evaluative reports raise a set of fascinating questions, which I do not take up in this chapter. For instance, how are messy observations translated into aestheticized evaluation reports? Through what criteria is the data analyzed and how is "truth" created? What techniques of accountability are at play? There is a growing literature on the modalities of report writing, auditing, and accountability in anthropology (e.g., see Maurer 2002; Stirrat 2000; Strathern 2000).

5. (Cross)Talking Development: State and Citizen Acts

1. *Scheduled castes* is the official term for Dalits, which has been in use since the colonial period.

2. Although my primary fieldwork area was in the Seelampur block (an administrative subdivision of the district of Begumpur), I took several trips to the adjoining Nizabad block as part of my institutional ethnography of the MS program.

3. In Hindi, the word *backward*, or *pichhde*, is often used when talking of people belonging to lower castes.

4. *Sarkar* can mean both the state and the government in Hindi.

5. The coding of development as material entitlements by rural subalterns was a very common practice in the area of eastern U.P. in which I conducted my fieldwork. Damyanti and other MS fieldworkers described to me the difficulties they often faced when initiating the program because MS, unlike other development programs, did not give people "things." They tried, at times unsuccessfully, to negotiate this obstacle by telling reluctant village women that resources, like money, did not last very long, but that the information they would get from MS would stay with them for a lifetime.

6. Sally Merry (2003, 344) discusses the use of rights talk by the battered women's movement in the United States, and argues that the ability to see oneself as a rights-bearing individual is facilitated by encounters with the legal system. I contend that in postcolonial contexts, development serves as a critical site for the adoption and articulation of a rights consciousness among subaltern subjects who may have little contact with the formal judicial state apparatus.

7. Coutin (2003) argues that state discourses in the United States define citizenship in a generic manner, as a public identity that is shared by individuals who are seen as legally identical and equal units.

8. Interestingly, some senior MS staff members also believed that their policy of paying village women chosen for leadership roles was faulty. They argued that giving people money to empower themselves was wrong and that such payments were creating tensions and hierarchies between clients.

9. In the United States minimum wage does not necessarily correspond to welfare. Low-paid workfare is seen as a neoliberal alternative to welfare. Thus, constructions of what counts, and does not count, as welfare are contextual and products of struggles won or lost.

10. The shift away from redistribution is a paradoxical move because the development resources that the state wishes to deny the dispossessed justify its very existence. Moreover, the Indian constitution guarantees its people the right to demand from the state entitlements such as education, water, and housing.

11. There has been a lengthy tradition of antiwelfarism and undeserving poor, coeval with the welfare state in the West. Those critiques are not directly relevant to the situation of the Indian postcolonial state, which, despite its socialist rhetoric, has never had large welfare bureaucracies like those in the West. The neoliberal re-spinning of these older critiques, however, is relevant in contemporary postcolonial contexts where officials use neoliberal rhetoric to explain the failure and curtailment of development programs.

12. Nancy Fraser (1989) discusses the two-tiered gendered nature of the welfare system in the United States, which implicitly differentiates between rights that are deserved and welfare assistance that is undeserved. Thus, masculine programs position their primarily male recipients as rights-bearers who earn their benefits, and feminine programs deem women and children as welfare beneficiaries who receive unearned charity handed out to them.

13. Curiously, however, Kumar also blended liberal welfare discourse with neoliberal antiwelfarism, in that he did position the state as a "good provider."

14. Dalit, a political and powerful term of identification, has replaced the earlier and more benign Harijan; Ajay, however, used the latter.

15. James Brow (1996) discusses how subaltern people in Sri Lanka differentiate between the bad state (local administrators) and the good state (urban-based, senior officials).

16. Some MS representatives also resorted to the same logic, as Damyanti did in Gauzpur. She positioned herself on the side of the informed and powerful harbingers of development. In fact she was one of the few MS employees who was criticized by some of her colleagues for forgetting her humble rural roots that made her a "person of the soil" [*mitti se judi hui*] and for pulling rank like bureaucrats [*adhikaaripan*].

17. Grassroots groups in India, such as the *Mazdoor Kisan Shakti Sangathan*, struggled (since the 1990s) against the unfair practice of withholding information by public authorities. Their efforts resulted in the passage of the Right to Information Act by the Indian government, which is a part of the fundamental rights under article 19(1)

of the Indian constitution. The act, which came into force in October 2005, details how citizens can obtain information (about laws, rights, accounts, and such) from state agencies and thus make administration more transparent and accountable (see http://www.humanrightsinitiative.org/programs/ai/rti/rti/what.htm; accessed August 2, 2006).

18. It seemed to me that subaltern subjects were at once accusing the familiar, local power players and the more abstract, faceless bureaucrats of corruption. Thus, on the one hand, the system itself may encourage dishonesty and, on the other, local elites exploit the system for their own selfish ends. This speaks of a more diffuse mistrust of governmental power. But many subaltern actors also spoke about a distant, abstract state as a more dependable caretaker. Even though the bureaucratic system was corrupt and corruptible, they were willing to put some trust in faceless senior officials who had the ability to make the system function as it was supposed to.

19. Unlike Gandhi, who saw no role for the state in social development, subaltern subjects define equitable and just development as the moral duty of the state.

6. Between Women? The Micropolitics of Community and Collectivism

1. The MS program in U.P. initially implemented the sakhi model (see Introduction). Accordingly, village women, who showed leadership potential, were designated sakhis and paid a nominal monthly stipend (Rs 200) for doing extra work such as calling village meetings and attending block-level meetings and training sessions. During 1998–1999, the sakhi model was being replaced by the sangha model because of the tensions that paid sakhi work was creating among MS collectives.

2. Most MS participants tended to be older women who had domestic female help (either daughters or daughters-in-law) and thus had time to participate in MS activities.

3. These women participated in the *chauthai* form of sharecropping, where they provided the labor and upper-caste landowners provided land and other inputs; women received 25 percent of the produce as payment for their labor.

4. Ration cards are government-issued documents that list basic household information on each family—this includes the total number of members in a household, their ages, and household income. These cards entitle families to subsidized monthly rations of staples, including sugar and kerosene oil. Those families living "below the poverty line" are issued special ration cards, which entitle them to 7 kilograms of wheat and 3 kilograms of rice per month in addition to sugar and oil (which are also received by those with "regular" ration cards).

5. Development, as Stacy Pigg (1997) has argued, is already a part of the social imaginary of village residents, regardless of the nature and success of their encounters with specific programs.

6. The village women I interacted with worked as full-time peasants on upper-caste–owned land. Yet they did not consider their labor real work. They equated real

work with a semipermanent or permanent *sarkari naukri* [government job] that paid steady cash wages.

7. The word *poonchwali* literally means "those with tails." Kevla explained that this term was seen as an insult by women because it equated them with cows—passive, inferior in terms of their mental and strategic capacities, and generally harmless.

8. Before the Indian government passed the seventy-third and seventy-fourth amendments to the constitution in mid-1990s, women had little representation in village councils. These two amendments ensure that one-third of the membership of village- and block-level elected councils is reserved for women. The purpose of these amendments was to increase women's political representation and participation. Many village women told me that they liked having women council members because women could better understand women's issues. Previously, they told me, men used to speak on women's behalf and decide on women-related matters in these meetings.

9. Spaces, in general, and public places, in particular, are not ungendered, as feminist geographers have shown (Massey 1994); nor are they equally accessible by differently positioned subjects. The Farmers' Assistance Center in Seelampur was a supposed gender-nonspecific public place, yet when Nimani's women tried to access it, their act was seen as transgressive and they were told to stay at home. Not only were farmers implicitly defined as men, the public Center was also marked a masculinized space where women ("nonfarmers") did not belong. Women, therefore, were reinstated in the privatized domestic spaces where they (naturally) belonged.

10. Those against this strategy argued that MS needed to address gender as a social relation and not work through women-only groups. They also stated that this was not simply a problem with MS, but a symptom of a more widespread confusion between women and gender within development. Although various agencies, including international development organizations, state bodies, and NGOs were talking the gender talk (which was in keeping with the transition from women to gender), they continued to implement "women's" programs under the "gender" rubric.

11. A few nonparticipants told me that they had chosen not to participate in MS because, lacking in female domestic help, they did not have any free time to devote to MS.

12. Some MS staff members were uncomfortable with the importance attached to the grant and peer-group savings/lending component of MS. Started in the mid-1990s, this component was supposed to be one among several MS activities; it was, however, fast becoming the primary activity among MS groups, taking time and effort away from other forms of empowerment.

13. The sakhi model is no longer in use as MS now works with the sangha model in its new program areas, to avoid the hierarchies that were created under the former model.

14. This honorarium, as many sakhis complained, was a woefully inadequate compensation for their lost agricultural labor and wages.

15. These tensions were revealed to me during a visit to Nilupur village. When I asked local participants about the goals of the MS program, I was met with silence. The participants looked over to their sakhi with anticipation, thinking that she would know how to respond; she, however, remained quiet. One MS woman looked me in the eye and remarked sarcastically, "This sakhi gets paid to forget!" This was a common refrain I heard in the Seelampur area.

16. Other members denied this charge and explained that Heeravati's loan requests were not approved because she did not attend meetings regularly, fought with the other members, and was thus not considered a "good" and "worthy" program participant.

17. In my focus on development as a ground for the production and negotiation of identities, I borrow from different bodies of anthropological and feminist work that examine other sites where identities and communities are produced and negotiated; for example, popular culture (Hall 1986; Hall 1989; Hall 1997; Mankekar 1993), the law (Collier, Maurer, and Suarez-Navaz 1995), and state policy (Butalia 1993; Menon and Bhasin 1993; Pathak and Sunder Rajan 1992; Sunder Rajan 2003).

18. For an excellent discussion of the centrality of statistics and enumeration to governmentality, see Hacking (1982).

19. Urvashi Butalia (1993) and Tanika Sarkar (1991 and 1995) discuss the problematic nature of women's agency in the context of the partition of India and women's participation in right-wing Hindu nationalist movements respectively (see also Sarkar and Butalia 1995). Nivedita Menon (2004) analyzes the dilemmas of women's agency and feminist activism in the context of legal reform, especially concerning female feticide and violence (rape, sexual assault, and harassment).

Conclusion

1. Written and directed by Ashutosh Gowariker, whose earlier production, *Lagaan*, was nominated for the Oscars in 2002 (in the best non-English-language films category), *Swades* was released in 2004. It fit both the mainstream and art genres of Indian films; it did not, however, do well commercially.

2. See http://nrega.nic.in/; accessed on August 15, 2006.

3. See Jandhyala (2001) for a critical discussion of these debates in India.

4. Writing about civil society, governance, and political participation in the context of e-governance and public-service reform in Britain, John Clarke (n.d., 13) uses the term "*demotic*, rather than democratic, modes of governance" to reference those political strategies that use populist and vernacular languages to speak "in the name (and sometimes voice) of 'ordinary people.'"

5. Subaltern talk and political society struggles powerfully instantiate how citizenship is "the symbolic circuit of the mobilizing of subalternity into hegemony" (Spivak 1999, 309).

Bibliography

Abrams, Philip. 1988. "Notes on the Difficulty of Studying the State." *Journal of Historical Sociology* 1, no. 1: 58–89.

Agarwal, Bina. 1988. *Structures of Patriarchy: State, Community and Household in Modernising Asia*. New Delhi: Kali for Women.

_____. 1994. *A Field of One's Own: Gender and Land Rights in South Asia*. Cambridge: Cambridge University Press.

Agnihotri, Indu, and Vina Mazumdar. 1995. "Changing Terms of Political Discourse: Women's Movement in India, 1970s–1990s." *Economic and Political Weekly* 30, no. 29: 1869–78.

Agrawal, Arun. 2001. "State Formation in Community Spaces? Decentralization of Control over Forests in the Kumaon Himalaya, India." *Journal of Asian Studies* 60, no. 1: 9–40.

Alavi, Hamza. 1972. "The State in Post-colonial Societies: Pakistan and Bangladesh." *New Left Review* I/74: 59–81.

Alexander, Jacqui M. 1997. "Erotic Autonomy as a Politics of Decolonization: An Anatomy of Feminist and State Practice in the Bahamas Tourist Economy." In *Feminist Genealogies, Colonial Legacies, Democratic Futures*, edited by M. Jacqui Alexander and Chandra T. Mohanty, 63–100. New York: Routledge.

Althusser, Louis. 1971. "Ideology and Ideological State Apparatuses (Notes towards an Investigation)." In *Lenin and Philosophy and Other Essays*, 127–86. New York: Monthly Review Press.

Alvarez, Sonia. 1998. "Latin American Feminisms 'Go Global': Trends of the 1990s and Challenges for the New Millennium." In *Cultures of Politics, Politics of Cultures: Re-visioning Latin American Social Movements*, edited by Sonia E. Alvarez, Evelina Dagnino, and Arturo Escobar, 293–324. Boulder: Westview Press.

Amin, Shahid. 1984. "Gandhi as Mahatma: Gorakhpur District, Eastern UP 1921–2." In *Subaltern Studies: Writings on South Asian History and Society, vol. III*, edited by Ranajit Guha, 1–61. New Delhi: Oxford University Press.

Anagnost, Ann. 1995. "A Surfeit of Bodies: Population and the Rationality of the State in Post-Mao China." In *Conceiving the New World Order: The Global Politics of Reproduction*, edited by Faye D. Ginsburg and Rayna Rapp, 22–41. Berkeley: University of California Press.

Appadurai, Arjun. 1993. "Number in the Colonial Imagination." In *Orientalism and the Postcolonial Predicament: Perspectives on South Asia*, edited by Carol A. Breckenridge and Peter van der Veer, 314–39. Philadelphia: University of Pennsylvania Press.

Arce, Alberto, and Norman Long. 1993. "Bridging Two Worlds: An Ethnography of Bureaucrat–Peasant Relations in Western Mexico." In *An Anthropological Critique of Development: The Growth of Ignorance*, edited by Mark Hobart, 179–208. New York: Routledge.

Austin, J. L. 1962. *How to Do Things with Words*. Edited by J. O. Urmson. New York: Oxford University Press.

Baden, Sally, and Anne Marie Goetz. 1997. "Who Needs [Sex] When You Can Have [Gender]? Conflicting Discourses on Gender at Beijing." In *Women, International Development, and Politics: The Bureaucratic Mire*, edited by Kathleen Staudt, 37–58. Philadelphia: Temple University Press.

Bardhan, Kalpana, and Stephan Klasen. 1999. "UNDP's Gender-Related Indices: A Critical Review." *World Development* 27, no. 6: 985–1010.

Bardhan, Pranab. 1984. *The Political Economy of Development in India*. Oxford: Basil Blackwell.

Barry, Andrew, Thomas Osborne, and Nikolas Rose. 1996. "Introduction." In *Foucault and Political Reason: Liberalism, Neo-Liberalism, and Rationalities of Government*, edited by Andrew Barry, Thomas Osborne, and Nikolas Rose, 1–18. Chicago: University of Chicago Press.

Basch, Linda, Nina Glick Schiller, and Cristina Szanton Blanc, eds. 1994. *Nations Unbound: Transnational Projects, Postcolonial Predicaments, and Deterritorialized Nation-States*. Langhorne: Gordon and Breach.

Basu, Amrita. 1995. *The Challenge of Local Feminisms: Women's Movements in Global Perspective*. Boulder: Westview Press.

Batliwala, Srilatha. 1994. *Women's Empowerment in South Asia: Concepts and Practices*. New Delhi: FAO (FFHC/AD) and ASPBAE.

———. 1997. "What Is Female Empowerment?" Paper presented at a seminar organized by the Swedish Association for Sexual Education and the Department of Demography, Stockholm University. Stockholm, Sweden, April 25.

Beeman, William. 1993. "The Anthropology of Theater and Spectacle." *Annual Review of Anthropology* 22: 369–93.

Beneria, Lourdes, and Gita Sen. 1982. "Class and Gender Inequalities and Women's Role in Economic Development: Theoretical and Practical Implications." *Feminist Studies* 8, no. 1: 157–76.

Bergeron, Suzanne. 2003. "Challenging the World Bank's Narrative of Inclusion." In *World Bank Literature*, edited by Amitava Kumar, 157–71. Minneapolis: University of Minnesota Press.

Bhabha, Homi. 1997. "Of Mimicry and Man: The Ambivalence of Colonial Discourse." In *Tensions of Empire: Colonial Cultures in a Bourgeois World*, edited by Frederick Cooper and Ann L. Stoler, 152–60. Berkeley: University of California Press.

Bhattacharjee, Ananya. 1997. "The Public/Private Mirage: Mapping Homes and Undomesticating Violence Work in the South Asian Immigrant Community." In *Feminist Genealogies, Colonial Legacies, Democratic Futures*, edited by Jacqui M. Alexander and Chandra T. Mohanty, 308–29. New York: Routledge.

Bose, Sugata. 1997. "Instruments and Idioms of Colonial and National Development: India's Historical Experience in Comparative Perspective." In *International Development and the Social Sciences: Essays on the History and Politics of Knowledge*, edited by Frederick Cooper and Randall Packard, 45–63. Berkeley: University of California Press.

Bose, Sugata, and Ayesha Jalal. 1998. *Modern South Asia: History, Culture, Political Economy*. New York: Routledge.

Boserup, Ester. 1970. *Women's Role in Economic Development*. New York: St. Martin Press.

Bourdieu, Pierre. 1977. *Outline of a Theory of Practice*. Translated by Richard Nice. Cambridge: Cambridge University Press.

_____. 1999. "Rethinking the State: Genesis and Structure of the Bureaucratic Field." In *State/Culture: State Formation after the Cultural Turn*, edited by George Steinmetz, 53–75. Ithaca: Cornell University Press.

Brass, Paul R. 1990. *The Politics of India since Independence*. Cambridge: Cambridge University Press.

Brow, James. 1996. *Demons and Development: The Struggle for Community in a Sri Lankan Village*. Tucson: University of Arizona Press.

Brown, Wendy. 1995. "Finding the Man in the State." In *States of Inquiry: Power and Freedom in Late Modernity*, 166–96. Princeton: Princeton University Press.

Bunch, Charlotte. 1990. "Women's Rights as Human Rights: Toward a Re-vision of Human Rights." *Human Rights Quarterly* 12, no. 4: 486–98.

Bunch, Charlotte, and Roxanna Carrillo. 1990. "Feminist Perspectives on Women in Development." In *Persistent Inequalities: Women and World Development*, edited by Irene Tinker, 70–82. New York: Oxford University Press.

Burchell, Graham. 1996. "Liberal Government and the Techniques of the Self." In *Foucault and Political Reason: Liberalism, Neo-liberalism and Rationalities of Government*, edited by Andrew Barry, Thomas Osborne, and Nikolas Rose, 19–36. Chicago: The University of Chicago Press.

Burchell, Graham, Colin Gordon, and Peter Miller, eds. 1991. *The Foucault Effect: Studies in Governmentality (With Two Lectures by and an Interview with Michel Foucault)*. Chicago: The University of Chicago Press.

Butalia, Urvashi. 1993. "Community, State and Gender: On Women's Agency during Partition." *Economic and Political Weekly* 28, no. 17: WS12–24.

_____. 1995. "Muslims and Hindus, Men and Women: Communal Stereotypes and the Partition of India." In *Women and the Hindu Right: A Collection of Essays*, edited by Tanika Sarkar and Urvashi Butalia, 58–81. New Delhi: Kali for Women.

Butler, Judith. 1994. "Gender as Performance: An Interview with Judith Butler," interviewed by Peter Osborne and Lynne Segal. *Radical Philosophy* 67: 32–9.

———. 1999. *Gender Trouble: Feminism and the Subversion of Identity*. New York: Routledge.

Buvinic, Mayra, Catherine Gwin, and Lisa Bates. 1996. *Investing in Women: Progress and Prospects for the World Bank*. Baltimore: The Johns Hopkins University Press.

Callon, Michel, ed. 1998. *The Laws of the Markets*. Oxford: Blackwell Publishers.

Cardoso, Fernando Henrique, and Enzo Faletto. 1979. *Dependency and Development in Latin America*. Berkeley: University of California Press.

Chakrabarty, Dipesh. 2000. *Provincializing Europe: Postcolonial Thought and Historical Difference*. Princeton: Princeton University Press.

Charlton, Sue Ellen M., Jana Everett, and Kathleen Staudt. 1989. *Women, the State, and Development*. Albany: State University of New York Press.

Chatterjee, Partha. 1986a. "The Moment of Manoeuvre: Gandhi and the Critique of Civil Society." In *Nationalist Thought and the Colonial World: A Derivative Discourse*, 85–130. Minneapolis: University of Minnesota Press.

———. 1986b. *Nationalist Thought and the Colonial World: A Derivative Discourse*. Minneapolis: University of Minnesota Press.

———. 1993. *The Nation and Its Fragments: Colonial and Postcolonial Histories*. Princeton: Princeton University Press.

———. 1998. "Development Planning and the Indian State." In *State and Politics in India*, edited by Partha Chatterjee, 271–97. Delhi: Oxford University Press.

———. 2004. *The Politics of the Governed: Reflections on Popular Politics in Most of the World*. New York: Columbia University Press.

Chaudhuri, Maitrayee. 1996. "Citizens, Workers and Emblems of Culture: An Analysis of the First Plan Document on Women." In *Social Reform, Sexuality and the State*, edited by Patricia Uberoi, 211–35. New Delhi: Sage Publications.

Chhachhi, Amrita. 1991. "Forced Identities: The State, Communalism, Fundamentalism and Women in India." In *Women, Islam and the State*, edited by Deniz Kandiyoti, 144–75. London: Macmillan.

Clark, Dana, Jonathan Fox, and Kay Treakle, eds. 2003. *Demanding Accountability: Civil-Society Claims and the World Bank Inspection Panel*. Lanham: Rowman and Littlefield Publishers, Inc.

Clarke, John. 2004. *Changing Welfare, Changing States: New Directions in Social Policy*. London: Sage Publications.

———. 2007. "Living with/in and against Neo-liberalism: Pursuing Ambivalence?" Paper presented at Transnational Governmentality in South East Europe Workshop, Translating Neo-liberalism on the Sovereign Frontier: Concepts, Cases, Contestations, Rabac, Istria, Croatia, June 1–3.

———. Governance Puzzles. n.d.

Clinton, Bill. 2006. "How We Ended Welfare, Together." *The New York Times*, August 22, A19.

Cohn, Bernard S. 1985. "The Command of Language and the Language of Command." In *Subaltern Studies IV: Writings on South Asian History and Society*, edited by Ranajit Guha, 276–329. Delhi: Oxford University Press.

_____. 1987. "The Census, Social Structure and Objectification in South Asia." In *An Anthropologist among the Historians and Other Essays*, 224–54. Delhi: Oxford University Press.

_____. 1996. *Colonialism and Its Forms of Knowledge: The British in India*. Princeton: Princeton University Press.

Collier, Jane F., Bill Maurer, and Liliana Suarez-Navaz. 1995. "Sanctioned Identities: Legal Constructions of 'Modern' Personhood." *Identities* 2, no. 1: 1–27.

Collier, Stephen J., and Aihwa Ong. 2005. "Global Assemblages, Anthropological Problems." *In Global Assemblages: Technology, Politics, and Ethics as Anthropological Problems*, edited by Aihwa Ong and Stephen J. Collier, 3–21. Malden: Blackwell Publishing.

Cooper, Frederick, and Randall Packard. 1997. "Introduction." In *International Development and the Social Sciences: Essays on the History and Politics of Knowledge*, edited by Frederick Cooper and Randall Packard, 1–41. Berkeley: University of California Press.

Corbridge, Stuart. 2007. "The (Im)Possibility of Development Studies." *Economy and Society* 36, no. 2: 179–211.

Corbridge, Stuart, and John Harriss. 2000. *Reinventing India: Liberalization, Hindu Nationalism and Popular Democracy*. Malden: Blackwell Publishing.

Coronil, Fernando. 1997. *The Magical State: Nature, Money, and Modernity in Venezuela*. Chicago: University of Chicago Press.

Corrigan, Philip, and Derek Sayer. 1985. *The Great Arch: English State Formation as Cultural Revolution*. Oxford: Basil Blackwell Ltd.

Coutin, Susan Bibler. 2003. "Cultural Logics of Belonging and Movement: Transnationalism, Naturalization, and U.S. Immigration Politics." *American Ethnologist* 30, no. 4: 508–26.

Cowen, Michael, and Robert Shenton. 1995. "The Invention of Development." In *Power of Development*, edited by Jonathan Crush, 27–43. London: Routledge.

Crenshaw, Kimberle. 1991. "Mapping the Margins: Intersectionality, Identity Politics, and Violence against Women of Color." *Stanford Law Review* 43, no. 6: 1241–99.

Cruikshank, Barbara. 1996. "Revolutions Within: Self-Government and Self-Esteem." In *Foucault and Political Reason: Liberalism, Neo-liberalism, and Rationalities of Government*, edited by Andrew Barry, Thomas Osborne, and Nikolas Rose, 231–52. Chicago: University of Chicago Press.

_____. 1999. *The Will to Empower: Democratic Citizens and Other Subjects*. Ithaca: Cornell University Press.

Crush, Jonathan. 1995. *Power of Development*. London: Routledge.

Dagnino, Evelina. 2005. "'We have all the rights, but . . .' Contesting Concepts of Citizenship in Brazil." In *Inclusive Citizenship: Meanings and Expressions*, edited by Naila Kabeer, 149–63. New York: Zed Press.

Das, Veena. 1976. "Indian Women: Work, Power, and Status." In *Indian Women: From Purdah to Modernity*, edited by B. R. Nanda, 129–45. New Delhi: Vikas Publishing House Pvt. Ltd.

———. 1995. "Communities as Political Actors: The Question of Cultural Rights." In *Critical Events: An Anthropological Perspective on Contemporary India*, 84–117. Delhi: Oxford University Press.

Das, Veena, and Deborah Poole, eds. 2004. *Anthropology in the Margins of the State*. School of American Research Advanced Seminar Series, ed. Richard M. Leventhal. Santa Fe: School of American Research Press.

de Alwis, Malathi. 1995. "Gender, Politics and the 'Respectable Lady.'" In *Unmaking the Nation: The Politics of Identity and History in Modern Sri Lanka*, edited by Pradeep Jeganathan and Qadri Ismail, 137–57. Colombo: Social Scientists' Association.

Dean, Mitchell. 1999. *Governmentality: Power and Rule in Modern Society*. London: Sage Publications.

———. 2001. "'Demonic Societies': Liberalism, Biopolitics, and Sovereignty." In *States of Imagination: Ethnographic Explorations of the Postcolonial State*, edited by Thomas B. Hansen and Finn Stepputat, 41–64. Durham: Duke University Press.

de Certeau, Michel. 1988. *The Practice of Everyday Life*. Translated by S. Rendall. Berkeley: University of California Press.

Deleuze, Gilles, and Félix Guattari. 1987. *A Thousand Plateaus: Capitalism and Schizophrenia*. Translated by Brian Massumi. Minneapolis: University of Minnesota Press.

Diamond, Elin. 1987. "Mimesis, Mimicry, and the 'True-Real.'" *Modern Drama* 32, no. 1: 58–72.

Ebron, Paulla A. 2002. *Performing Africa*. Princeton: Princeton University Press.

Elson, Diane. 1988. "Market Socialism or Socialization of the Market?" *New Left Review* 172: 3–44.

———. 1992. "From Survival Strategies to Transformation Strategies." In *Unequal Burden: Economic Crises, Persistent Poverty, and Women's Work*, edited by Lourdes Beneria and Shelley Feldman, 26–48. Boulder: Westview Press.

Elyachar, Julia. 2002. "Empowerment Money: The World Bank, Non-Governmental Organizations, and the Value of Culture in Egypt." *Public Culture* 14, no. 3: 493–513.

———. 2005. *Markets of Dispossession: NGOs, Economic Development, and the State in Cairo*. Durham: Duke University Press.

Escobar, Arturo. 1995. *Encountering Development: The Making and Unmaking of the Third World*. Princeton: Princeton University Press.

Esteva, Gustavo. 1992. "Development." In *The Development Dictionary: A Guide to Knowledge as Power*, edited by Wolfgang Sachs, 6–25. Atlantic Highlands, New Jersey: Zed Books Ltd.

Evans, Peter B., Dietrich Rueschemeyer, and Theda Skocpol, eds. 1985. *Bringing the State Back In*. Cambridge: Cambridge University Press.

Everett, Jana. 1989. "Incorporation versus Conflict: Lower Class Women, Collective Action, and the State in India." In *Women, the State, and Development*, edited by Sue Ellen M. Charlton, Jana Everett, and Kathleen Staudt, 152–76. Albany: The State University of New York Press.

Ferguson, James. 1994. *The Anti-Politics Machine: "Development," Depoliticization, and Bureaucratic Power in Lesotho*. Minneapolis: University of Minnesota Press.

_____. 2002a. "Discussant Comments." Panel Session "Staging Development." American Anthropological Association Meetings, New Orleans, November 24.

_____. 2002b. "Global Disconnect: Abjection and the Aftermath of Modernism." In *The Anthropology of Globalization: A Reader*, edited by Jonathan X. Inda and Renato Rosaldo, 136–53. Malden: Blackwell Publishing.

Ferguson, James, and Akhil Gupta. 2002. "Spatializing States: Toward an Ethnography of Neoliberal Governmentality." *American Ethnologist* 29, no. 4: 981–1002.

Ferguson, Kathy E. 1984. *The Feminist Case against Bureaucracy*. Philadelphia: Temple University Press.

Finnemore, Martha. 1997. "Redefining Development at the World Bank." In *International Development and the Social Sciences: Essays on the History and Politics of Knowledge*, edited by Frederick Cooper and Randall Packard, 203–227. Berkeley: University of California Press.

Fisher, William F. 1997. "Doing Good? The Politics and Antipolitics of NGO Practices." *Annual Review of Anthropology* 26: 439–64.

Foucault, Michel. 1980. *Power/Knowledge: Selected Interviews and Other Writings (1972–1977)*, edited by Colin Gordon. Translated by Colin Gordon, Leo Marshall, John Mepham, and Kate Soper. New York: Pantheon Books.

_____. 1982. "On the Genealogy of Ethics: An Overview of Work in Progress." In *Michel Foucault: Beyond Structuralism and Hermeneutics*, edited by Hubert L. Dreyfus and Paul Rabinow, 229–52. Chicago: University of Chicago Press.

_____. 1990. *The History of Sexuality: An Introduction*. Translated by Robert Hurley. New York: Vintage Books.

_____. 1991. "Governmentality." In *The Foucault Effect: Studies in Governmentality*, edited by Graham Burchell, Colin Gordon, and Peter Miller, 87–104. Chicago: University of Chicago Press.

_____. 1995. *Discipline and Punish: The Birth of the Prison*. Translated by Alan Sheridan. New York: Vintage Books.

Fox, Jonathan A., and L. David Brown. 1998. "Introduction." In *The Struggle for Accountability: The World Bank, NGOs, and Grassroots Movements*, edited by Jonathan A. Fox and L. David Brown, 1–47. Cambridge: MIT Press.

Fox, Richard G. 1989. *Gandhian Utopia: Experiments with Culture.* Boston: Beacon Press.

Frank, Andre Gunder. 1969. *Capitalism and Underdevelopment in Latin America: Historical Studies of Chile and Brazil.* New York: Monthly Review Press.

Frankenberg, Ruth, and Lata Mani. 1993. "Crosscurrents, Crosstalk: Race, 'Postcoloniality' and the Politics of Location." *Cultural Studies* 7, no. 2: 292–310.

Fraser, Nancy. 1989. "Women, Welfare, and the Politics of Need Interpretation." In *Unruly Practices: Power, Discourse, and Gender in Contemporary Social Theory,* 144–60. Minneapolis: University of Minnesota Press.

Freire, Paulo. 1970. *Pedagogy of the Oppressed.* Translated by Myra Bergman Ramos. London: Penguin Books.

Fuller, C. J., and Veronique Benei, eds. 2000. *The Everyday State and Society in Modern India.* New Delhi: Social Science Press.

Gal, Susan, and Gail Kligman. 2000. *The Politics of Gender after Socialism: A Comparative-Historical Essay.* Princeton: Princeton University Press.

Gandhi, M. K. 1997. *Hind Swaraj and Other Writings.* Edited by Anthony J. Parel. Cambridge: Cambridge University Press.

Gandhi, Nandita, and Nandita Shah. 1992. *The Issues at Stake: Theory and Practice in the Contemporary Women's Movement in India.* New Delhi: Kali for Women.

Garain, Swapan. 1994. "Government–NGO Interface in India: An Overview." *Indian Journal of Social Work* 55, no. 3: 337–46.

Gardner, Katy, and David Lewis. 1996. *Anthropology, Development and the Post-Modern Challenge.* Chicago: Pluto Press.

Geertz, Clifford. 1973. "Deep Play: Notes on a Balinese Cockfight." In *The Interpretation of Cultures,* 412–53. New York: Basic Books.

———. 1980. *Negara: The Theatre State in Nineteenth-Century Bali.* Princeton: Princeton.

Gibson-Graham, J. K. 1996. *The End of Capitalism (As We Knew It): A Feminist Critique of Political Economy.* Malden: Blackwell Publishing.

Gilroy, Paul. 1993. *Small Acts: Thoughts on the Politics of Black Cultures.* London: Serpent's Tail.

Global Exchange. 2005. "Reality Tours." Electronic document. www.globalexchange.org/tours/faq.html (accessed on September 13, 2005).

Gluckman, Max. 1958. "Analysis of a Social Situation in Modern Zululand." Rhodes-Livingstone Paper 28. Manchester: Manchester University Press.

Goffman, Erving. 1973. *The Presentation of Self in Everyday Life.* Woodstock: The Overlook Press.

Goode, Judith. 2002. "From New Deal to Bad Deal: Racial and Political Implications of U.S. Welfare Reform." In *Western Welfare in Decline: Globalization and Women's Poverty,* edited by Catherine Kingfisher, 65–89. Philadelphia: University of Pennsylvania Press.

Gordon, Linda, ed. 1990. *Women, the State, and Welfare*. Madison: University of Wisconsin Press.

Government of India. 1974. *Towards Equality: Report of the Committee on the Status of Women in India*. Delhi: Department of Social Welfare.

_____. 1988. *Mahila Samakhya: Program for Education for Women's Equality*. New Delhi: Ministry of Human Resource Development: Department of Education.

_____. 1991. *Mahila Samakhya—Education for Women's Equality*. New Delhi: Ministry of Human Resource Development, Department of Education.

_____. 1997. *Mahila Samakhya (Education for Women's Equality): Ninth Plan Document 1997–2002*. New Delhi: Ministry of Human Resource Development, Department of Education.

Gramsci, Antonio. 1971. *Selections from the Prison Notebooks*. Edited and translated by Quintin Hoare and Geoffrey Nowell Smith. New York: International Publishers.

Grewal, Inderpal. 2005. *Transnational America: Feminisms, Diasporas, Neoliberalisms*. Durham: Duke University Press.

Grillo, R. D. 1997. "Discourses of Development: The View from Anthropology." In *Discourses of Development: Anthropological Perspectives*, edited by R. D. Grillo and R. L. Stirrat, 1–33. Oxford: Berg.

Grillo, R. D., and R. L. Stirrat, eds. 1997. *Discourses of Development: Anthropological Perspectives*. Oxford: Berg.

Guha, Ranajit. 1983. *Elementary Aspects of Peasant Insurgency in Colonial India*. Delhi: Oxford University Press.

Gupta, Akhil. 1995. "Blurred Boundaries: The Discourse of Corruption, the Culture of Politics, and the Imagined State." *American Ethnologist* 22, no. 2: 375–402.

_____. 1997. "Agrarian Populism in the Development of a Modern Nation (India)." In *International Development and the Social Sciences: Essays on the History and Politics of Knowledge*, edited by Frederick Cooper and Randall Packard, 320–44. Berkeley: University of California Press.

_____. 1998. *Postcolonial Developments: Agriculture in the Making of Modern India*. Durham: Duke University Press.

_____. 2001. "Governing Population: The Integrated Child Development Services Program in India." In *States of Imagination: Ethnographic Explorations of the Postcolonial State*, edited by Thomas B. Hansen and Finn Stepputat, 65–96. Durham: Duke University Press.

Gupta, Akhil, and James Ferguson. 1997. "Discipline and Practice: 'The Field' as Site, Method, and Location in Anthropology." In *Anthropological Locations: Boundaries and Grounds of a Field Science*, edited by Akhil Gupta and James Ferguson, 1–46. Berkeley: University of California Press.

Gupta, Akhil, and Aradhana Sharma. 2006. "Globalization and Postcolonial States." *Current Anthropology* 47, no. 2: 277–307.

Hacking, Ian. 1982. "Biopower and the Avalanche of Printed Numbers." *Humanities in Society* 5, no. 3 & 4: 279–95.

Hall, Stuart. 1986. "Popular Culture and the State." In *Popular Culture and Social Relations*, edited by Tony Bennett, Colin Mercer, and Janet Woollacott, 22–49. Milton Keynes: Open University Press.

______. 1989. "Cultural Identity and Cinematic Representation." *Framework* 36: 68–81.

______. 1997. "Old and New Identities, Old and New Ethnicities." In *Culture, Globalization and the World-System: Contemporary Conditions for the Representation of Identity*, edited by Anthony D. King, 41–68. Minneapolis: University of Minnesota Press.

Hall, Stuart, and David Held. 1990. "Citizens and Citizenship." In *New Times: The Changing Face of Politics in the 1990s*, edited by Stuart Hall and Martin Jacques, 173–88. New York: Verso.

Hansen, Thomas Blom, and Finn Stepputat, eds. 2001. *States of Imagination: Ethnographic Explorations of the Postcolonial State*. Durham: Duke University Press.

Harriss, John. 2002. *Depoliticizing Development: The World Bank and Social Capital*. London: Anthem Press.

Harvey, David. 2005. *A Brief History of Neoliberalism*. Oxford: Oxford University Press.

Haynes, Douglas, and Gyan Prakash. 1991. "Introduction: The Entanglement of Power and Resistance." In *Contesting Power: Resistance and Everyday Social Relations in South Asia*, edited by Douglas Haynes and Gyan Prakash, 1–22. Oxford: Oxford University Press.

Herzfeld, Michael. 1992. *The Social Production of Indifference: Exploring the Symbolic Roots of Western Bureaucracy*. Chicago: The University of Chicago Press.

Hindess, Barry. 2004. "Liberalism—What's in a Name?" In *Global Governmentality: Governing International Spaces*, edited by Wendy Larner and William Walters, 23–39. London: Routledge.

Hirshman, Mitu. 1995. "Women and Development: A Critique." In *Feminism/Postmodernism/Development*, edited by Marianne H. Marchand and Jane L. Parpart, 42–55. New York: Routledge.

hooks, bell. 1984. *Feminist Theory: From Margin to Center*. Boston: South End Press.

Horwitz, Simca. 2003. *Empowerment on the Agenda: Women and the World Bank's Changing Development Discourse*. Senior Essay. Wesleyan University, CT.

Human Rights Watch. 1999. *Broken People: Caste Violence Against India's "Untouchables."* New York: Human Rights Watch.

Jaggar, Alison M. 1983. *Feminist Politics and Human Nature*. Totowa: Rowman & Allanheld.

Jalal, Ayesha. 1995. *Democracy and Authoritarianism in South Asia: A Comparative and Historical Perspective*. Cambridge: Cambridge University Press.

Jandhyala, Kameshwari. 2001. "State Initiatives: Towards Equality: A Symposium on Women, Feminisms and Women's Movements." *Seminar* 505: 31–35.

———. *Empowering Education: The Mahila Samakhya Experience*, n.d. http://unesdoc.unesco.org/images/0014/001467/146780e.pdf (accessed on August 2, 2005).

Jaquette, Jane S. 1990. "Gender and Justice in Economic Development." In *Persistent Inequalities: Women and World Development*, edited by Irene Tinker 54–69. New York: Oxford University Press.

John, Mary E. 1996. "Gender and Development in India, 1970–1990s: Some Reflections on the Constitutive Role of Contexts." *Economic and Political Weekly* 31, no. 47: 3071–77.

———. 1999. "Gender, Development, and the Women's Movement: Problems for a History of the Present." In *Signposts: Gender Issues in Post-Independence India*, edited by Rajeswari Sunder Rajan. New Delhi: Kali for Women.

Joseph, Gilbert M., and Daniel Nugent, eds. 1994. *Everyday Forms of State Formation: Revolution and the Negotiation of Rule in Modern Mexico*. Durham: Duke University Press.

Kabeer, Naila. 1994. *Reversed Realities: Gender Hierarchies in Development Thought*. New York: Verso.

———. 2001. "Resources, Agency, Achievements: Reflections on the Measurement of Women's Empowerment." In *Discussing Women's Empowerment: Theory and Practice*, SIDA Studies No. 3, edited by Anne Sisask, 17–57. Stockholm: SIDA.

Kabeer, Naila, and Ramya Subrahmanian, eds. 1999. *Institutions, Relations and Outcomes: A Framework and Case Studies for Gender-aware Planning*. New Delhi: Kali for Women.

Kahn, Joseph. 2000. "International Lenders' New Image: A Human Face." *The New York Times*, September 26, A5.

Kamat, Sangeeta. 2002. *Development Hegemony: NGOs and the State in India*. New Delhi: Oxford University Press.

Kardam, Nuket. 1991. *Bringing Women In: Women's Issues in International Development Programs*. Boulder: Lynne Reinner Publishers.

———. 1997. "The Adaptability of International Development Agencies: The Response of the World Bank to Women in Development." In *Women, International Development, and Politics: The Bureaucratic Mire*, edited by Kathleen Staudt, 136–50. Philadelphia: Temple University Press.

Kaviraj, Sudipta. *Democracy and Development in India*. n.d.

Keck, Margaret E., and Kathryn Sikkink. 1998. *Activists Beyond Borders: Advocacy Networks in International Politics*. Ithaca: Cornell University Press.

Khan, Azeez M. 1997. *Shaping Policy: Do NGOs Matter? Lessons from India*. New Delhi: Society for Participatory Research in Asia.

Khilnani, Sunil. 1999. *The Idea of India*. New York: Farrar, Straus and Giroux.

Klein, Naomi. 2003. "Now Bush Wants to Buy the Complicity of Aid Workers." *The Guardian*, June 23 http://www.guardian.co.uk/society/2003/jun/23/disasterresponse.internationalaidanddevelopment (accessed on October 9, 2004).

Kohli, Atul. 1990. *Democracy and Discontent: India's Growing Crisis of Governability*. Cambridge: Cambridge University Press.

Kondo, Dorinne. 1997. *About Face: Performing Race in Fashion and Theater*. New York: Routledge.

Kothari, Rajni. 1986. "NGOs, the State and World Capitalism." *Economic and Political Weekly* 21: 2177–82.

Krishnaraj, Maithreyi. 1988. *Women and Development: The Indian Experience*. Pune, India: Shubhada Saraswat Prakashan.

Lenin, V. I. 1943. *State and Revolution*. New York: International Publishers.

Leve, Lauren G. 2001. "Between Jesse Helms and Ram Bahadur: Participation and Empowerment in Women's Literacy Programming in Nepal." *Polar: Political and Legal Anthropology Review* 24, no. 1: 108–28.

Li, Tania Murray. 2007. "Practices of Assemblage and Community Forest Management." *Economy and Society* 36, no. 2: 263–93.

Long, Norman. 1992. "Introduction." In *Battlefields of Knowledge: The Interlocking of Theory and Practice in Social Research and Development*, edited by Norman Long and Ann Long, 3–15. New York: Routledge.

Ludden, David. 1992. "India's Development Regime." In *Colonialism and Culture*, edited by Nicholas B. Dirks, 247–87. Ann Arbor: The University of Michigan Press.

Lukes, Steven. 1974. *Power: A Radical View*. London: Macmillan.

Lutz, Catherine A., and Jane L. Collins. 1993. *Reading National Geographic*. Chicago: University of Chicago Press.

MacKinnon, Catharine A. 1982. "Feminism, Marxism, Method, and the State: An Agenda for Theory." *Signs* 7, no. 3: 515–44.

———. 1989. *Toward a Feminist Theory of the State*. Cambridge: Harvard University Press.

Macpherson, Crawford B. 1964. *The Political Theory of Possessive Individualism: Hobbes to Locke*. Oxford: Oxford University Press.

Malhotra, Anju, Sidney Schuler, and Carol Boender. 2002. *Measuring Women's Empowerment as a Variable in International Development*. Washington, DC: The World Bank.

Mani, Lata. 1989a. "Contentious Traditions: The Debate on Sati in Colonial India." In *Recasting Women: Essays in Colonial History*, edited by Kumkum Sangari and Sudesh Vaid, 88–126. New Delhi: Kali for Women.

———. 1989b. "Multiple Mediations: Feminist Scholarship in the Age of Multinational Reception." *Inscriptions* 5: 1–23.

Mankekar, Purnima. 1993. "National Texts and Gendered Lives: An Ethnography of Television Viewers in a North Indian City." *American Ethnologist* 20, no. 3: 543–63.

Marglin, Frederique Apffel, and Stephen A. Marglin, eds. 1990. *Dominating Knowledge: Development, Culture, and Resistance*. Oxford: Clarendon Press.

Massey, Doreen. 1994. *Space, Place, and Gender*. Minneapolis: University of Minnesota Press.

Mathur, Kanchan. 1999. "From Private to Public: The Emergence of Violence Against Women as an Issue in the Women's Development Programme, Rajasthan." In *Institutions, Relations and Outcomes: A Framework and Case Studies for Gender-aware Planning*, edited by Naila Kabeer and Ramya Subrahmanian, 288–311. New Delhi: Kali for Women.

Maurer, Bill. 2002. "Anthropological and Accounting Knowledge in Islamic Banking and Finance: Rethinking Critical Accounts." *Journal of the Royal Anthropological Institute* 8, no. 4: 645–67.

Mendelsohn, Oliver, and Marika Vicziany. 1998. *The Untouchables: Subordination, Poverty and the State in Modern India*. Cambridge: Cambridge University Press.

Menon, Nivedita. 1996. "The Impossibility of 'Justice': Female Foeticide and Feminist Discourse on Abortion." In *Social Reform, Sexuality and the State*. Contributions to Indian Sociology, edited by Patricia Uberoi, 369–92. New Delhi: Sage Publications.

_____. 2004. *Recovering Subversion: Feminist Politics Beyond the Law*. New Delhi: Permanent Black.

Menon, Ritu, and Kamla Bhasin. 1993. "Recovery, Rupture, Resistance: Indian State and Abduction of Women during Partition." *Economic and Political Weekly* 28, no. 17: WS2–11.

Menon-Sen, Kalyani. 2001. "The Problem: Towards Equality: A Symposium on Women, Feminisms and Women's Movements." *Seminar* 505: 12–15.

Merry, Sally E. 2003. "Rights Talk and the Experience of Law: Implementing Women's Human Rights to Protection from Violence." *Human Rights Quarterly* 25, no. 2: 343–81.

Mies, Maria. 1982. *The Lace Makers of Narsapur: Indian Housewives Produce for the World Market*. London: Zed Press.

Miliband, Ralph. 1969. *The State in Capitalist Society*. New York: Basic Books.

Miller, Daniel. 2002. "Turning Callon the Right Way Up." *Economy and Society* 31, no. 2: 218–33.

Mitchell, Timothy. 1988. *Colonising Egypt*. Cambridge: Cambridge University Press.

_____. 1991. "America's Egypt: Discourse of the Development Industry." *Middle East Report* 21, no. 2: 18–36.

_____. 1999. "Society, Economy, and the State Effect." In *State/Culture: State Formation after the Cultural Turn*, edited by George Steinmetz, 76–97. Ithaca: Cornell University Press.

_____. 2000. "The Stage of Modernity." In *Questions of Modernity*. Contradictions of Modernity, edited by Timothy Mitchell, 1–34. Minneapolis: University of Minnesota Press.

_____. 2002. *Rule of Experts: Egypt, Techno-Politics, Modernity*. Berkeley: University of California Press.

Mohanty, Chandra Talpade. 1991. "Under Western Eyes: Feminist Scholarship and Colonial Discourses." In *Third World Women and the Politics of Feminism*, edited by Chandra T. Mohanty, Ann Russo, and Lourdes Torres, 51–80. Bloomington: Indiana University Press.

______. 2002. "'Under Western Eyes' Revisited: Feminist Solidarity through Anticapitalist Struggles." *Signs* 28, no. 2: 499–535.

Molyneux, Maxine. 1985. "Mobilisation without Emancipation? Women's Interests, the State and Revolution in Nicaragua." *Feminist Studies* 11, no. 2: 227–54.

Moore, Donald S. 1999. "The Crucible of Cultural Politics: Reworking 'Development' in Zimbabwe's Eastern Highlands." *American Ethnologist* 26, no. 3: 654–89.

Moore, Sally F. 1977. "Political Meetings and the Simulation of Unanimity: Kilimanjaro 1973." In *Secular Ritual*, edited by Sally F. Moore and Barbara G. Myerhoff, 151–72. Amsterdam: Van Gorcum.

Moore, Sally F., and Barbara G. Myerhoff. 1977. "Introduction: Secular Ritual: Forms and Meanings." In *Secular Ritual*, edited by Sally F. Moore and Barbara G. Myerhoff, 3–24. Amsterdam: Van Gorcum.

Morris, Rosalind. 1995. "All Made Up: Performance Theory and the New Anthropology of Sex and Gender." *Annual Review of Anthropology* 24: 567–92.

Moser, Caroline O. N. 1993. *Gender, Planning, and Development: Theory, Practice and Training*. New York: Routledge.

Mouffe, Chantal. 1992. "Feminism, Citizenship, and Radical Democratic Politics." In *Feminists Theorize the Political*, edited by Judith Butler and Joan W. Scott, 369–84. New York: Routledge.

Murphy, Josette. 1995. *Gender Issues in World Bank Lending*. Washington, DC: The World Bank.

Nagar, Richa, and Saraswati Raju. 2003. "Women, NGOs and the Contradictions of Empowerment and Disempowerment: A Conversation." *Antipode* 35, no. 1: 1–13.

Nandy, Ashis. 1983. *The Intimate Enemy: Loss and Recovery of Self under Colonialism*. Delhi: Oxford University Press.

______. 1989. "The Political Culture of the Indian State." *Daedalus* 118, no. 4: 1–26.

______. 1992. "State." In *The Development Dictionary: A Guide to Knowledge as Power*, edited by Wolfgang Sachs, 264–74. Atlantic Highlands: Zed Books Ltd.

Narayan, Deepa. 2002. *Empowerment and Poverty Reduction: A Sourcebook*. Washington, DC: The World Bank.

Navaro-Yashin, Yael. 2002. *Faces of the State: Secularism and Public Life in Turkey*. Princeton: Princeton University Press.

Ong, Aihwa. 1999. *Flexible Citizenship: The Cultural Logics of Transnationality*. Durham: Duke University Press.

______. 2006. *Neoliberalism as Exception: Mutations in Citizenship and Sovereignty*. Durham: Duke University Press.

Orloff, Ann S. 1999. "Motherhood, Work, and Welfare in the United States, Britain, Canada, and Australia." In *State/Culture: State Formation after the Cultural Turn*, edited by George Steinmetz, 76–97. Ithaca: Cornell University Press.

Osanloo, Arzoo. 2006. "Islamico-civil 'Rights Talk': Women, Subjectivity, and Law in Iranian Family Court." *American Ethnologist* 33, no. 2: 191–209.

Overholt, Catherine A., et al. 1991. "Gender Analysis Framework." In *Gender Analysis in Development Planning*, edited by Aruna Rao, Mary B. Anderson, and Catherine A. Overholt, 9–20. West Hartford: Kumarian Press.

Oxaal, Zoe, and Sally Baden. 1997. *Gender and Empowerment: Definitions, Approaches and Implications for Policy*. Report no. 40. Brighton: Institute of Development Studies.

Paley, Julia. 2001. *Marketing Democracy: Power and Social Movements in Post-Dictatorship Chile*. Berkeley: University of California Press.

Pathak, Zakia, and Rajeswari Sunder Rajan. 1992. "Shahbano." In *Feminists Theorize the Political*, edited by Judith Butler and Joan W. Scott, 257–79. New York: Routledge.

Pearson, Ruth, Ann Whitehead, and Kate Young. 1981. "Introduction: The Continuing Subordination of Women in the Development Process." In *Of Marriage and the Market: Women's Subordination Internationally and Its Lessons*, edited by Kate Young, Carol Wolkowitz, and Roslyn McCullagh, ix–xix. London: Routledge.

Peck, Jamie. 2004. "Geography and Public Policy: Constructions of Neoliberalism." *Progress in Human Geography* 28, no. 3: 392–405.

Peet, Richard, and Michael Watts. 1996. *Liberation Ecologies: Environment, Development, Social Movements*. London: Routledge.

Perry, Richard W. 1996. "Rethinking the Right to Development: After the Critique of Development, After the Critique of Rights." *Law and Policy* 18, no. 3 & 4: 225–49.

Phelan, Peggy. 1993. *Unmarked: The Politics of Performance*. New York: Routledge.

Philipose, Pamela. 2001. "International Dimensions: Towards Equality: A Symposium on Women, Feminisms and Women's Movements." *Seminar* 505. http://www.india-seminar.com/2001/505/505%20pamela%20philipose.htm (accessed on October 15, 2004).

Pigg, Stacy Leigh. 1997. "'Found in Most Traditional Societies': Traditional Medical Practitioners between Culture and Development." In *International Development and the Social Sciences: Essays on the History and Politics of Knowledge*, edited by Frederick Cooper and Randall Packard, 259–90. Berkeley: University of California Press.

Piven, Frances Fox. 1990. "Ideology and the State: Women, Power, and the Welfare State." In *Women, the State, and Welfare*, edited by Linda Gordon, 250–64. Madison: The University of Wisconsin Press.

Piven, Frances Fox, and Richard A. Cloward. 1971. *Regulating the Poor: The Functions of Public Welfare*. New York: Pantheon Books.

Pletsch, Carl E. 1981. "The Three Worlds, or the Division of Scientific Labor, circa 1950–1975." *Comparative Studies in Society and History* 23, no. 4: 565–90.

Poulantzas, Nicos. 1973. *Political Power and Social Classes*. London: New Left Books.

Putnam, Robert. 1993. *Making Democracy Work: Civic Traditions in Modern Italy*, Princeton: Princeton University Press.

Rahnema, Majid. 1997. "Towards Post-Development: Searching for Signposts, a New Language and New Paradigms." In *The Post-Development Reader*, edited by Majid Rahnema and Victoria Bawtree, 377–403. London: Zed Books.

Ramachandran, Vimala. 1995. *En-gendering Development: Lessons from Some Efforts to Address Gender Concerns in Mainstream Programmes and Institutions in India.*

Razavi, Shahrashoub, and Carol Miller. 1995. *From WID to GAD: Conceptual Shifts in the Women and Development Discourse.* Occasional Paper. Geneva: United Nations Research Institute for Social Development.

Rofel, Lisa. 1999. *Other Modernities: Gendered Yearnings in China after Socialism.* Berkeley: University of California Press.

Rose, Nikolas. 1990. *Governing the Soul: The Shaping of the Private Self.* London: Routledge.

______. 1996. "Governing 'Advanced' Liberal Democracies." In *Foucault and Political Reason: Liberalism, Neo-liberalism and Rationalities of Government*, edited by Andrew Barry, Thomas Osborne, and Nikolas Rose, 37–64. Chicago: The University of Chicago Press.

______. 1999. *Powers of Freedom: Reframing Political Thought.* Cambridge: Cambridge University Press.

Rostow, Walt Whitman. 1971. *The Stages of Economic Growth: A Non-Communist Manifesto.* New York: Cambridge University Press.

Rowlands, Jo. 1998. "A Word of the Times, but What Does it Mean? Empowerment in the Discourse and Practice of Development." In *Women and Empowerment: Illustrations from the Third World*, edited by Haleh Afshar, 11–34. New York: St. Martin's Press, Inc.

Rudolph, Lloyd, and Susanne H. Rudolph. 1987. *In Pursuit of Lakshmi: The Political Economy of the Indian State.* Chicago: University of Chicago.

Sachs, Wolfgang. 1992. "Introduction." In *The Development Dictionary: A Guide to Knowledge as Power*, edited by W. Sachs, 1–5. Atlantic Highlands: Zed Books Ltd.

Sangari, Kumkum, and Sudesh Vaid. 1989. "Recasting Women: An Introduction." In *Recasting Women: Essays in Colonial History*, edited by Kumkum Sangari and Sudesh Vaid, 1–26. New Delhi: Kali for Women.

Sarkar, Tanika. 1991. "The Woman as Communal Subject: Rashtrasevika Samiti and Ram Janmabhoomi Movement." *Economic and Political Weekly* 26, no. 35: 2057–62.

______. 1995. "Heroic Women, Mother Goddesses: Family and Organization in Hindutva Politics." In *Women and the Hindu Right: A Collection of Essays*, edited by Tanika Sarkar and Urvashi Butalia, 181–215. New Delhi: Kali for Women.

Sarkar, Tanika, and Urvashi Butalia. 1995. "Introductory Remarks." In *Women and the Hindu Right: A Collection of Essays*, edited by Tanika Sarkar and Urvashi Butalia, 1–9. New Delhi: Kali for Women.

Sassen, Saskia. 1998. *Globalization and Its Discontents: Essays on the New Mobility of People and Money.* New York: The New Press.

Sathin Union Representative. 1994. "State's Role in Women's Empowerment: For Better or for Worse." *Economic and Political Weekly* 29, no. 51–52: 3187–90.

Sayer, Derek. 1994. "Everyday Forms of State Formation: Some Dissident Remarks on 'Hegemony.'" In *Everyday Forms of State Formation: Revolution and the Negotiation of Rule in Modern Mexico*, edited by Gilbert M. Joseph and Daniel Nugent, 367–77. Durham: Duke University Press.

Schechner, Richard. 1988. *Performance Theory*, revised and expanded edition. New York: Routledge.

Scott, David. 1999. "Colonial Governmentality." In *Refashioning Futures: Criticism after Postcoloniality*, 23–52. Princeton: Princeton University Press.

Scott, James C. 1977. *The Moral Economy of the Peasant: Rebellion and Subsistence in Southeast Asia*. New Haven: Yale University Press.

_____. 1985. *Weapons of the Weak: Everyday Forms of Peasant Resistance*. New Haven: Yale University Press.

_____. 1990. *Domination and the Arts of Resistance: Hidden Transcripts*. New Haven: Yale University Press.

_____. 1998. *Seeing Like a State: How Certain Schemes to Improve the Human Condition Have Failed*. New Haven: Yale University Press.

Sen, Gita, and Caren Grown. 1987. *Development, Crises, and Alternative Visions*. New York: Monthly Review Press.

Sen, Siddhartha. 1993. "Defining the Nonprofit Sector: India." *Working Papers of the Johns Hopkins Comparative Nonprofit Sector Project, no. 12*, edited by Lester M. Salamon and Helmet K. Anheier. Baltimore: The Johns Hopkins Institute of Policy Studies.

Serageldin, Ismael. 1998. *Culture and Development at the World Bank*. Washington, DC: World Bank.

Sharma, Aradhana. 2006. "Crossbreeding Institutions, Breeding Struggle: Women's Empowerment, Neoliberal Governmentality, and State (Re)Formation in India." *Cultural Anthropology* 21, no. 1: 60–95.

Sharma, Aradhana, and Akhil Gupta. 2006. "Introduction: Rethinking Theories of the State in an Age of Globalization." In *The Anthropology of the State: A Reader*, edited by Aradhana Sharma and Akhil Gupta, 1–41. Malden: Blackwell Publishing.

Shiva, Vandana. 1988. *Staying Alive: Women, Ecology and Development in India*. New Delhi: Kali for Women.

Shrestha, Nanda. 1995. "Becoming a Development Category." In *Power of Development*, edited by Jonathan Crush, 266–77. New York: Routledge.

Singh, Manmohan. 2007. Prime Minister's Independence Day Address. http://pib.nic.in/release/release.asp?relid=29937 (accessed on August 24, 2007).

Sivaramakrishnan, K. 2000. "Crafting the Public Sphere in the Forests of West Bengal: Democracy, Development and Political Action." *American Ethnologist* 27, no. 2: 431–61.

Sivaramakrishnan, K., and Arun Agrawal. 2003. *Regional Modernities: The Cultural Politics of Development in India*. New Delhi: Oxford University Press.

Skocpol, Theda. 1979. *States and Social Revolutions: A Comparative Analysis of France, Russia, and China*. Cambridge: Cambridge University Press.

Sparr, Pamela, ed. 1994. *Mortgaging Women's Lives: Feminist Critiques of Structural Adjustment*. Atlantic Highlands: Zed Books.

Spivak, Gayatri Chakravorty. 1988a. "Can the Subaltern Speak?" In *Marxism and the Interpretation of Culture*, edited by Cary Nelson and Lawrence Grossberg, 271–313. Urbana: University of Illinois Press.

______. 1988b. "Subaltern Studies: Deconstructing Historiography." In *Selected Subaltern Studies*, edited by Ranajit Guha and Gayatri Chakravorty Spivak, 3–34. New York: Oxford University Press.

______. 1999. *A Critique of Postcolonial Reason: Toward a History of the Vanishing Present*. Cambridge: Harvard University Press.

Staudt, Kathleen, ed. 1997. *Women, International Development, and Politics: The Bureaucratic Mire*. Philadelphia: Temple University Press.

Steinmetz, George, ed. 1999a. *State/Culture: State-Formation after the Cultural Turn*. Ithaca: Cornell University Press.

______. 1999b. "Introduction: Culture and the State." In *State/Culture: State-Formation after the Cultural Turn*, edited by George Steinmetz, 1–49. Ithaca: Cornell University Press.

Stirrat, R. L. 2000. "Cultures of Consultancy." *Critique of Anthropology* 20, no. 1: 31–46.

Stoler, Ann L. 1995. *Race and the Education of Desire: Foucault's History of Sexuality and the Colonial Order of Things*. Durham: Duke University Press.

______. 2004. "Affective States." In *A Companion to the Anthropology of Politics*, edited by David Nugent and Joan Vincent, 4–20. Malden: Blackwell Publishing.

Strathern, Marilyn. 2000. *Audit Cultures: Anthropological Studies in Accountability, Ethics and the Academy*. New York: Routledge.

Stree Shakti Sanghatana. 1989. *"We Were Making History": Women and the Telangana Uprising*. London: Zed Books, Ltd.

Sunder Rajan, Rajeswari. 2003. *The Scandal of the State: Women, Law, and Citizenship in Postcolonial India*. Durham: Duke University Press.

Susser, Ida. 1982. *Norman Street: Poverty and Politics in an Urban Neighborhood*. New York: Oxford University Press.

Taussig, Michael T. 1997. *The Magic of the State*. New York: Routledge.

Taylor, Diana. 1997. *Disappearing Acts: Spectacles of Gender and Nationalism in Argentina's "Dirty War."* Durham: Duke University Press.

Tennekoon, Serena. 1988. "Rituals of Development: The Accelerated Mahavali Development Program of Sri Lanka." *American Ethnologist* 15, no. 2: 294–310.

Tinker, Irene, ed. 1990. *Persistent Inequalities: Women and World Development*. Oxford: Oxford University Press.

Townsend, Janet, Gina Porter, and Emma Mawdsley. 2004. "Creating Spaces of Resistance: Development NGOs and their Clients in Ghana, India and Mexico." *Antipode* 36, no. 5: 871–89.

Trouillot, Michel-Rolph. 2003. "The Anthropology of the State in the Age of Globalization: Close Encounters of the Deceptive Kind." In *Global Transformations: Anthropology and the Modern World*, 79–96. New York: Palgrave Macmillan.

Turner, Victor. 1982. *From Ritual to Theatre: The Human Seriousness of Play*. New York: Performing Arts Journal Publications.

_____. 1988. *The Anthropology of Performance*. New York: Performing Arts Journal Publications.

Uberoi, Patricia. 1996. "Introduction: Problematising Social Reform, Engaging Sexuality, Interrogating the State." In *Social Reform, Sexuality and the State*, edited by Patricia Uberoi, ix–xxvi. New Delhi: Sage Publications.

United Nations. n.d. http://www.un.org/millenniumgoals/ (accessed on September 9, 2006).

Wallerstein, Immanuel. 1995. "The Insurmountable Contradictions of Liberalism: Human Rights and the Rights of Peoples in the Geoculture of the Modern World-System." *South Atlantic Quarterly* 94, no. 4: 1161–78.

Walley, Christine. 2003. "Our Ancestors Used to Bury Their 'Development' in the Ground: Modernity and the Meanings of Development within a Tanzanian Marine Park." *Anthropological Quarterly* 76, no. 1: 33–54.

_____. 2004. *Rough Waters: Nature and Development in an East African Marine Park*. Princeton: Princeton University Press.

WDP Fact Finding Team. 1992. "Development for Whom? Critique of Rajasthan Programme." *Economic and Political Weekly* 27, 5: 193–98.

Weber, Max. 1968. "Bureaucracy." In *Economy and Society: An Outline of Interpretive Sociology*, vol. 2, edited by Guenther Roth and Claus Wittich, 956–1005. New York: Bedminster Press.

Wieringa, Saskia. 1995. *Subversive Women: Women's Movements in Africa, Asia, Latin America and the Caribbean*. New Delhi: Kali for Women.

Wilber, Charles K., and Kenneth P. Jameson. 1973. "Paradigms of Economic Development and Beyond." In *The Political Economy of Development and Underdevelopment*, edited by Charles K. Wilber, 3–27. New York: Random House.

Wolfensohn, James. 1995. *Women and the Transformation of the 21st Century*. http://www.worldbank.org/html/extdr/hnp/hddflash/conf/conf004.html (accessed on December 8, 2006).

_____. 1997. "The Challenge of Inclusion." Speech delivered at the 1997 Annual Meetings of the Board of Governors. Hong Kong, China. http://www.imf.org/external/am/speeches/pdf/PR04E.pdf (accessed on December 7, 2006).

World Bank. 1999. *World Development Report*. Washington, DC: World Bank.

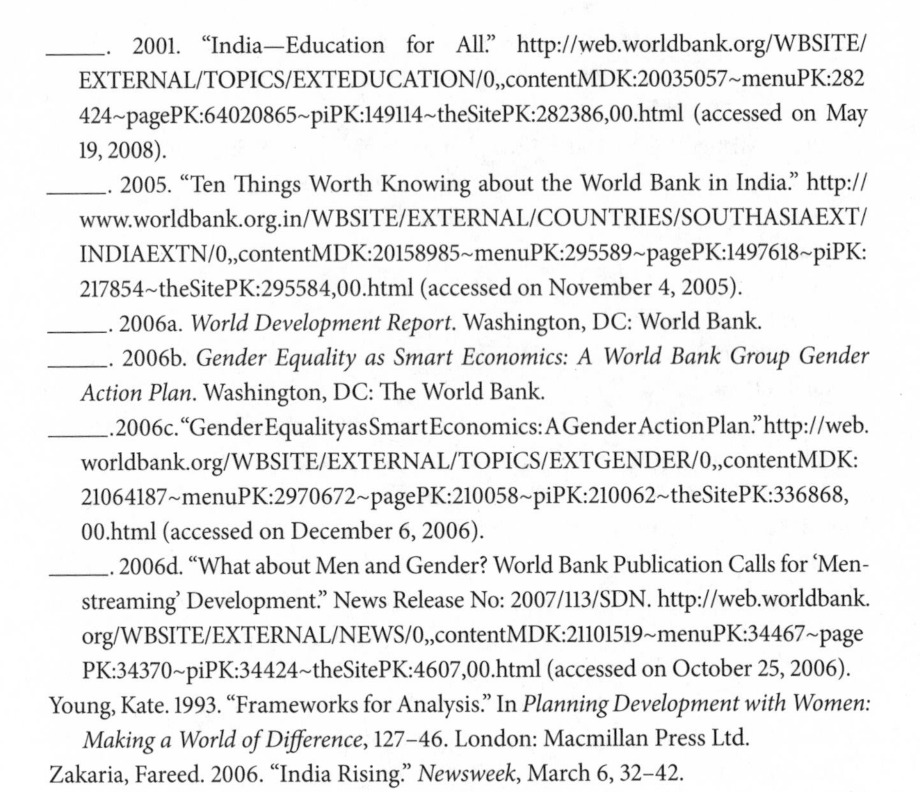

———. 2001. "India—Education for All." http://web.worldbank.org/WBSITE/EXTERNAL/TOPICS/EXTEDUCATION/0,,contentMDK:20035057~menuPK:282424~pagePK:64020865~piPK:149114~theSitePK:282386,00.html (accessed on May 19, 2008).

———. 2005. "Ten Things Worth Knowing about the World Bank in India." http://www.worldbank.org.in/WBSITE/EXTERNAL/COUNTRIES/SOUTHASIAEXT/INDIAEXTN/0,,contentMDK:20158985~menuPK:295589~pagePK:1497618~piPK:217854~theSitePK:295584,00.html (accessed on November 4, 2005).

———. 2006a. *World Development Report*. Washington, DC: World Bank.

———. 2006b. *Gender Equality as Smart Economics: A World Bank Group Gender Action Plan*. Washington, DC: The World Bank.

———. 2006c. "Gender Equality as Smart Economics: A Gender Action Plan." http://web.worldbank.org/WBSITE/EXTERNAL/TOPICS/EXTGENDER/0,,contentMDK:21064187~menuPK:2970672~pagePK:210058~piPK:210062~theSitePK:336868,00.html (accessed on December 6, 2006).

———. 2006d. "What about Men and Gender? World Bank Publication Calls for 'Men-streaming' Development." News Release No: 2007/113/SDN. http://web.worldbank.org/WBSITE/EXTERNAL/NEWS/0,,contentMDK:21101519~menuPK:34467~pagePK:34370~piPK:34424~theSitePK:4607,00.html (accessed on October 25, 2006).

Young, Kate. 1993. "Frameworks for Analysis." In *Planning Development with Women: Making a World of Difference*, 127–46. London: Macmillan Press Ltd.

Zakaria, Fareed. 2006. "India Rising." *Newsweek*, March 6, 32–42.

Index

ARADHANA SHARMA is assistant professor of anthropology and feminist, gender, and sexuality studies at Wesleyan University.